LEARNING TO LEARN IN HIGHER EDUCATION

NEW PATTERNS OF LEARNING SERIES
Edited by P.J. Hills, University of Leicester

AN INTRODUCTION TO EDUCATIONAL COMPUTING
Nicholas John Rushby

PREPARING EDUCATIONAL MATERIALS
N.D.C. Harris

THE ORGANISATION AND MANAGEMENT OF EDUCATIONAL TECHNOLOGY
Richard N. Tucker

ADULT LEARNING
R. Bernard Lovell

EVALUATING INSTRUCTIONAL TECHNOLOGY
Christopher Kay Knapper

ASSESSING STUDENTS, APPRAISING TEACHING
John C. Clift and Bradford W. Imrie

STUDENT LEARNING IN HIGHER EDUCATION
John D. Wilson

LEARNING AND VISUAL COMMUNICATION
David Sless

RESOURCE-BASED LEARNING FOR HIGHER AND CONTINUING EDUCATION
John Clarke

Learning to Learn in Higher Education

Jean Wright

CROOM HELM
London & Canberra

Croom Helm Ltd, 2-10 St John's Road, London SW11
British Library Cataloguing in Publication Data

Wright, Jean
Learning to learn in higher education - (New patterns of learning series)
1. Study, Method of - Research
I. Title II. Series
378.1'7'02812

ISBN 0-7099-2744-4

Printed and bound in Great Britain

CONTENTS

To DAVID with deep appreciation for his understanding and encouragement

NEW PATTERNS OF LEARNING

THE PURPOSE OF THIS SERIES

This series of books is intended to provide readable introductions to trends and areas of current thinking in education. Each book will be of interest to all educators, trainers and administrators responsible for the implementation of educational policies and programmes in higher, further and continuing education.

The books are designed for easy access of information and contain bibliographies of key works to enable the reader to pursue selected areas in more depth should he or she so wish.

This book examines the way in which students learn how to learn and looks at the individual learner as a person with a separate and developing perception of his learning environment.

Jean Wright is University Counsellor at the University of Reading.

P.J. Hills
Leicester

ACKNOWLEDGEMENTS

Gratitude brings to mind the following names: Professor Peter Hall, Department of Human Geography, Professor Peter Dunn and Dr Gerry Hamilton, Department of Engineering, Dr Viv Greenhalgh, Open University, and Miss Josephine Wright. I am especially indebted to those colleagues who, by their writing or by their criticism of mine, by their encouragement and in more subtle ways, have not only influenced the form and content of this book but have helped to maintain the inward pressures which have brought it to completion.

My gratitude is also due to Mr Gordon Smith who arranged for the typing of the first version of the manuscript and much of the retyping of the final manuscript, to Mrs G. Long and Mrs M. Cutts for retyping and checking, and to the Executive Committee at the Reading University Students' Union for their help. I would also like to thank all those who kindly granted permission to reprint material which appeared in this volume: Dr Chris Lucas, Director of the Student Health Service, University College, Dr Dia Hounsell, University of Lancaster, and Mrs Gill Sturidge, University of Reading.

Finally, I would like to thank the students and young people who have taught me so much.

J.W.

'Knowledge is not a loose leaf notebook of facts. Above all it is a responsibility for the integrity of what we are, primarily of what we are as ethnic creatures. The personal commitment of a man to his skill, the intellectual commitment and the emotional equipment working together as one, has made the Ascent of Man.'

(Bronowski, 1976)

PREFACE

'The most socially useful learning in the modern world is learning about the process of learning, a continuing openness to experience and incorporation into oneself of the process of change' (Rogers, 1969).

This book sets out to examine the way students learn 'how to learn' in higher education institutions, and in so doing asks administrators and academic staff to consider each individual learner as a person with a separate perception of his learning environment and a developing sense of his own identity. In doing so it calls into question the hidden agendas, motives and prejudices, and examines the institutions' ability to be open to new experiences and to incorporate into itself the process of change.

Learning which involves change, whether for the individual or the institution, is threatening and tends to be resisted since it questions current value systems; but it is far more dangerous to cling to ineffective and out-of-date methods.

To be able to take this risk an individual has to have a firm sense of his own identity so that he feels secure inside himself and is self-confident. He also deserves support in order to achieve this, as does a patient in therapy, who is also involved in change.

First, this book seeks to examine the individual as he develops as a learner through the educational system, seeing the stifling of his creative potential in all but the most progressive of senior schools and the focus on structure and rote learning in order to obtain the qualifications necessary for progression to higher education.

Secondly, it considers the situation in higher education today. It calls on administrators and academic staff to reconsider the goals of higher education so that the development of the student's identity and his motivation and intellect are equally valued.

In order to be able to realise his academic potential a student needs to develop as a creative and autonomous learner with a well-developed sense of his own identity, but the development of these personal characteristics is usually given low priority in academic institutions.

It is argued that a self-motivating confident student makes better use of his academic potential and hence obtains a higher level degree. He is also better able to develop a flexible approach to 'learning to learn'.

The developing of 'learning to learn' facilities is discussed - how these are administered and how 'learning to learn' resource centres can be established.

Members of academic staff are expected to be able to facilitate learning, to relate comfortably to students, to arouse curiosity, to encourage creativity, to communicate ideas and concepts and to allow spontaneous discussion. This is in addition to their primary task of carrying out research, administrative and tutorial functions. This is a very exacting role for which inadequate training is provided.

In examining the students' experiences of 'learning to learn', the book will look at particular educational establishments, such as the School for Independent Studies at Lancaster University, which seeks to encourage creativity and autonomous learning.

Whether a graduate continues into post-graduate studies or obtains a professional job or joins the ranks of the unemployed, the ability to be a creative, self-motivating confident person is equally important. Hudson (1979) says that 'the skills needed are not the traditional hard techniques of the past, but rather imagination and creative understanding coupled with judgement - the qualities associated with the "divergent mind" of the arts graduate rather than the scientist'. We shall challenge the concept that study skills can be taught like a course in self-improvement and examine the whole concept of 'learning to learn' in higher education as it is understood by different cultures. Like businesses, British universities now need to attract foreign 'customers' in order to remain economically viable. The overseas student from a different higher educational system finds difficulty in adjusting to the British university. Factors other than scholarship are being considered by the overseas funding authorities. The provision of group and individual counselling, 'learning to learn' resource centres, group and individual language tuition and English conversation schemes are likely to attract more overseas students to British universities. Academic staff administrators and counsellors, more than ever before, need to pool their resources and develop an eclectic approach.

However, before we consider the way to respond to the present-day situation in higher education, we should consider the curious, creative, imaginative, pre-school child who has not yet been inhibited by formal education.

J.W.

REFERENCES

Bronowski, J. (1976) 'The Ascent of Man' BBC, London, p. 438

Hudson, L. (1979) 'Contrary Imaginations', Penguin, London, pp. 49-67

Rogers, C. (1969) 'Freedom to Learn', Columbus Oxio, Melville

1 THE MODELS OF PRE-UNIVERSITY LEARNING

Over the last decade the arguments have been expounded between examination-focused syllabus teaching and the development of creative learning environments, yet neither 'school' has shown any great concern for the concept of 'learning to learn'. Few of us are teachers but all of us are learners. The learning to learn process in initiated by the fostering of creative learning through the school experience not instead of but parallel with the syllabus-bound formal teaching.

Even the more progressive schools are concerned with control more than learning, with teachers' objectives and with manipulating children to achieve these objectives. In the planning of the curriculum teachers do not look at the skills that are needed to learn (thereby incorporating method and content), but rather teach the content on an examination-based syllabus. Research into the curriculum has been carried out by the Department of Education and Science, and the Schools Council has now produced a document called 'The Practical Curriculum'. However, even this does not suggest incorporating study skills at primary, junior and senior school level. The National Foundation for Educational Research is proposing to study this aspect of learning to learn, but there is often a delay of several years after the publication of the result of their studies before proposals become regular practice in the schools.

However formal or informal the teaching methods - and changes of headmaster have often resulted in swings from one extreme to another - the incorporation of 'the project' has given rise to the ideal framework for the development of study skills in school. Children are infinitely curious creatures and naturally want to learn - particularly if the title of the topic is of their own choice. In carrying out topic work pupils learn how to use the library, how to take notes, how to write creatively, all skills that they would require in higher education. From the commencement of full-time education children are expected to write formal essays (known as compositions) and, although they are given basic instructions on 'how to plan an essay', they often have no idea of the skills required to write creatively. When laboratory work is introduced in secondary schools it is essential for pupils to understand the purpose of practicals and how to take notes from practicals, but this instruction is virtually never provided.

THE DEVELOPMENT OF CREATIVE LEARNING

The Concept

The idea of creativity, imagination and spontaneity has always been viewed as something of lesser value by the hard scientists and others. Liam Hudson in 'The Cult of the Fact' refers to the Oxford Philosophers thus:

> Looking back, the context they created seems one concerned, almost to the point of obsession, with the question of intellectual control. The concern for logic, the avoidance of feeling, the idea of clarity, the hostility to metaphysics, the assumption that confusion dissolves if examined with sufficient dispassion; all these seem to have been carried over into philosophy from the classical training that so many of the older philosophers had enjoyed - a training designed by the Victorians as a means of translating tradesmen's sons into colonial administrators and gentlemen (Hudson, 1972).

The attitude is that the Arts are of less importance that the Sciences, the emotional of less importance than the intellectual, so that the sensuous subjects such as Art, Poetry or Music are relegated to optional subjects in the school curriculum. Maslow (1975) writes that the most impressive evidence of creativity resulting from peak experiences comes

> from studying autobiographies of scholars to whom a scrupulous respect for evidence is second nature; a scientist like Julian Huxley, a historian like Arnold Toynbee, or an arch empiricist like Arthur Koestler. In 'Arrow in the Blue' Koestler feels how, at the age of fourteen, a 'mystic elation', a 'spontaneous illumination', made him consciously dedicate his life to science and to trying to solve the 'unbearable riddle' of infinity.

C.S. Lewis in his autobiography 'Surprised by Joy' had 'peak experiences' in his childhood and again was engulfed with this intense transcendental feeling when he read 'Siegfried and the Twilight of the Gods' at a later age. He felt the

> pure 'Northernness' engulfed me: a vision of huge, clear spaces hanging above the Atlantic in the endless twilight of a Northern Summer, remoteness, severity ... (Lewis, 1955)

Pafford (1975) alluded to this experience of Lewis's in his appraisal of students' methods of learning - he feels that

> this renaissance of 'Joy' had, or so it seems from what Lewis goes on to say, four important results: results that may be paralleled in many other people's experience. In the first

> place, this new imaginative intoxication, this vision of 'pure Northernness' led to a feverish search for and voracious devouring of everthing connected remotely with Wagnerian mythology, both literature and music. It led, it would be fair to say, to a rapid widening of intellectual and aesthetic horizons: it acted as a powerful stimulant to the thirst for knowledge; it set flowing a stream of mental energy and enthusiasm which was to spread far beyond the original narrow confines of its source. To borrow A.N. Whitehead's phrase, it acted as a patent example of what he calls the 'Romance Stage' in the cyclic process of education or what Sir Percy Nunn, in a similar analysis of the rhythm of learning, called the 'Wonder Stage'. If such experiences of 'Joy' are at all common, they would seem to have a very real educational significance ...

I can recall such exquisite moments from my own experience - a silent night's train ride from Bergen to Oslo amid the purple brooding mountains with lakes which are shrouded with circling mist. At another time, an apparently motionless pond, heavy with the heat of summer and swarming with insect life - in the depths of a forest. These led to me pursuing everything connected with natural history and the environment.

How then shall teachers in urban schools, with pupils from high-rise flats and underprivileged homes, generate curiosity and nurture their imaginations?

The Process

There are many definitions of the creative process, which has been investigated by psychologists since the 1950s. These have stemmed from attempts to define it as a thinking skill, subdivided into sub-skills which can be improved by training and practice. In contrast, psychoanalytic theory regards creativity as an illusive phenomenon. Recent psychoanalytic theory has emphasised the complex personal nature of creative thought and suggested that it occurs when conscious and pre-conscious processes interact to produce creative insights.

Koestler maintains that creative thinking normally occurs in 'frames of reference' which are the habitual methods used to code and interpret the world around us. He suggests that

> major creative breakthroughs have occurred by the perception of commonality between apparently incompatible frames of reference, and cites Gutenberg's invention of the printing press to illustrate this. Apparently unrelated experiences enabled Guntenberg to achieve his creative breakthrough: an observation of the repeated picture motif on playing cards, his knowledge of the production of coins using small replaceable seals and a casual observation in Summer of grapes being pressed (Turner, Renshaw and Sinclair, 1977).

I would suggest that the creative process can be broken down into five stages:

(a) curiosity
(b) a spontaneous and imaginative style
(c) an analytical and critical approach
(d) the courage to be independent and different from others
(e) a commitment to hard and persistent work.

Curiosity and a Spontaneous and Imaginative Style

The pre-school child is intensely curious about his environment and by the time he starts school he has learnt how to live in his home, church, play group, or wherever he spends his waking hours. The play group or nursery school also gives him the opportunity to socialise with his peers and to relate to an authority figure other than the parents.

Due, however, to real and sometimes to imaginary dangers, it is unlikely that many urban pre-school children have had an opportunity to explore alone outside their own homes. The child of professional parents and some others already has a built-in advantage over the deprived child by experiencing home activities such as books, learning an instrument, finger painting and family leisure activities such as sailing or hill walking etc. These pre-school experiences educate the 'whole person' and act as an educational advantage throughout his school career. By exercising his talents he is able to develop a sense of his identity and thus he is able to take what <u>he</u> wants from the formal education. In the West, children rarely experience the deep continuous immersion in a tactile sensual environment which occurs in primitive tribes like the Yanoonamo tribe in the Amazon visited by Alec Shoumatoff or the Yequana tribe in South America described by Jean Liedloff in her book 'The Continuum Concept'.

> Between birth and the voluntary commencement of crawling, the Yequana infant is carried everywhere, aware of the sight, sound, taste, smell and touch of his mother's body and bathed daily in the river with sensuous enjoyment (Liedloff, 1975).

He later experiences the smell of cooking and the woodfire, the feeling of the hot sun and the chill rain on his bare skin. Depsite the fact of his growing up suffering from disease and malnutrition he also grows up a sensuous fulfilled human being, living in harmony with nature with none of the neurosis and sexual inhibitions of so-called 'civilised man'.

> His self reliance and self confidence grows with a speed, depth and breath which would seem prodigious to anyone who has known only civilised children deprived of the complete 'in-arms' experience (Liedloff, 1975).

This is further emphasised by Winnicott (1971) when he states that:

> It is in playing and only playing that the individual child or adult is able to be creative and to use the whole personality, and it is only in being creative that the individual discovers the self.

An Analytical and Critical Approach

Margaret Donaldson considers that the pre-school child's first step is the step of conceptualizing language - becoming aware of it as a separate structure, freeing it from its embeddedness in events' (Donaldson, 1978). She refers to a book reporting the work of Barbel Inhelder and her colleagues:

> at one point in the book in which they report their findings, they discuss the question of differences between children from different kinds of homes and whether linguistic skill is relevant. They go on to deny that 'language as such' has anything to do with success, but they say that they have noticed certain differences in 'attitude towards the words of the experimenter' (Donaldson, 1978).

For example children from more privileged backgrounds are more likely to pay scrupulous attention to the words of the question, reflecting on them and analysing them before answering. By contrast, the less privileged children have a strong tendency to substitute a 'more natural' question for the one the experimenter had asked and therefore answer the question incorrectly in the eyes of the experimenter. This is another example where the types of 'learning environment' at home can be a positive advantage or disadvantage.

The Courage to Be Different from others

Developing a sense of one's own identity and thus becoming oneself is probably the most important learning activity that a child can carry out.

Alison Stallisbrass describes oneself as:

1. Becoming a fully-functioning human being, capable of awareness and responsiveness on the sensory-motor and emotional planes.
2. Developing the natural aptitude and character and the vision that is latent in every individual.
3. Developing spontaneity - by which I mean the ability to respond in a manner that is true to oneself as an integrated whole so that, instead of reacting compulsively to this or that force, one has 'free will' (Stallisbrass, 1977).

If the child and the adolescent has the freedom to develop in a supportive but not over-protective environment, he will naturally develop a sense of his own identity and with it self-confidence. He will then maximise his learning potential, and have the confidence to develop an improved 'learning to learn' style.

A Commitment to Hard and Persistent Work

During the course of junior and secondary school education the teacher has specific goals to achieve so that there is a change from 'person-orientated learning' to 'learning the curriculum'. This no longer utilises the natural resources of the child unless the teacher can combine project work and other open-discovery activities with the curricula activity. Pafford (1975) says that:

> Education is almost exclusively concerned with man's verbalising and conceptualising proclivities; it develops them to a precocious and unbalanced degree and the veil of words and concepts eclipses the vividness of perception known to the innocent age of the child... When it is almost exclusively intellectual, education neglects knowledge that is not prepositional; meaning that is not conceptualised; thinking that is not discursive; symbols that do not function like the symbols of mathematics or science, coherence - as in works of art - that is not the coherence of logical relations. It cannot comprehend reason of the heart as well as of the head: above all such an education cannot tolerate browsing, rambling, idleness, daydreams, reverie and contemplation, and yet it is at these times when we are least self-consciously purposive that we are most likely to know transcendent ecstacy and awe. Wordsworth's picture of the mis-educated product of such a system is of a horrifying vain and corpse-like prig without reverie, humility or joy and locked in the pinfold of his own conceit.

The Relationship Between IQ and Creativity

It has been found with the IQ test that the expected standard response gets the highest score but real genius gives an individual creative response and, therefore, achieves a lower IQ score. Hudson (1979) discusses this in 'Contrary Imagination'. Getzels and Jackson (1962) in exploring gifted children raised the issue of whether it is 'emotional or motivational pathology or distinctive intellectual ability that accounts for the superior scholastic ability of our creative students, despite their relatively lower I.Q.'

In addition to the advantage that children from over-privileged homes have in examinations, because of their superior linguistic skills, Eell, David *et al.* (1951) looks at another variable, that of culture. He argues

> that behaviour requisite for successful achievement on intelligence test items is, to a very great extent, culturally learned, and that the cultural background of the high-status child, as compared with that of a low-status child, is more adequate preparation for appropriate response to a test which is highly saturated with 'middle-class' symbols, problems, vocabulary and objects.

This situation, according to Davis, creates a bias in favour of high-status pupils which leads to higher test scores, on average, for the pupil from high socio-economic levels. A highly creative child from an ethnic minority group could be disadvantaged.

Creativity and the Examination System

The CSE examination has an emphasis on project work which allows the pupil to be creative, but when the typical CSE candidate leaves school he is likely to be employed in routine factory work that does not demand creativity. The increase in unemployment gives rise to a further dimension: the number of unemployed school leavers in the UK was 217,000 out of 750,713 school leavers in June 1980 (29 per cent). Perhaps teachers should realise that they are educating many pupils for unemployment and revise their courses accordingly. This group need to have a sense of their own identity, self-confidence and the ability to function creatively to withstand the frustrations of their depressing situation, but also they need to be prepared for a variety of jobs when they eventually start work.

The 'O' and 'A' level examinations, with the exception of the Nuffield school projects, require mainly rote learning although these students hope to progress into higher education where they will need different learning techniques.

STUDY SKILLS IN SIXTH FORM COLLEGES

There is an almost complete lack of any studies relating to 'learning how to learn at university' in sixth form colleges.

The National Foundation for Educational Research has been investigating the efficacy of study skills programmes for 16-19 year-olds in schools. They are studying 100 such programmes in depth on a three-year project which will be completed in February 1982. Such programmes have been instigated by head teachers or teachers of General Studies courses.

The focus in sixth froms is on processing pupils through the entrance examination into higher education. Teaching staff have very little wish to be involved in running 'learning to learn' workshops when they have no training or experience in this field. Often the concept of running a workshop, instead of giving a lesson, is a daunting experience. Staff argue that there is no time to include such workshops in the normal timetable.

Most secondary school teachers get their satisfaction from the examination successes of their pupils, and their teaching prowess is also assessed on this. It would take a fundamental change in the attitudes of the whole secondary school teaching hierarchy for teachers to concern themselves with preparing their pupils to learn at university. Parents generally agree with the teachers, often feeling that higher education is a 'good thing' - particularly if they are professional families. Higher education is connected with social status as well as future employment possibilities. We may not have yet reached the situation where higher education is a preferable alternative to facing unemployment, as it is in Italy, but it is something to be aware of. Many pupils, however, from over-protected and over-guided homes pass into higher education, without any sense of vocation or motivation, merely because the parents want them to.

A recent survey of 24 secondary comprehensive schools in Cheshire and Nottinghamshire, carried out for the British Library by Irving and Snape (1979), showed that at sixth-form level children were expected to develop the skills needed for independent study without any special teaching. This report reinforced the findings of a report published by the Schools Council on 'The Effective Use of Reading'. It shows that secondary school children in the UK are rarely, if ever, taught the advanced reading skills needed for different kinds of academic study.

SELECTION FOR HIGHER EDUCATION

Securing a place on a course of higher education in the UK is nearly always dependent on good examination grades, not on personality factors. Even in selection for medical school, where the doctor-patient relationship is ultimately part of the treatment, 'A' level grades are the main determinant for entry. This also applies to Law and Veterinary Science and other professional training.

Alwyn Smith, writing in 'The Times Higher Education Supplement' in April 1981, proposed changes in the training of medical students, who in the past have been trained to treat disease rather than people. Attention was also drawn to this problem by Ian Kennedy in the Reith Lectures in 1981 when he pointed out that doctors have been trained 'to think of themselves as a scientist problem-solver, raised in an environment of white coats and machinery where people are being constantly monitored and measured'.

The NHS 'from the cradle to the grave' provides total care, and when one looks at the increase in geriatric and psychiatric patients it is obvious that these need care not problem-solving. This needs a radical change in medical student training.

If changes do occur then we may have a more human and less technological approach to training future doctors and the selection procedures will change to be more in line with this aim. Selection on interview is not a foolproof method but it is a useful indication and it is disquieting to realise that at some universities veterinary students, for example, are admitted without interview.

It is essential however for certain groups, such as mature students, that a full personal as well as academic interview takes place.

Experimental Selection

Perhaps, as Nicholas Malleson suggested in 1965 we have to

> try selecting some university entrants on different criteria altogether, on creative ability and inventive productivity, regardless of the level of their formal examination attainment. Once examination results were set aside, it would only be the school who could make an assessment, however subjective, of a child's creative potential. The suggestion is that some Universities should enter into agreements with particular Headmasters. They could guarantee to accept an agreed number of children from each on his recommendation alone, unquestioningly. In doing this they would restore to him the freedom to educate those he chooses as widely and creatively as he wants. This could revive the great virtue of the traditional Public Schools ... absolute confidence and security of future opportunity. With that there would be a marvellous adventure in creative teaching that different schools of all kinds could undertake.

Malleson continued: 'A number of Oxford and Cambridge Colleges have each made arrangements with the West Riding Grammar Schools to start this experiment in selection ...' This could be tried experimentally by other universities.

The Situation Abroad

Many other countries have open entry and broad admission but then protect standards by a heavy examination failure rate at the end of the first year. It is not possible simply to compare cross-culturally, even in Europe, without taking a wide variety of socio-economic as well as academic factors into account. Edwards and Roberts (1980) state that:

> In the U.K. in the half century before 1960, the professional, administrative, managerial and technical classes were expanding at an annual rate of about 2.4 per cent per annum, which was very close to the secular rate of expansion of student numbers ... For example in Britain the participation rate in all forms of full time higher education among the sons of senior professions rose from about 40% in the 50's to about 80% in the

70's. In the case of University enrolment alone it rose from 25.7% in 1957 to 57.5% in 1976. The social differentials remain much the same since the participation rate of sons of unskilled workers rose from about .5% to just over 1% in the same period while their daughters remained at less than half that level.

The same social trends dominated in Germany and France and produced top social participation rates of the same or an even higher order. The much greater overall expansion rate over the century in the USA is, on the other hand, the result of a broader social participation in higher education, and the same may well be true of Japan as well as Soviet Russia.

The awarding of grants is a very significant factor. In France, the higher education system is divided between 250 Grandes Ecoles, 76 universities and 56 university institutes of technology. Grants are not awarded to undergraduates. In the university sector alone, the 'drop-out' rate of sometimes 50 per cent in the first year at university has to be seen against the hardship of trying to be full-time worker and full-time student.

Selection is being slowly introduced into the university sector. Though traditionally free and open to all holders of the baccalaureat, special selection takes place prior to entry to certain establishments.

In Italy where grants are awarded and there is open entry, there is general unrest in the university sector which is resulting in closures to some departments. Students are admitted for entry to courses in Medicine and Law where the supply of qualified graduates far outstrips the demand. If one considers Psychology for example, the Department of Psychology at the University of Padua had 10,000 registered students, and at the University of Rome there are 12,000 students with inadequate provision and academic staff subjected to intolerable pressures. When, after four years' tuition, these students have qualified, the chances of being employed as a psychologist in Italy are minimal. There is no selection and the government awards grants to all.

In the United States the state university has open admission but

> In the 1st year it weeds out many of the incompetent who may number a third or more of those entering class ... A second answer is to side track unpromising students rather than have them fail. This is the 'soft' response: never to dismiss a student but to provide him with an alternative. One form of it in some state universities is the detour to an extension division or a general college, which has the advantage of appearing not very different from the main road. Sometimes 'easy' fields of study, such as education, business administration, and social science are used as alternatives to dismissal (Clark, 1959).

The situation among the students in South African universities is rapidly changing. A report by Yach in 1978 gave evidence to substantiate the hypothesis that when higher education is used as a means of retaining social and economic status, the student has no real motivation or sense of vocation, eventually reaches a crisis of identity and effectively drops out.

The situation in developing countries is very different with fierce competition for places at universities such as the University of Hong Kong and the Chinese University in the new territories. This strong desire for higher education as the gateway to a better job and better standard of living is reflected in a coversation I had a few years ago with the Registrar of the Chinese University. I was enquiring about the 'drop out' rate and was met by non-comprehension. Further explanation elicited the response: 'The only way a student would drop out would be if he unfortunately died during his academic career.' A similar story could be repeated in many developing countries.

The failure and drop-out rate is smallest where the competition for places is keenest and based on selection. How then do we explain the 'drop-out' rate in the UK in a system based on selection, and where 80% of these students come from the advantaged homes of the senior professional classes? These UK students have also experienced careers advice in their sixth form but perhaps the drop-out rate has been so high because, as Abraham Maslow describes:

> In our schools, however, many vocational counsellors have no sense of possible goals of human existence, or even of what is necessary for basic happiness. All that this type of counsellor considers is the need of the society for aeronautical engineers and dentists. No one ever mentions that if you are unhappy with your work, you have lost one of the most important means of self-fulfilment (Maslow, 1975).

Table 1.1: Comparative Data on European University Systems

Country	Open Entry	Selection by examination	Drop-out Rate (%)
France			50
Italy			50
UK			14

Source: France - French Secretariat for State for Universities; Italy - Ministry of Education, Rome; UK - University Grants Committee.

So selection on academic achievement is not the total answer. There are other factors relating to the invidiual to be considered such as:

(a) a sense of identity
(b) the discovery of vocation
(c) motivation
(d) self-confidence
(e) the ability to adapt to change.

The UK universities' attempt to assist the potential 'drop-out' by their network of caring agencies is often seen by other countries as perpetuating the over-protectiveness which is the hallmark of child-rearing in this country. Certainly it is sometimes an onerous task as a university counsellor to work with a first-year student whose development has been almost entirely cerebral.

Unless these personal characteristics can be developed by the schools before the student embarks on higher education, the caring facilities developed in higher education institutions can only partially make good the deficit.

REFERENCES

Clark, B.R. (1959) The Cooling-out Function in Higher Education, 'The American Journal of Sociology', vol. 65, p. 571

Donaldson, M. (1978) 'Children's Minds', Collins, London, p. 89

Edwards, E.G. and Roberts, I.J. (1980) Significance and Limitations of the Robbins Principle in D. Billings (ed.), 'Indicators of Performance', SRHE, Guildford, Surrey

Eell, K., David, A. *et al.* (1951) 'Intelligence and Cultural Differences', University of Chicago, Illinois, as quoted in R. Hess, Controlling Culture Influence in Mental Testing: An Experimental Test, 'Journal of Educational Research', vol. 49 (1955), p. 53

Getzels, J.W. and Jackson, P.W. (1962) 'Creativity and Intelligence', John Wiley and Sons, London and New York, p. 27

Gibbs, G. Morgan, A. and Tayler, L. (1980) 'Understanding Why Students Don't Learn', Study Methods Group Report, no. 5, Institute of Educational Technology, Open University, Milton Keynes, p. 6

Heywood, J. (1971) A Report on Student Wastage, 'University Quarterly', vol. 25, pp. 189-237

Hudson, L. (1972) 'The Cult of the Fact', Jonathan Cape (Paperback), London, p. 35

Hudson, L. (1979) 'Contrary Imagination', Penguin, London

Inhelder, B., Sinclair, H. and Bovet, M. (1974) 'Apprentissage ETV Structures de la Connaissance', Presses Universitaires de France, Paris

Irving, A. and Snape, W.H. (1979) 'Educational Library Use in Secondary Schools', Report No. 5467, The British Library, London

Lewis, C.S. (1955) 'Surprised by Joy', Collins, London, p. 62 (Twentieth edn, 1979)
Liedloff, J. (1975) 'The Continuum Concept', Duckworth, London, p. 49
Lunzer, E. and Gardiner, K. (eds.) (1979) 'The Effective Use of Reading', The Schools Council Report for The Schools Council, Heinemann Educational, London
Malleson, N. (1965) Creativity in Education - An Experiment, 'Universities Quarterly', vol. 20, no. 1, p. 107
Maslow, A. (1975) Title Unquoted as quoted in Pafford, p. 172
Pafford, M. (1977) Inglorious Wordsworth in N. Entwistle and D. Hounsell (eds.), 'How Students Learn', Institute for Research and Development in Post-Compulsory Education, University of Lancaster
Stallisbrass, A. (1977) 'The Self Respecting Child', Pelican, London, p. 217
Turner, L., Renshaw, P. and Sinclair, K.E. (1977) Guided Discovery Learning and Fostering Creativity, 'Sydney Micro Skills Series No. V Handbook', Sydney University Press, Sydney
Winnicott, D.W. (1971) 'Playing and Reality', Tavistock Publications, London, p. 54
Yach, D. (1978) Paper submitted to the Conference on Student Counselling and Guidance, IRTAC, Greece

2 DIFFERENT STYLES OF LEARNING IN HIGHER EDUCATION AND THEIR EFFECT ON THE STUDENTS

EXPECTATION AND REALITY

The scene is any university campus at the beginning of the academic year.

First-year students are being disgorged out of parents' cars - their possessions, a repetitive heap of books, guitars, clothes etc. Having only visited the campus once before, if at all, and probably without any experience of being away from home, each one hopes to be able to organise his time, manage his financial affairs, carry on a well-balanced social life and get involved with his course of studies. He hopes in fact to take on the identity of a student at X University.

Liam Hudson tells of his metamorphosis at Cambridge.

> For such bodies as King's possess astonishing powers of assimilation; they take the talented but insecure, and turn them effortlessly into scholars and gentlemen. As a newcomer, you boggle at the transformation; yet, unwittingly, you are already subject to it. Clever boys from ordinary suburban homes - even more recently, rough young lads from the Commonwealth - are taken up and metamorphosed. Within a few years, they are virtually indistinguishable from the college's Old Etonians (Hudson, 1972).

For students who have experienced a similar initiation at a public or direct grant school the experience is not dissimilar, but outside 'Oxbridge' induction is experienced quite differently.

Traditionally, the 'Freshers' week, which is organised by the Students' Union Executive, is to be experienced passively, and it is only recently at the University of Reading that there has been a change to activities of a more participatory nature. Workshops have been introduced about learning and about the linguistic/cultural interface - where feelings and attitudes, as well as ideas, can be discussed.

At a time when the student's perception of his new academic environment is interacting with the student's perception of self, it may be helpful for him to discuss affective feelings in a cognitive setting. This experience is particularly important for overseas students.

The other unresolved problem is that the induction and administrative procedures are varied and numerous, so that it can be almost a week before the student attends his first lecture and can begin to relate to his chosen department.

By this time the student will have been exhorted to consult a multitude of caring agencies, amongst them the education counsellor, should his transition to higher education be traumatic.

Students have a concern for their fellow men - witness the development of Student Union Welfare Officers, the Junior Common Room Executive Officers in halls of residence, the Students' Samaritan Service 'Night Line'. They befriend the dependent and lonely, and back up the establishment services, such as personal tutors, wardens and university counsellors. Many are crisis intervention services.

However, a significant number of first-year students need long-term help. These are students who are academically able, often from advantaged homes, but who are deficient in one of the individual characteristics which they need to cope with a course in higher education.

It is perhaps interesting at this stage to reflect on the fact that in the United Kingdom at a time when the age of consent and the voting age were lowered to 18 years (Family Reform Act, 1969, operational 1970, and Representation of the Peoples Act, 1969) and students were rejecting the idea of wardens and tutors acting in loco parentis, the National Union of Students (at their annual conference in 1969) passed a resolution 'pressing for Counselling Services to be established in each higher education institution - staffed by fully trained personnel' (Milner, 1974). It is not so strange a development when one realises that a counsellor, who is often a lay psychotherapist, is concerned with bringing about change in the individual so that he can cope with his own life, rather than just dispensing guidance and advice.

The Learners' Subjective Experience of the Learning Environment

If we accept the hypothesis that the university is there for the learner and not the learner for the university, then we must be concerned about how the learner experiences his learning environment. This means not only how he perceives the demands of the curriculum, and the teaching and assessment in each of his departments, but also involves other factors relating to the personality of the learner and the teacher.

The Student's Perception of Himself

All that is known about the individual learner when he arrives at a higher education establishment is

(a) the standard he achieved in his 'A' levels
(b) a report on his interview, if he had one

(c) a list of the interests and hobbies he chose to put on his UCCA form
(d) the headmaster's report that would show only why he should be acceptable to higher education.

Each individual is the result of his own character, and the influence of his previous home and learning environments. How he learns in his new environment will depend not only on his mental but on his personality factors, and on whether he has successfully dealt with the normal development crises as they occur in his life - the ability to cope with authority, to exercise control both physical and later verbal, and to achieve a sense of his own identity, including his sexual and work identity.

It is also important for him to know how his personal and academic life affect one another - if he has a sense of vocation or at least some motivation.

These are factors and there are others which will influence the way that all students will approach their learning experiences, but no systematic testing or assessment takes place at the commencement of their academic career.

THE STUDENT'S PROFILE

The factors that are already 'known' about the student make up his 'intellectual profile'. The medical file transferred to the University Health Centre by the student's previous General Practitioner - coupled with any questions he answers for the college doctor - make up his 'physical profile'. In my opinion it is therefore essential to interview and devise a questionnaire that will establish the student's 'personality profile'. These three profiles could together give a true picture of the student as learner as he embarks on his university career.

Edward Jones, at the University of Buffalo, USA, investigated the personal environmental factors and methods of study of students who were under-achieving - to see whether there were any areas of significance - having matched them for occupation of parents, aptitude tests and homes using non-English language, etc. against superior students. He found that:

> The capable student is more independent; he has been brought up in a house with relatively little discord and he has been encouraged in hobbies which are off the track of athletics or mass receptiveness, as in listening to the radio. He has been an active participator in some interests (Jones, 1955).

Table 2.1: Results of Jones's Research at the University of Buffalo, USA

Areas of Greatest (Significant) Difference	Matched Superior (%)	Probation (%)
Homes reported as tense, disturbed or often not quiet	9	35
His study time has been watched or directed by parents much of the time	32	58
Hobbies (not music or sport) individually run by self	60	35
Home life autocratically dominated by a parent	14	37
Major difficulty with high school study concentration	6	29
Hobbies, none or merely gangs with athletic sports	12	34
Areas of Some Difference		
Above-average worry index	43	25
Definite chores required in home when young	68	51
Kept problems to himself, not discussed in home	17	29
Low self-confidence indications	36	20
Good understanding with father; can talk things over	36	23
Outside work or family demands are disturbing	17	3
Above-average range of fiction books read in past 2 years	9	20

Notes: The student who is under-achieving is asked to report to his academic adviser - this usually accounts for about 5-8 per cent of the student population.

In order to analyse the personal factors it would be necessary to ask certain questions, such as:

(a) To what extent have you learned to be alone in studying and with hobbies?

(b) What would you like to do that is different from others and that you can practise and excel at?
(c) Do you seem to get conflicting ideas from your parents, and, if so, have you tried talking it over with them calmly?

The answers to these questions will indicate whether the student is mature, with a strong sense of his identity.

The Definition of an Advantaged Home

It is clear from the results of this survey that students from professional or semi-professional homes are classified as 'advantaged' because these homes are likely to have

(a) been financially satisfactory
(b) encouraged creativity
(c) exposed the child to the world of books
(d) encouraged him in his school studies.

However these factors only relate to 'social advantage'. The more important factor that can only be discovered by careful interviewing and questioning relates to whether the home is 'emotionally advantaged'. This I would define as a home

(a) without serious discord
(b) that has first nurtured the child
(c) that has helped him to pass comfortably through the normal stages of development
(d) that has allowed him to establish his own identity, including a sense of vocation and self-confidence, before he commences higher education.

By this definition the student from an emotionally and socially advantaged home is most likely to achieve his academic potential - the emotional factor being far the greater in importance.

The Effect of Social Factors

There has been considerable research carried out over the years in schools to show the relationship between academic attainment and social factors such as father's occupation, parents' education, position in family and size of family. In higher education there have been a few but significant studies. Results of research by Hopkins, Malleson and Sarnoff (1958) and Malleson (1959) showed 'that professional workers' children who had been educated at public schools were found to fail more regularly than did students from other backgrounds'. Hopkins, Malleson and Sarnoff (1958) showed that, compared with a control group, a significantly higher percentage of students who failed had parents who had been to university. McCracken (1969) found a similar effect for students with graduate parents.

The chidren of professional people are likely to be influenced by their parents' and teachers' expectation that they will automatically progress to university if they are academically able. If they are likely to fail their qualifying entrance examination (the 'A' level) their parents would arrange private tuition. The alternatives to full-time higher education are hardly ever discussed and it is seldom that the student in such a family has the confidence or the maturity to make a decision that would be in conflict with his parents.

The working-class pupil living in an under-privileged home after experiencing disturbed psychological behaviour is at an educational disadvantage. If he is admitted to higher education he is however probably more intelligent than the student from a professional background. As Entwistle and Hounsell (1977) go on to point out, 'it appears that the students most at risk will be those who have come from professional families'.

The student from a working-class background is usually more independent, mature and motivated than the student from a professional-class family. These personal attributes are needed if the student is to achieve academic success. The working-class student may have a certain narrowness of vocabulary and lack certain social graces, making initial problems of transition, but he is better able to organise his time and get involved with his studies than the student from a professional background. I would suggest that the student from a professional home may be socially but not emotionally advantaged.

Academic staff may wish to dismiss as irrelevant the effect of development factors, or suspect anything that relates to the emotions. They prefer to concentrate on the intellect in which area they are experts. This concept that what a student _is_ affects him as a learner is not always acknowledged.

THE NEED TO ESTABLISH IDENTITY

In his book 'The Adolescent Predicament', John Mitchell points out that:

> Identity questions are especially troublesome for young people because our society has raced beyond the comparative simplicity of a bygone era, construing in its wake a technically complex and essentially impersonal society. The person, _as a person_, is losing significance; for youth this is disastrous because their egocentrism rebels against self negation and their sense of importance thrives upon acknowledgement.
>
> When youth does not have a clear intuition as to what life holds in store for them, they get edgy, bristling with uneasiness. Adults are the same, but are more accustomed to it, and, in some instances, anaesthetised against the reality of it (Mitchell, 1975).

The ever-rising level of graduate unemployment leads to even greater insecurity.

THE STUDENTS' PERCEPTION OF THE LEARNING PROCESS

Paul Ramsden at the University of Lancaster administered a questionnaire to second-year students in six university departments and the School of Independent Studies in 1976, and set out to 'identify the components of the learning environment from the students point of view. Using a combination of interviews and questionnaires it was possible to isolate eight dimenstions which students use to describe the characteristics of the academic departments which affect their learning' (Ramsden, 1979). These are given below:

Dimensions of Learning Environments
1. Relationship with Students - Closeness of lecturer/student relationship; help and understanding shown to students.
2. Commitment to Teaching - Commitment of staff to 'improving teaching' and to teaching students at a level appropriate to their correct understanding.
3. Workload - Pressure placed on students in terms of demands of syllabus and assessment tasks.
4. Formal Teaching Methods - Formality or informality of teaching and learning, e.g. lectures versus individual study.
5. Vocational Relevance - Perceived relevance of course to students' careers.
6. Social Climate - Frequency and quality of academic and social relationship between students.
7. Clear Goals and Standards - Extent to which standards expected of students are clear and unambiguous.
8. Freedom in Learning - Amount of discretion possessed by students in choosing and organising academic work.

Ramsden showed the close relationship between how students perceive their learning environment and the way they set about learning. The most significant factor in that environment is the teacher and the way the work is assessed. If the teacher is enthusiastic and committed the student can develop a deep understanding of fundamentals and a deep-level approach to studying. In considering the dimensions of learning environments six out of the eight variables relate directly to the teacher - his personality and his ability to create an effective learning environment. Martin Covington and Richard Berry feel that 'the process of establishing a "freedom to learn" has an almost exact counterpart in effective child rearing practices'.

> Teachers too must accept their students for what each has achieved thus far, for the potential each brings to the learning place, and for what each can become. Second, like effective parents, teachers must also set limits of conduct and

> establish reasonable standards. Every student is capable of responding to some level of excellence and should be held to these standards. And, finally, there is a matter of allowing each student considerable latitude to pursue these standards at his own rate and on his own terms (Covington and Berry, 1976).

Ramsden goes on to question whether in a competitive society, such teaching is possible. Gardner feels that 'individuals at every level will realise their full potentialities, perform at their best and harbour no resentment towards any other level' (Gardner, 1961). It should be possible for good teachers to value each student as a unique person, thereby helping them to develop a sense of identity and the self-confidence that is a vital factor in academic excellence. It is only then that they will view other students as friends rather than competitors and work co-operatively with them.

THE REALITY OF THE LEARNING EXPERIENCE

Whilst acknowledging the validity of the research, one has to focus on the actual learning experience of a first-year Arts student in a higher education institution set against Ramsden's 'Dimensions of Learning Environment'.

Relationship With Students - Closeness of Lecturer/Student Relationships, Help and Understanding Shown to Students

In practice it is very difficult for first-year Arts students and teachers to develop a close relationship when they are taught in three separate departments, mainly in large formal teaching situations. It is not really until the second year in most institutions that most students experience regular small-group teaching. Science students, with their practical laboratory work, experience more informal staff/student contact from the beginning of their courses. Their syllabus-determined science subject needs far greater contact time than the amorphous lecture and tutorial essay approach of the Arts subjects. If the United Kingdom with her comparatively small staff/student ratio has to admit the impracticability of close staff/student relationships in the first year, the sheer enormity of classes in other countries such as France, Italy, Australia or the USA and the use of closed-circuit television would emphasise the feeling of anonymity even further. In addition, members of academic staff may live in other parts of the city or, in the case of France and Italy, in another city and have no private office in the institution where they can be available to students. The other important factor is the teacher's ability to relate to people in general and students in particular, when he has been engaged all his adult life primarily in private study and research.

Students often fail to realise that whilst the schoolteachers' primary task is teaching, the member of academic staff's primary task is research. His promotion prospects are linked to his research publications and in the present economic climate could even affect his present tenure. Should he neglect this he could be doing a disservice not only to himself but also to his own family.

The evaluation of creative teaching ability is admittedly difficult; few serious attempts have so far been made to work out appropriate criteria. Promotion, however, is not the only form of reward; most teachers place a high value on job satisfaction.

Commitment to Teaching - Commitment of Staff to Improve Teaching and to Teaching Students at a Level Appropriate to Their Current Understanding

In any institution the staff who are committed to teaching are often easily identified. They involve themselves in new lecture courses and follow-up courses, in in-service training and are members of the senate sub-committee on training and other appropriate bodies. They act as mentors and supervisors of new academic staff in their first year's probation and work closely with educational counsellors in presenting learning to learn workshops. The reality is that the committed teacher accounts for only a certain percentage of the academic staff but his influence is out of all proportion to his number.

It is difficult to identify and define the qualities which make a competent teacher, whether in a school or university. The assessment, whether by supervisor or pupil, is too subjective.

An attempt was made in 1951 by Jenson at the University of California, based on the critical incidents techniques used in industrial research by Flanagan (1949). It consisted of reports of 'observable teacher behaviour or activity that may make the difference between success and failure in teaching. The respondents were teachers, administrators and teachers-in-training. A critical incident should describe what some teacher did in a specific situation at a specific time - something the teacher did that seemed markedly effective or ineffective'.

In addition, participants were asked to respond to six situations or questions. The results were analysed and tabulated under the personal, professional and social qualities that contributed to effective and ineffective teaching (see Appendix III, pp. 187-9). A variation of this technique could form a useful contribution to the new lecturers' courses in universities.

Workload - Pressure Placed on Students in Terms of Demands of the Syllabus and Assessment Tasks

The workload of different courses varies tremendously in British universities. This is even found when comparing the courses of different departments in the same faculty. The learner, however, seems to expect this and only discusses this as a problem when his own personal life is taking up a disproportionate amount of his attention. If a heavy workload cannot be avoided it can be made bearable by excellent staff/student relationships.

In assessing the instruction of reading groups conducted by 40 female elementary teachers, Aspy and Roebuck (1972) investigated the relationships between teachers' classroom behaviour and their students' levels at cognitive functioning. They found 'that a teacher's increased positive regard for students is translated into classroom behaviour which elicits higher levels of cognitive functioning from the students'.

Formal Teaching Methods - Formality or Informality of Teaching and Learning, E.g. Lectures Versus Individual Study

Entwistle and Hounsell (1977) have shown that:

> any account of recent innovations in teaching and in higher education encompass a bewildering range of approaches. For example, in the Nuffield Foundation's recent survey, 'The Drift of Change' (Becher et al., 1975), one finds tightly controlled programmes of study, such as the Keller Plan, alongside unstructured small group tutorial techniques. Both of these contrasting approaches are thought to improve student's learning.

Vocational Relevance - Perceived Relevance of Course to Student's Careers

With the exception of certain professional training it is very unlikely that sutdents have a clear vocational objective after graduation, and the increasing unemployment is not likely to improve this situation. In every course there is invariably a period of stagnation or boredom on the part of the student and a long-term goal is the much needed motivation as a means of overcoming this problem.

If the teacher makes analogies relating to the 'real' world outside university, and in particular to the student's possible career, the meaning underlying mathematical obstraction is made clear and learning is enhanced.

Social Climate - Frequency and Quality of Academic and Social Relationships Between Students

Higher education delays maturity by keeping students financially dependent on their parents and secludes them in what they perceive as 'one-class' societies. Academic staff, mature undergraduates and post-graduates may make up at least 30 per cent of the total population of the university, but the student halls of residence and students' unions are almost entirely occupied by 18-22 year-olds.

The student needs to relate to his peer group in order for normal adolescent growth to take place. During his time at university a student lives in groups, in his hall, in his department, in his clubs and societies, and these clubs fulfil his adolescent needs for recognition, belonging, esteem and affiliation. Mitchell (1975) points out that by meeting together in this way: 'Adolescents preserve their fluctuating sense of identity and integrity by forming a unifying alliance against adults in general and impersonal authority in particular.'

If the student is able to function effectively in his peer group he will have a good emotional equilibrium and his learning will be enhanced.

Clear Goals and Standards - Extent to Which Standards Expected of Students Are Clear and Unambiguous

Many students suffer unnecessary anxiety because they have no idea of the academic standards expected of them in the first year. They need adequate feedback at an early stage and departmental tests throughout the first year. They are often confused when they realise that the academic standard of the first-year examinations is not dissimilar to 'A' levels but that the approach is different. This means that having an 'A' level in a subject such as Economics can be a disadvantage.

Freedom in Learning - Amount of Discretion Possessed by Students in Choosing and Organising Academic Work

In most universities in the United Kingdom the students are expected to adhere to the set undergraduate course and final-year project work is the only opportunity to engage in intellectual self-directed exploration.

There have been many instances over the years where the absence of self-directed learning - what is described as 'course-based' rather than 'interest-based' learning - has led many of the most creative students to consult the counselling service about withdrawal. They have then been challenged to stay within the system and work towards changing the system instead of opting out. In case this sounds reactionary I will quote a case history of one such student.

This student was a mature person, with a well-developed sense of his own identity, self-confident, well motivated, and with a clearly perceived vocational goal. We found that he was capable of introducing project work into the first-year curriculum and of persuading the lecturers to make their analogies more relevant, and of improving the relationship between staff and first-year undergraduates - all functions relevant to an improvement in the learning environment. It is accepted that many first-year students in Britain are not motivated to study on their courses. The introduction of project work in the first year would, I suggest, increase their motivation.

NEW STYLES OF LEARNING

During the last decade there has been a variety of new approaches to learning and teaching in further and higher education. For significant learning to take place students need to take responsibility for their own learning, exercising their own choice at subject, method and learning through their less successful attempts. This is shown by Entwistle and Hounsell (1977), Beach (1874) and Powell (1974). Not only is learning maximised but also 'discovering learning methods that fester creativity stimulate a high level of intrinsic motivation in the student' (Brumer, 1960).

Despite this, the unstructured small-group learning experience, as pioneered and described by Rogers (1969), causes much initial anxiety and some criticism. It is not the learning experience that some students want. In describing an experience of such a group Samuel Tenebaum reports that two students wanted the teacher (Rogers) to provide them with a rounded-out piece of merchandise which they could commit to memory and then give back to an examination. They would then have the assurance that they had learnt what they should... For the authoritative person who puts his faith in neatly piled facts, this method, I can believe, can be threatening.

For many overseas students the small-group learning experience provokes anxiety. They do not like to challenge or even question the teacher's authority. Their transition to the concept of self-directed learning is only accomplished by the close and time-consuming support of the academic teacher.

The different approaches to teaching and learning can be reviewed on a continuous spectrum from leaderless discussion groups to programmed learning and related to educational theorists and theory. The method selected needs to be suited to the culture and personality of the student, to the course material, and also to the learning style and personality of the teacher, but so often it is an administrative decision.

Counselling has the same wide spread of methodology from the non-directive counselling of Rogers's humanist approach to the behavioural theory of Skinner (1963). Perhaps teachers, like counsellors, need to develop an approach geared to the needs of the individual learner.

In evaluating methods of instruction and relating them to academic success it is important to realise that the course can often cause problems that are not related to lack of appropriate study skills, emotional or psychological problems, how they perceive the learning environment, lack of maturity or motivation. Students may find, for example, that:

Psychology is a Science not an Arts subject.

Engineering has very little to do with tuning up cars.

Studying Music means also studying more 'humdrum' subjects.

The theoretical level of university Mathematics is too intellectually difficult.

'Professional subjects' can be rather boring.

But unless the relationships between staff and students are very close it is often difficult to realise that lack of academic progress can sometimes be due to intellectual difficulties or difficulties with the course generally.

Table 2.2 shows the different methods of instruction used in higher education.

Table 2.2: Different Approaches to Teaching Showing the Wide Range of Instruction Methods and Associated Learning Theories

Exploratory learning emphasising freedom and self-expression; evaluation retrospective and subjective

Method of Instruction	Associated Learning Theorists	Type of Theory
Leaderless discussion groups Co-operative projects Free background reading	Rogers Maslow	Humanist
Individual project work	Bruner	Cognitive
Tutor-led discussions	Perry	Developmental
Tutor-led seminars	Marton	
Learning cells	Ausubel	Cognitive
Lectures Hand-outs and guided reading Computer-managed learning	Broadbent Lindsay and Norman Pask	Information Processing
Keller-plan courses	Gagne	Task Analysis
Programmed learning Computer-assisted instruction	Skinner	Behaviourist

Tight control of content and method; outcomes measured psychometrically and related to pre-determined specific objectives

Source: Entwistle and Hounsell, 1977

It is important to distinguish between autonomous and self-directed learning.

The main difference between autonomous and self-directed learning, according to Carver and Dickinson (1980), is that autonomy is one of the many possibilities within self-directed learning. Autonomy represents the upper limit of self-directed learning in that all educational choices are made by the learner independently of teacher and institution.

> Autonomy implies self-direction. All learning must take place within some organisational framework of aims, objectives, syllabuses, materials, activities, etc. In autonomous learning that framework is self-selected and self-imposed, whereas in a traditional formal course it is, at least partly, imposed by the establishment. If it is self-imposed, and if the learner implements the plans and discussions without the help from a teacher or an institution, then he is also autonomous.

EXAMPLES

The Independent Studies Degree at Lancaster University

The School of Independent Studies at Lancaster University gives students an opportunity for independent learning. Barbara Senior describes the method by which

> the students work out what subject areas and topics they wish to pursue and also the ways and means by which they will pursue them. Students control the allocation of their time and the pace at which they work. They also decide what learning facilities they will use, and the ways that they will be assessed... Students do not begin to study in an independent manner such as that described above until the second year of their degree course... Students wishing to participate in Independent Studies are encouraged to examine problems relevant to their own experiences and interest (Senior, 1980).

These students must be strongly motivated and reasonably self-confident with a sense of their own identity, if they are to embark on studies that cause them to be socially, and to a certain extent academically, isolated. Their academic tutor would be fulfilling a role similar to that of a supervisor to a post-graduate student. This development at Lancaster is more in line with Maslow's (1977) vision:

> The ideal college would be a kind of educational retreat in which you could try to find yourself; find out what you like and want: what you are and are not good at. People would take various subjects, attend various seminars, not quite sure of where they were going, but moving towards the discovery

of vocation, and once they found it, they could then make good use of technological education. The chief goals of the ideal age, in other words, would be the discovery of identity, and with it the discovery of vocation.

There are now a number of self-directed learning courses being run at colleges and polytechnics.

Flexistudy at the Barnet College, Hertford

This is home study with occasional tutorials and the availability of telephone contacts including telephone conference calls, which link up several students to the tutor for a telephone tutorial. Students study for professional examinations, for certain 'O' level courses, for study skills courses and for Open University preparation courses.

The college which provides the course material, a library and audio-visual centre started this scheme in 1977. It is now considering the possibility of a directed private study link course with the Middlesex Polytechnic.

The Self-directed Part-time Course in Counselling at South-West London College

This course which has evolved over the last five years in intended to give training to practising counsellors. The staff act as a learning resource and students are expected to determine their own study objective.

The Assistant Private Study Course in Quarrying at Doncaster Metropolitan Institute of Higher Education, South Yorkshire

This is an opportunity for working managers to study by correspondence, with weekend tutorials, for the professional examinations of the Institute of Quarrying. It has been running since 1972 and has attracted more than 700 students.

Flexastudy at Redditch College, Hereford and Worcester

Students attend the college and study for professional examinations working from the printed word, with a tutor always available to assist with difficulties and the assessment of written work. This system allows a student to attend in periods of his choice - subject to college vacations and vacancies - and to work at a pace which suits him.

Correspondence Schools

A research project on various aspects of two-way communication in correspondence education was carried out by Baath (1976) at the Department of Education at the University of Lund, Sweden.

The aim was to get a deeper theoretical insight into some of the vital methodological problems of correspondence education and to offer written recommendations.

The research was carried out mainly by means of studies of relevant literature and experiments of different kinds, and through questionnaires which were distributed to 21 institutions in ten European countries. John Baath interpreted the results of the main questionnaire in the light of the theoretical approaches of Moore, Gaff and Peters.

> Moore's (1975, 1976, 1977) concept of correspondence education is as a form of independent study with students characterised by autonomy.
> Gaff (1970) views correspondence education as essentially directed and controlled self teaching.
> Peters (1971, 1973) sees correspondence education as an industrialised form of teaching.
> Most of the schools allow their students considerable freedom and that, plus the capacity of most postal students-tutor dialogue and the low submission rate of assessments means that this method of study is suited to fairly autonomous students (Baath, 1976).

In contrast some institutions introduce compulsory tutorials - which could be irksome to highly independent learners. As one might have expected, the traditional attitude of the colleges led to a complete resistance to any suggestions that tutors could be replaced by multiple-choice questions and computers. It is clear, however, that the researchers and the institutions focused on the academic teaching role of the tutors and not on the academic/personal role that is so vital as a resource for independent learners. It is not the frequency of contact but the fact that the resourse exists that is the important factor.

Correspondence study, particularly when linked with other independent study methods, is a low-cost solution to continuing education.

The Open University

The Open University which opened in January 1971 derived from (a) the educational television experiments conducted by the National Extension College, London and the University of Nottingham, and (b) the massive study of the potentiality of degrees and certificates through correspondence study conducted under direction of E.G. Wedell and the University of Manchester.

The Open University employs a co-ordinated mixture of instructional techniques including:

(a) Television and radio programmes
(b) Correspondence and home study programme

(c) Regular meetings with tutors in the local study centres or by telephone-linked tutorials on self-help tutorial groups
(d) Short-duration summer schools.

The clientele are normally aged over 21 in full-time employment or working at home. No formal requirement is necessary for entry as a student. Although students work at home at their own pace the learning is 'course' not 'person' orientated, and the emphasis has been not 'on the individual student's educational priorities but on those of the course team' (Cross and Ransome, 1977).

There has now been an experimental move towards more genuinely independent study, by the introduction in 1979 of a:

> fourth-level full credit course in the Faculty of Technology, consisting solely of a project to be carried out by the student... Students who have progressed this far in the Open University have in the main shown their maturity in study (Spear, 1977).

These projects are similar to the final-year projects of university students and can really be equated with autonomous learning. The aim however is 'not to prepare a student for a Ph.D. and further research' but to fit him for the world of work where 'design and decision-making permeate the whole of technology'.

Developments in Other Countries

'The unique and disquieting feature in the correspondence educating process is that the learner is at a distance from the teacher for much, most or even all of the time' (Sims, 1977).

Many other countries apply Open University methods to distance education and adapt it to their culture. This has been a two-way benefit. As De Rolph (1972) pointed out when discussing the setting up of the North American Open University (NAOU): 'It is a means for the British to underwrite the costs of production of materials. It is felt that the American Universities or higher education systems will probably join HAOU to utilise these expensive materials.'

The Open University Centre for International Co-operation of Services (OUCICS) provided: (a) consultations abroad - for institutions in Kenya, Columbia, Venezuela, Pakistan, Iran and Saudi Arabia, and many others; (b) a regular study programme comprising seven courses on various aspects of distance learning; and (c) a documentation centre to collect and codify distance learning throughout the world.

The vice-chancellor reported in 1979 that the centre had to close for lack of funds. The vice-chancellor's office assumed responsibility for international activity. The Open University works more closely with the British Council who administers overseas visits and consultations on their behalf and maintains the close links with North American countries, but in practical terms the Open University responds to individual overseas visits but no longer runs courses in distance learning. It has, however, been possible for the documentation centre to continue.

Courses of independent study have been established in many other countries. As an example, let us look at courses in colleges in the USA. Courses of independent study and individualised education programmes were established 'in some college curricula extension courses, and the US Armed Forces Institute, which provided courses for 130,000 service men' (Korst, 1977). Arising from 'a workshop on individualised medical education which was held in 1973 by the Association of American Medical Colleges the University of Wisconsin Medical School set up an independent study programme for an additional 30 students in the class admitted in 1973'. The course has now been accepted as a continuing part of the medical school curriculum and provides a more flexible track for some students.

This course is important in that it provides an opportunity for independent study within a formal system, thus giving the student an element of choice.

Research

Holmberg (1980) reports the research carried out by Glatter and Wedell (1971) in a questionnaire sent to 20,000 students where the response rate was 60 per cent. More than 50 per cent answered that they had chosen correspondence study because it 'makes it easier for you to work at your own pace than if you went to class!' More than one-third of the respondents stated that they preferred studying on their own to 'studying in a class with people'.

In Flinck's (1979) study of 4,000 students of European distance study institutions the three most important reasons why students examined had chosen correspondence education were:

83% - the freedom offered to pace their study as they wanted.
73% - the support in planning the study and assessing progress provided (in relation to completely unaided study).
63% - 'I like working by myself'.

These adult students are strongly motivated; have the confidence to cope with self-directed learning and often have a well-developed work identity.

In a study of Open University students Holmberg (1980) found that '75% declared that they studied in order to qualify for promotion'.

Perhaps the long-term unemployed would benefit by studying for an Open University degree. The interaction between the tutor and the Open University student is of great importance in itself. Their relationship should focus on facilitating learning and not on that teaching which only reinforces the printed word and audio instruction. 'Normally personal consultations along the lines of Oxbridge tutorials and discussion groups organised or formed spontaneously, appear to be the most valuable supporting function of face to face sessions' (Holmberg, 1980). Supervision, however, must be seen by the students to be effective. As Welsh's (1979) monograph on 'The First Year of Post Graduate Research Study' shows, the supervisor and student may see the role of supervisor quite differently, which leads to dissatisfaction.

HOW IMAGINATIVE TEACHING IS REWARDED

A greater concern for the quality of teaching, and hence a more informed reliance on the available support services (such as tutors for university teaching methods, educational counsellors and media services), is likely to be stimulated if some overt recognition for imaginative teaching effort is accorded to academics by their departments and by the universities and polytechnics as a whole.

Greenway and Harding (1978) in their recent book on 'The Growth of Policies for Staff Development' discuss how staff are viewed by their institutions at the present time.

> Financial constraint has required an approach to controlled decision-making which was unthought of and unthinkable even as recently as five years ago. Resources used to be so abundant that they were not referred to by that all-embracing name. It would have been somewhat unseemly to have referred to staff - who are, after all, people - as 'resources'. How different in 1977! Staff are resources because they cost money: it is therefore important that they be chosen carefully and nurtured well in order that maximum benefit may be gained from them. But even though staff may be regarded, when necessary, as units in a barter type of economy (one lecturer's post could be exchanged for six pieces of equipment or so many square metres of space) they have a remarkably resilient habit of remaining individual people with feelings, skills, motivations, anxieties and aspirations. Since 1971 staff development has been focussing more and more on teachers as people and recognising the symbiotic relationship between the institution's support for the individual and the individuals' support for the institution.

The present financial crises in universities which makes teachers feel like dispensable pawns, is a destructive process.

It will now be becoming clear to the reader that the teacher, his personality, expertise and attitude is crucial to the learning process. The teacher is not just another resource, his role is that of stimulating the student in teaching the student how to develop and enrich his own potential for learning by learning to learn. This means that his true value as a resource is not just the impact of the moment but the ever-widening influence of a pebble tossed into the ocean.

REFERENCES

Aspy, D.N. and Roebuck, F.N. (1972) An Investigation of the Relationship between Students' Levels of Cognitive Functioning and the Teacher's Classroom Behaviour, 'Journal of Educational Research', vol. 65, no. 8, p. 365

Baath, J. (1976) Postal Contacts and Some Other Means of Two-way Communication: Practice and Opinions on a Number of European Correspondence Schools, Dept of Education, University of Lund, Sweden

Barnet College of Further Education (1978 and 1980) Flexistudy: A Manual for Local Colleges, 'National College Extension Reports', series 2, no. 4

Beach, L.R. (1974) Self-directed Student Groups and Culture Learning, Higher Education Bulletin, no. 3, pp. 187-200, as quoted in Entwistle and Hounsell, pp. 163-71

Becher, A., et al. (1975) The Drift of Change, An interim report of the Group for Research and Innovation in Higher Education, The Nuffield Foundation, London, as quoted in Entwistle and Hounsell, London

Bruner, J. (1960) 'The Process of Education', Harvard University Press as quoted in R.C. Turner, P. Renshaw and K.E. Sinclair, Guided Discovery Learning and Fostering Creativity Series 1-5, Sydney University Press, Sydney, 1977

Carver, D. and Dickinson, L. (1980) 'Autonomy: Self Direction and the Affective Domain in Language Learning in Schools', Proceedings of the Scottish Centre for Education Overseas, Moray House, College of Education, Edinburgh, Ch. 3, pp. 1-2

Covington, M.C. and Berry, R.G. (1976) 'Self Worth and School Learning', Holt, Rinehart and Winston, New York, p. 145

Cross, N. and Ransome, S. (1977) Survey of a Project Based Course, 'Teaching at a Distance', no. 8, pp. 59-61

De Rolph, J. (1972) The Open University - Tomorrow's Higher Education, 'Adult Leadership' (March), vol. 20, part 9, p. 330

Entwistle, N.J. and Hounsell, D. (1977) How Students Learn: Implications for Teaching in Higher Education in N. Entwistle and D. Hounsell (eds.), 'How Students Learn', Institute for Research and Development in Post-Compulsory Education, University of Lancaster, pp. 175 and 179

Entwistle, N.J. and Wilson, J.D. (1977) 'Degrees of Excellence: the Academic Achievement Game', Hodder and Stoughton, Sevenoaks, Kent, p. 24

Flanagan, J.C. (1949) 'Critical Requirements for Research Personnel', American Institute for Research, Pittsburgh, as quoted in Jensen
Flinck, R. (1979) The Research Project on Two-way Communication in Distance Education: In Our View, EHSC working document, Liberhermods, Malmo, Sweden, as quoted in Holmburg
Gardner, J.W. (1961) 'Can We be Equal and Excellent Too?', Harper and Row, New York, p. 33
Glatter, R. and Wedell, E.G. (1971) 'Study by Correspondence: An Enquiry into Correspondence Study for Examination for Degrees and Other Advanced Qualifications', Longman, London, as quoted in Holmburg
Graff, K. (1970) Voraussetzungen erfolgriechen Fernstudiums, Dorgestellt am Beispiel des schwedischen Fernstudiensystems, Lüdke Hamburg
Greenway, H. and Harding, A. (1978) 'The Growth of Policies for Staff Development', SRHE, Guildford, Surrey
Holmburg, B. (1980) Aspects of Distance Education, 'Comparative Education', vol. 16 (June) no. 2, pp. 108 and 112
Hokins, J., Malleson, N. and Sarnoff, I. (1958) Some Non-Intellectual Correlates of Success and Failure among University Students, 'British Journal of Educational Psychology', vol. 28, pp. 25-36
Hudson, L. (1972) 'The Cult of the Fact', Jonathan Cape, London, p. 50
Jenson, A. (1951) Determining Critical Requirements for Teachers, 'Journal of Experimental Education', University of California, LA, vol. XX, pp. 79-85
Jones, E. (1955) The Probation Student: What He Is Like And What Can Be Done, 'Journal of Educational Research', vol. 49
Korst, D.R. (1977) The Independent Study Programme at the University of Wisconsin Medical School, 'Journal of Medical Education', vol. 52 (May), p. 405
Mackenzie, O. and Christensen, E.L. (eds.), 'The Changing World of Correspondence Study', Pennsylvania State University Press
McCracken, D. (1969) University Student Performance (The Changing Patterns Over Medical Social Factors Over Three Years and Their Correlations With Examination Results), Report of the Student Health Department, University of Leeds
Malleson, N. (1959) University Students 1953, 1 - Profile, 'University Quarterly, vol. 13, pp. 287-98
Maslow, A. (1977) Goals and Implications of Humanistic Education in Entwistle and Hounsell, p. 162
Milner, P. (1974) 'Counselling in Education', J.M. Dent and Sons Ltd, London, as quoted in J.E. Wright, An Approach to Psycho-sexual Counselling, 'International Journal for the Advancement of Counselling', Martinus Nijhoff, The Hague, vol. 3, no. 2
Mitchell, J.J. (1975) 'The Adolescent Predicament', Holt, Rinehart and Winston, Toronto, pp. 17, 149-53

Moore, M.G. (1975) Cognitive Style and Telemathic (Distance) Teaching, 'ICCE Newsletter', p. 5

Moore, M.G. (1976) Investigation of the Interaction between the Cognitive Style of Field Independence and Attitudes to Independent Study Among Adult Learners Who Use Correspondence Study and Self-directed Independent Study, Dissertation, the University of Wisconsin

Peters, O. (1971) Theoretical Aspects of Correspondence Instructions in Mackenzie and Christensen

Peters, O. (1973) Die diaktische Struktur des Fernunterrichts. Untersuchungen zu einer industrialisierten Form des Lehrens und Lernens, 'Tübinger Beitrage zum Fernstudium', vol. 7, Beltz, Weinheim

Powell, J.P. (1974) Small Group Teaching Methods in Higher Education, 'Educational Research', vol. 16, no. 3, as quoted in Entwistle and Hounsell, p. 179

Ramsden, P. (1979) Student Learning and Perceptions of the Academic Environment, 'Higher Education', vol. 8, pp. 411-27

Rogers, C. (1969) 'Freedom to Learn - A View of What Education Might Become', Columbus Ohio, Melville

Senior, B. (1980) The Open University Degree and Independent Studies, 'Teaching at a Distance', The Open University, vol. 8

Sims, R.S. (1977) 'An Inquiry into Correspondence Education Processes, Policies, Principles and Practices in Correspondence Education', CICCE-UNESCO, unpublished

Skinner, B.F. (1963) 'Behaviourism at Fifty', 'Science', vol. 140, pp. 951-8

Spear, R. (1977) A Full Credit Project in Technology, 'Teaching at a Distance', no. 8 (March), pp. 54-8

Welsh, J. (1979) 'The First Year of Post Graduate Research Study', SRHE, Guildford, Surrey

3 THE CRITERIA FOR 'LEARNING TO LEARN'

Most of the research carried out has concentrated on the learning strategies that should be adopted in order to be competent in certain learning activities such as 'note-taking'. Recently it has been emphasised that the student should adopt a different learning strategy to master different courses or even parts of a course, but the aim has always been success in the examination and in the obtaining of a degree. It presupposes that this alone is the aim of every student at university.

Since 1810, there has been a proliferation in Britain of study skills manuals, usually describing the learning strategies that the author and his colleagues have themselves found effective. In Britain between 1900 and 1924 15 manuals were published, the first one being 'The Improvement of the Mind' by Isaac Watts, published in 1810. The study skills strategies described have always focused on the text, the lecture, the course, the examination - hardly ever on the Learner.

Exceptions are rare pearls. One is the book 'On Becoming an Educated Person' by Voeks (1979) which spends the first 33 pages discussing 'Why Go to College?'. It considers not institutions but the individual student and shows how he can be in control of his own personal development. Voeks says that: 'Universities and colleges furnish opportunities... no college or university can give one education... Education is an on-going process and the result of that process, built day by day through the way you live.'

It has been recognised that, in order to develop as a self-directed learner, the student needs to have a sense of his own identity, from which comes a sense of vocation and self-confidence, and the same can be said for 'learning to learn'.

A student who has reached this stage of personal development has the confidence to develop a learning strategy closely related to why he is carrying out a particular learning activity at a particular time and to consider the broader issues of why he is at university and what his purpose is in studying a particular course.

A mature, confident student will be able to look self-critically at his learning strategies - to experiment with alternatives and to adopt flexible learning strategies which may be suitable for particular courses, or even parts of courses. If he lacks this maturity and self-confidence he may cling rigidly to an obsolete learning style, even if he knows that it is ineffective.

THE INTELLECTUAL DEVELOPMENT OF THE STUDENT

Each student on entering university has a unique intellectual, physical and personality profile at a particular stage of development which determines the way he perceives his environment. This is important in an academic setting as it determines the way he experiences and records his lectures, tutorials etc., each student utilising an individual and personalised structure.

Utilising Perry's (1970) cognitive framework, this intellectual development of the student's perception of his learning environment can be analysed in the following ways.

Position 1 - Basic Duality

The child at this basic stage divides his world into polar spheres of right and wrong knowledge, conduct and values, in particular segregating the secure familiar world from the frightening chaos outside. This personal world of the child is extended into the intellectual environment; the child learns morality by rote as a set of non-related responses and procedures dictated by an external authority.

Position 2 - Multiplicity Pre-legitimate

From the simple black and white world of Position 1, the student moves into the more uncertain stage of Position 2 where he starts to question and have his own ideas, thus producing a more complex situation. This may occur as a radical rejection of all the authoritative conditioning of his youth; however, such a violent step often leaves the student awash and isolated with no framework to stimulate further growth. The more fertile route is where the student accepts authority per se but agrees to differ in some areas as he begins to discover and assert his own identity.

Position 3 - Multiplicity Subordinate

Having begun to evaluate his own ideas the student again presents the problem of moral duality to reduce the anxiety-producing uncertainty. However, he is faced with the problem that even authority does not know the true answer and his anxiety is exaggerated rather than reduced.

Position 4 - Multiplicity Correlate

The answer which the student advocates again depends on the balance between radical opposition to authority and liberal adherence to a situation similar to Position 2.

Position 5 - Relativism Correlate, Competing or Diffuse

In order to develop further, the student needs to substitute the violent dualism of his views for the previously subordinate subtle relativism. This relativism becomes the major context within which dualism stands as a special case.

Position 6 - Commitment Foreseen

By establishing relativism as the major context one is faced with an infinite choice of knowledge and values. Since Erikson (1959) sees the concepts of 'I know' and 'I value' as contingent and their continuity as vital to one's sense of identity, relativism embodies these concepts with such uncertainty that the student finds his identity intolerably threatened.

Positions 7, 8 and 9 - Developing Commitment

In the next stages the student's development gradually stabilises as he develops a fuller identity and sense of responsibility for that identity (Position 7). The university context provides the stages for the move from Position 1, the development from hard dualism to reflective individualism - 'can he claim to be who he thinks he is? He must if he is to live heartily, but with how much certainty?' (Perry, 1970).

He must have the strength to have faith in himself. Main (1980) in referring to Perry's stages of cognitive development says that

> When a student reaches the third stage of relativism he realises that knowing and valuing are both relative in time and circumstance. The individual is faced with the responsibility for change and commitment: a student who accepts this third level generally shows a strong sense of his own identity and worth. He is in command of his own learning.

Conversely from my own experience I have found that when a student presents to me or to his tutor a 'study skills' problem, it may be found that this is deeply rooted in a crisis of identity and confidence.

STUDY SKILLS IN THE SIXTH FORM AND STUDY SKILLS AT COLLEGE

The varied learning strategies needed to cope with differing courses in higher education are very different from the skills required to cope with 'A' level studies; hence even the 'successful' school learner needs to re-examine his learning strategies when he first arrives at university.

The skills required for the different courses vary enormously. There is more change for the Arts student in the skills he needs to research his material and write creatively. There is a very high content of mathematics in all Science and Engineering courses and these still require students to memorise - by rote - the new equations and symbols. The skill that is common to all courses is that of organising one's time. In the absence of this the student attempts to study - for better or worse - and then becomes entrenched in his own effective or non-effective methods. In all probability the transition to university and the absence of close staff/student contact and feedback will result in the new student clinging to his previous learning methods - whether or not it suits the situation. Gibbs (1980) notes that:

> We have had students who know that the way they take notes is ridiculous and useless, but who lack the confidence to abandon their note taking technique for another which they know will be more useful. In our experience, the less happy and secure a student is in his existing habits, the less likely he is to abandon them in the hope that some new technique will improve things.

THE DEVELOPMENT OF THE STUDENT AT UNIVERSITY

Two major longitudinal studies in this area were conducted in British universities in recent years, examining the 'changes in students' explorations over the course of their studies' (Gibbs, Morgan and Tayler, 1980). Beatty (1978), for example, interviewed students over the three years of their courses about why they were studying, in order to glean an understanding of their study habits and use of reference facilities. From her work emerged the notion of a 'study contract', comprising the student's aims and the methodology of achieving these aims whilst at university, which the student makes on entering university.

> Students come to University with ideas of what it will be like and with aims at various stages of development. Through interaction with others and experience of the University and course, they develop a study stragegy, tentative at first, which is consistent with their aims and self-identity. This organisation of attitude and study patterns soon affects educational outcomes in the form of essay marks but also in knowledge gained etc. This provides the student with objective and subjective feedback on the effectiveness of their strategy and allows them to reinterpret and perhaps redesign the Study Contract by changing strategy or perhaps aims in order to be consistent once more (Beatty, 1978).

The problem with this model is that is presupposes that the student receives feedback so that he can reassess his learning strategy and that he has the self-confidence to cope with the uncertainty of changing such methods. In the first part of the

Christmas term the feedback is often negligible. Second-year students were able to recognise and reappraise the feelings they had expressed when they were shown their last year's transcripts, and, most importantly, they could explain how things had changed and how they now saw them.

These approaches were themselves varied as the student moved through his degree course rather than being 'static mental characteristics' (Mathias, 1978). During the progress of their university career, students can change several times between course of interest focus - this depends on their position in terms of their personal development and how they perceive their learning environment at any moment in time.

The Influence of Academic Staff

The previous chapter showed how the academic staff can affect the students' attitude towards learning a particular course. The teacher who encourages the students to develop a learning strategy appropriate to their own purpose and personality is the teacher who can allow his students to align with a rival school of thought in his discipline.

Hudson (1972) feels that his intellectual training amounted to indoctrination. 'For affection, respect and fear of being bullied or rejected are all powerful agents of persuasion. If a teacher successfully transmits his own beliefs about the limits of legitimate inquiry, he is, de facto, an indoctrinator'.

There are, however, teachers who by the nature of their personality find it easy to be a learning resource for their students - to offer them their own way of thinking, their special experience and knowledge, their accessibility to special services or materials, and yet who allow the students to refuse or accept the offers as they see fit.

The Criteria for Academic Success

One of the most persuasive reasons for students to develop effective learning strategies is that research has shown that it is a major factor in academic success.

Yi-Guang Lin and McKeachie (1970) studied the academic performances of extremely anxious students at the University of Michigan. They found that: 'Student study habits contributed to academic achievement independently of college aptitude, particularly for women.' Lavin (1965) observes that: 'In field investigations, such as research on academic achievement, it is, of course, always difficult to establish casual interpretations because it is not possible to control extraneous factors with the precision often attainable in the laboratory setting.' On the other hand, in discussing the research of Masters and Johnson, Farber (1966) 'condemns the artificiality of the laboratory setting'.

Universities would like to be able to predict the characteristics of the successful students. Perhaps the word 'successful' and 'unsuccessful' need amplifying. The student who obtains a 2.2 class degree but who expected a 2.1 may feel unsuccessful but in the eyes of the institution is still a success. And how do we classify a student who gets a 2.1 degree but who is totally disenchanted with the course and intends to seek employment totally outside his discipline? Certainly the institution would again view him as a success.

In an enquiry by Entwistle and Wilson in 1977:

> The subjects used were the total intake to the Arts (N = 639) and Science (N = 376) Faculties at Aberdeen University. Three sets of data were collected; firstly for nearly all the students their actual and potential academic records were compiled as background information, the latter using headmasters' estimates. 61% (N = 624) were tested on variables of ability, personality and attitudes on entering their first year at University. Finally the same students were tested in their third year using a postal questionnaire. The latter enabled data on their degree performance related to personality, motivation and study methods to be collated.
>
> The two key conclusions show that
>
> (a) from the analysis of first year students, the rating of 'lack of mature outlook' accounts for half of the degree failures of the sample data
>
> (b) the third year questionnaire showed that high scores on the scales of motivation and study methods were associated with good degree performance for both sexes, with the result on motivation for women just failing to reach significance.

Using the above study as a pilot, Entwistle (1977) performed a larger follow-up study of the Lancaster area, encompassing seven universities plus colleges of education and polytechnics. Using a similar compendium of tests for first and third years (admission date of first year being 1968) ' it was possible to examine changes in personality, attitudes and values during higher education as well as to detect the factors which were related to degree results in six contracting areas of study'. The analysis of these results provides significant variables which, where the positive loading is high, may be used as 'indicators of success'. The findings support several previous investigations illustrating consistent and usually statistically significant correlations between degree results and such factors as 'A' level grades, study methods, hours worked (i.e. study skills factors), as well as introversion, motivation and self-ratings of 'hard working' and 'sociability' (i.e. personality factors).

Most of the research has been undertaken by educational researchers so that it is interesting to read a review of the educational researches by a team of student health doctors who reported that: 'In a wide ranging review of the literature relating to college failure and spanning a twenty five year period, Sexton found many inconsistencies' (Crown, Lucas and Supramaniam, 1973). Sexton (1965) concluded however 'that one trait could be easily identified, immaturity in attitude, operation and outlook. This immaturity manifested itself either in over-demanding dependence on parents or others, or as rebellion against authority and resistence to study.'

Figure 3.1

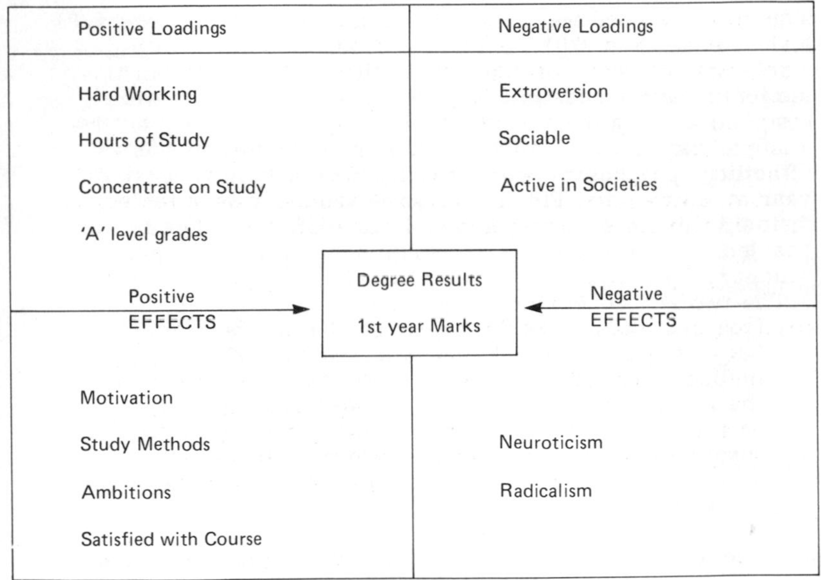

Source: Entwistle and Wilson, 1977.

It is difficult in research studies to define 'good' study methods. Do we mean suitable learning strategies for a particular course or do we mean learning strategies that consider the personality and motivation of the learner, or can we devise a strategy that takes both factors into account? We know that with the exception of 'organisation of time' it is not possible to 'teach' particular learning strategies that will ensure academic success in all disciplines. We can, however, help students to develop a self-questioning approach to their own learning tasks.

DIMENSIONS OF LEARNING TO LEARN

The dimensions that students use to describe the characteristics which affect their 'learning to learn' are the same as those described for learning:

(a) close staff/student relationships;
(b) staff prepared to commit themselves to helping students to find effective study skills;
(c) staff prepared to discover the skills needed for particular courses and discuss them with students;
(d) students introduced to a wide variety of study-skill resources, workshops, discussions, audio-visual methods in learning to learn resource centres, individual help, study manuals;
(e) the relevance of learning to learn in academic courses to the relevance of learning how to develop learning strategies in all new experiences in life generally; and
(f) students being encouraged to develop their social relationships with other students on the same course, to discuss their approaches to the learning tasks of the courses. As one is aware, student 'self-help' learning groups are a possible learning strategy to adapt for revision.

The Important of Motivation

Freeman (1972) tells us that:

> Universities have always placed great emphasis on learning for learning's sake - for them being interested in the subject is sufficient motivation. But most of us have a more mundane reason for study. Quite often the reason is to get a better job. It is one of the most powerful draws for keeping you at your studies!!

Some students find it hard to study because of absence of short- or long-term goals. A student may have developed a strong sense of vocation or at least a work identity before starting his course in higher education. If not, it may be beneficial for him to seek vocational counselling during the first year.

Deese and Deese (1979) in their book 'How to Study' have set out a questionnaire on 'Motivation for College'. The questionnaire is designed to help students think about motivation and give them some insights into it. The instructions state:

> Read carefully through each group of items; then mark them in importance by using 1 for the phrase that best applies to you, 2 for the phrase that applies next best and so on -
>
> I I came (or will come) to college
> - because I know what I want to be and college preparation is necessary for it
> - my father wanted me to, even though I didn't
> - I thought it would be a lot of fun
> - I wanted to gain a better knowledge and understanding of the world I live in

- many of my friends did and I wanted to be with them
- I wanted to get away from home
- I am particularly interested in athletics and student activities
- a college degree seems indispensable in this day and age
- I like to study and am particularly interested in certain subjects

II I wanted to make grades that are good enough to
- meet degree requirements
- let me participate in extra curricular activities
- put me in the honours list and give me special recognition
- make an outstanding record in college

III My motivation for making grades is to
- prove to myself that I am learning something
- secure a good job recommendation
- please my family
- do better than my competitors
- live up to my reputation of being a good student
- be respected by my teachers

IV I sometimes didn't study when I started because
- I was upset about my personal problems
- I simply can't get interested in entire subjects
- I am too involved in extra curricular activities
- I am bothered by illness and poor health
- I get distracted by things going on around me
- I tend to keep putting off work
- I am easily tempted to do more interesting things

The questionnaire is intended as an 'awareness raising' strategy and not intended for interpretation by a teacher or counsellor. It could however be used as a basis for a discussion group with new or intending students.

Wankowski (1973), in his study of the factors leading to success and failure in a random sample of Birmingham University students who entered in 1964-5 and completed their studies by 1970, found that:

> Flexibility in adopting new ways of dealing with academic learning is positively correlated with goal orientation (motivation) in the male population. In male and female populations flexibility scores increasingly consistently with the level of degree achievement, suggesting that high achievers tend to be less rigid in their attitude to tuition and more ready to change.

'Motivation can have a strong biasing effect on measurement of I.Q. higher than a certain level' (Hudson, 1979).

There are many different ways for students to become motivated to do a particular course. It might be

(a) as a result of a series of discussions with a careers adviser in the sixth form at school
(b) modelling on a parent, for example the tradition of medicine or music in families
(c) the translation of a 'peak experience' into a career - for example, the boy who spends his time 'studying' wild life in ponds might take a degree in marine biology
(d) becoming infected with the enthusiasm of a teacher or inspired by an autobiography.

This later influence is especially important in young children where 'likings for subjects of study are often derived from likings for people who teach these subjects' (Mace, 1973).

This is actually seen in higher education where the first-year student, still fairly dependent and in need of close staff/student relationships and feedback, is contemplating withdrawal from the university. If he seeks help from the counselling service, the counsellor can help him to establish a close tutor/tutee relationship which may result in the student becoming committed to his course.

When discussing the student's motivation for his intellectual studies we must not forget the personal and physical concerns. As Borgen and Seaborne (1969) point out:

> Motivated states do not occur singly, but co-exist and interact, they also have different time scales of operation. The condition that keeps a student at work to gain a degree exists alongside, now a need for food, now an urge to see a film, or to take exercise.

Fear as a Motivating Factor

For many students fear plays a central part in motivating a student's approach to his studies:

(a) fear of facing a seminar unprepared
(b) fear of facing his tutor with an overdue essay uncompleted
(c) fear of failing his examinations, which keeps him revising on a sunny day.

Fear can be, according to Cofer and Appley (1968), 'an acquired drive', but they emphasise that 'This state appears to be less a drive than an emotional response elicited in specific situations.'

Mowrer (1939) made an important contribution to the theoretical understanding and study of fear as an acquired drive. He believed that 'Just as pain can be used as a drive to procedure learning through escape, so anxiety can be used to produce learning. Hence these anxiety-reducing responses are learned by the ordinary re-inforcement principle of tension reduction.'

In discussing the applicability of learning 'theories' and

learning principles, Hilgard and Bower (1975) postulate that the

> Anxiety level of the individual learner may determine whether certain kinds of encouragement to learn will have beneficial or detrimental effects. The generalisation appears justified that, with some kinds of tasks, high anxiety learners perform better if not reminded of how well (or poorly) they are doing, while low anxiety learners do better if they are interrupted with comments on their progress.

This is directly related to attempts to assist learners in the development of more effective learning strategies. It is often the highly anxious student who comes for help with 'study problems' or who attends voluntary 'learning to learn' workshops run by educationalists or counsellors. We should, however, be concerning ourselves with how we can arouse the low anxiety learners to a greater awareness, so that they can assess their learning strategies critically and experiment with alternatives.

To be effective this fear or anxiety-arousal strategy must be carried out by the teaching staff whose academic authority will in itself be a significant factor. The staff must, of course, have a 'personality profile' of the individual student and be aware of the existing anxiety level of the student.

In arousing fear and anxiety care has to be taken not to increase the level of highly anxious students since the reduction of anxiety in this type of student is necessary in the development of more effective study methods. An obvious example is the student who suffers from extreme examination anxiety (who may even be 'examphobic') to such an extent that he finds it impossible to revise.

The Resistance to Change

Many 'low-anxiety' learners have accepted their academic performance level and 'accommodated' to it. There is often an absence of motivation and risk avoidance.

I would suggest that there is a clear analogy between this situation in higher education in developed countries and the villages in the Third World. The rural poor have often, as Galbraith (1980) so eloquently describes, 'accepted their situation and accommodated to it'. The work of rural development has shown 'the most effective work of the agencies was with a minority of farmers, and, it was noticed, not without some sense of guilt and failure, that these were usually the most progressive and prosperous, the ones who seemed least to need help'.

In running 'learning to learn' workshops across the disciplines, or in individual departments, I have often found that the audience consists of the students who are the over-anxious, high achievers, often with reasonably good study habits - the ones who seemed to need the help least.

THE LINK BETWEEN CONTENT AND SKILLS

Gibbs (1980) makes a plea for the process of studying and the subject matter studied to be more closely integrated. He states that 'Courses put on by Counselling Centres are attended by the over-anxious and highly efficient and are perceived by many students with suspicion, or simply ignored as irrelevant.' Galbraith (1980), however, states that the primary aim of overseas aid is to 'combat accommodation - to seek to enlarge the number of people who, resisting or refusing accommodation, are motivated to escape the equilibrium of poverty'. The secondary aim is to facilitate that escape.

In higher education teachers are seeking to find ways to enlarge the number of students who are motivated to reject accommodation and to escape the equilibrium of poverty. Before this seems too fanciful or even blasphemous to speak of the hungry millions in the same breath as well-fed university students - the word 'hunger' relates to men's minds as well as their stomachs.

To counter 'accommodation' in any setting is never easy. 'Why stir people up and cause discontent?' The agricultural extension worker cannot guarantee the rural poor a better life. The university teacher cannot guarantee the student a better learning style and academic performance. The methods by which 'accommodation' is broken are - according to Galbraith - 'trauma and education'. In the past it has often been by trauma - famine, military degradation, pogroms, forced expulsion of conforming or non-conforming ethnic or religious groups. None of these means recommends itself as a civilised procedure. What remains is education.

So often for the student it is the trauma - the possibility of examination failure (the 'forced expulsion' Galbraith refers to) - that makes him decide to look critically at his learning methods. He often hopes that, in a little over four weeks, he can develop new and effective learning strategies that will guarantee immediate examination success - not appreciating that when he first adopts new learning methods he may initially do less well in that area of study.

We, the administrators, the teachers, the counsellors, are left, like Galbraith, with 'education'; but in the same way as the agricultural extension worker and the government officials responsible for overseas aid we resist the new educational methods and cling to the accepted, though ineffectual methods of giving advice to those who respond - those who need it least.

In the higher education institution the enlightened teachers face the resistance to this new concept of 'learning to learn' by some senior academic staff and some students. These are the students who would prefer a brief 'study skills' lecture to the painful process of evolving a learning strategy that would in the long run be more effective.

In a recent unpublished study of all institutions of higher education, Robin Willis-Lee of the University of Birmingham asked: 'What were the attitudes to facilities for assisting students learning and the involvement of advising bodies?' The replies make interesting reading. A selection are given here:

> With regard to attitudes of different bodies; it is probably fair to say that opinions vary widely with many people being utterly convinced of the importance of such help, while others feel that, seeing that they had no help at University and yet survived, everybody should be able to survive under their own steam.
>
> Facilities for help with learning problems and study skills are probably not considered to be essential by the majority of academic staff here.
>
> None of the official bodies of the University have been involved in these programmes, and it is probably true to say that on the whole the academic and administrative staff are indifferent to them.
>
> In general terms the College probably publicly recognises study skills as desirable if not essential, while in some quarters, perhaps privately, lies the feeling that it is not even desirable (Willis-Lee, 1981).

The need is recognised by some staff, but there are others who argue that any student entering higher education should already possess these basic skills in learning and in work presentation. If not, he or she has no place in an institution of this kind.

In the face of the despair that I feel at the utterances of such meritorious men from the universities, I turn to Kuhn (1962) for a hope of change:

> normal science, presupposes a conceptual and instrumental framework or paradigm accepted by an entire scientific community; that the resulting mode of scientific practice inevitably evokes 'crisis' which cannot be resolved within this framework; and that science returns to normal only when the community accepts a new conceptual structure which can again govern its search for novel facts and for more refined theories.

In the context of 'learning to learn' I would replace the word 'science' with 'education'.

THE STATE OF LEARNING TO LEARN AT THE PRESENT TIME

I would suggest that the concept of 'study skills' in higher education is 'in crisis'. Throughout all universities academic staff and counsellors are applying 'learning to learn' methods which affect relatively small numbers; these often, as I have already stated, attract the very students who least need help and the results of their effects are rarely evaluated.

One exception was Gibbs (1980) who carried out a survey in 1978 which provided evidence that about 50 per cent of 1,000 teachers, mainly in higher education, who held copies of his 'learning to learn' manual were making use of the group approach that he pioneered in the Open University. Ratings supplied by tutors at 110 sessions indicated that they were felt to be lively and easy to run. It is always difficult to assess the effect of a new approach where changes in students are likely to be gradual rather than immediate.

Evaluation by individual counsellors and teachers is nearly always made on completion of a course by means of simple questionnaires. Evaluation would have more validity if it monitored students' changes in learning strategies after a period of at least a year.

If the institutions of higher education are to accept that they are not just centres for teaching academic excellence but also exist to facilitate learning and appropriate learning strategies, it will require the emergence of new paradigm. But as Kuhn (1962) so rightly states:

> At the start a new candidate for paradigm may have few supporters, and on occasion the supporters' motives may be suspect. Nevertheless, if they are competent, they will improve it, explore its possibilities, and show what it would be like to belong to the community guided by it. And as that goes on, if the paradigm is one destined to win its fight, the number and strength of the persuasive arguments in its favour will increase. More scientists will be converted, and the explorations of the new paradigm will go on. Gradually the number of experiments, instruments, articles and books based on the paradigm will multiply. Still more men, convinced of the new view's fruitfulness, will adopt the new mode of practising normal science, until at last only a few elderly hold-outs remain. And even they, we cannot say, are wrong. Though the historian can always find men - Priestley, for instance - who were unreasonable to resist for as long as they did, he will not find a point at which resistence becomes illogical or unscientific. At most he may wish to say that a man who continues to resist after his whole profession has been converted, ipso facto, has ceased to be a scientist.

Kuhn shows how change comes about in academic bodies. Change in institutions is something I will explore in Chapter 9.

THE HISTORIC DEVELOPMENT OF STUDY SKILLS IN THE UNITED STATES OF AMERICA

As far back as 1927, Woodrow, followed closely by Sleight, was showing that:

> Learning is not a uniting ability to be strengthened by mental gymnastics in the way that arm muscles are strengthened by regular exercise with dumb-bells. Studies of our learning show that intelligent teaching of general principles can achieve what unenlightened drill does not (Hunter, 1957).

The Text is the Task

For more than 100 years American teachers were focusing on the text and the problems of rapid reading rather than on analysing the academic skills that were required for college courses. Therefore in the minds of teachers 'study skills' and 'rapid reading' are synonymous.

Joval in 1878 was probably one of the first to explore systematically the role of eye movement in reading. 'The first set of Harvard Reading Films were developed in 1938 by Walter Deerbottom, a Professor at the Harvard Graduate School of Education. It showed a page of text in a series of jumps in mimicry of the action of the eye' (Hodgins, 1971). In 1946 Perry and Whitlock on behalf of the Bureau of Study Counsel offered this every year to 30 of the least able students at Harvard. At the present time 500 students enrol each year for a crash programme, meeting five days a week for four weeks. The students in 1946 were no different from the students in 1980 who find on entering university that the change in quantity of reading is nowhere near as shocking as the change in quality and direction required. Even in stable, well-motivated students, Hodgins (1971) tells us that 'the anxiety involved in changing reading procedures may involve exchanges between student and teacher as profound as any in a therapist/patient relationship'.

Educational research has shown that personal factors are as important as the particular mechanical device (such as tachistoscopes, pacers, accelerators, motion picture films, automatic film strip, projectors, book-centred techniques, study-skill programmes, skimming and scanning techniques, etc.) in improved reading performance.

Most programmes lead to improved ability in certain skills but there is no conclusive evidence indicating that such increased ability is transferred and applied to other skills. This is substantiated by Wilson and Einbecker (1974) in a survey of 898 students out of a total population of 7,859 from four junior colleges.

Similarly, Rosen (1967), following a comprehensive review on rapid reading programmes, found little definite scientific evidence to justify the random use of machines and devices for improving rates of reading with undifferentiated groups of students. He emphasised that more research was necessary to fully investigate the value of such materials and programmes. For rapid reading skills to be of any value when analysing the rate of reading it should always be considered in conjunction with comprehension. Students should be able to be flexible and adapt their rate to purpose, content and type of materials. Such factors should be taken into consideration by any teacher and counsellor who includes rapid reading courses as part of a 'learning to learn' programme.

Several studies have investigated different aspects of these study skills. Marvel (1959), taking as his subjects high school sophomores, found that motivational factors related to encouragement and urging, rather than any tachistoscopic training, were the most significant influence in improving both reading rate and permanency of rate. Glock (1949), working with three groups of college students, found that although controlled eye-movement practice was the most effective method of training students to improve the rate of comprehension, the major benefit from these types of training depended on the ease by which the subjects were motivated. The most significant variables, however, were teacher variables (which would affect student learning to learn and motivation) rather than the actual training method used.

Much effective work has been carried out over the years by counsellors setting up remedial programmes to deal with the study problems that arise from a broad-based entry to higher education. In the last few years, however, questions of accountability have been raised.

> A recent survey of efforts in the U.S.A. to help students overcome learning difficulties, reports that one State Board has refused to reimburse state colleges and universities for their expenditure on such programmes, arguing that the taxpayers should not be charged a second time for something they have already paid the High Schools to accomplish (Roueche and Snow, 1977).

DEVELOPMENT IN BRITAIN

Whilst this work has been developing in the USA it had very different beginnings in Britain.

Without the hindsight that research would give, educationalists - like all good academics - rushed into print. The result was a quantity of study skills manuals and 'do-it-yourself' cook-books.

Even now, the written word is a favourite form of 'instruction' with institutions - some departments even producing their own booklets. This is the work of caring, concerned teachers who want to help their students but might only be reproducing the study methods that they themselves found effective. The Chinese philosopher Mencius also had this criticism to make of writing: 'it ignores the tao [way]; it takes up one point and disregards a hundred others' (Goody and Watt, 1962).

Accountability is usually only prevalent in time of financial stringency, so it is interesting to note that, a decade ago, when 'Higher Education joined electronics and natural gas to be one of Britain's leading growth industries' (Johnson, 1977), questions began to be asked about the problems of student 'drop-out'. This resulted from the recommendation of the Robbins' Report (1963) which stated that ' it should be an essential part of the responsibility of any University towards the student, to investigate problems of student wastage and failure'.

Only the student health pioneer Nicholas Malleson had - as far back as 1957 - distinguished between 'students presenting anxiety over study in contrast to students who suffer apathetic withdrawal' (Crown, Lucas and Supramaniam, 1973).

Ryle, Director of the University Health Centre at the University of Sussex - writing about student casualties in 1969 - related lower intellectual ability with wastage. More significantly he reported on a study (carried out by Ryle and Lunghi, 1968) of under-achieving students. This accounted for 10 per cent of one year's intake at the University of Sussex. In his conclusions he made a clear division between (a) those with emotional and psychiatric problems; and, (b) those emotionally able, somewhat extrovert students who show a propensity to 'drop-out' and to 'under-achieve'. He does not appear to suggest that lack of appropriate study skills might be a contributary factor.

Study Skills Courses

Ryle's conclusion is surprising as it was

> in the middle of the 1960s that the Students' Union at the University of Sussex became interested in the possibility that students might derive benefit from using the rapid reading courses that were then available. They examined several and decided that the course designed by Tony Buzan was the most appropriate for students and accordingly invited him to present it at Sussex (Chibnall, 1979).

This course, which was recorded on television in 1971, and is sold as a 'package' to other institutions, was administered and taught by the Media Service Unit using some university staff and also some outside teachers as the need arose. Since then other staff have presented lectures and courses on study problems derived from their experience and interest, often disagreeing with Buzan's method.

One of the earliest pioneers in this field of educational research was Janek Wankowski who established the University of Birmingham Educational Services Unit in 1963 in response to

Robbins. He has worked clinically as an educational counsellor concurrently with his educational research, so that both have benefited. In 1968, Wankowski defined four areas that contribute to wastage and failure:

(a) Uncertainty of future goals
(b) Lack of interest in the course
(c) Persuasion to enter university
(d) Study difficulty.

The Concept of Learning to Learn

All research up until this time had been academic-goal focused - factors relating to examination success or failure, as it was not until the 'explosion' of the Open University that Gibbs and Nortledge (1977) introduced the concept of 'learning to learn' as opposed to 'study skills'.

A comprehensive one-week study skills course was run for a number of years by Brian Helviglaarsen (who was closely connected with Tony Buzan) at the University of East Anglia. This was independent of the university and attracted students from other higher education institutions, and also people from industry and commerce. Gibbs (1977) felt that these courses were 'aimed at the collection, packaging and re-gurgitating of information and rely on idealised models of study behaviour which may not represent realistic attitudes for students'. Through the use of structural groups, Gibbs helps students articulate their own perceptions of their study tasks and develop a questioning self-analytic attitude to studying, whilst they are in a process of change and development. His group work acknowledges the influence of Rogers (1969) and Kelly (1955).

Kelly's theory of personal constructs suggests that the acceptance of new ideas and 'construct systems' is based on cautious negotiation.

> No matter how well a construct system had been thought out by the teacher, no matter how clearly and logically presented, a student needs time to try it out if he is going to make it part of his active thinking process, rather than simply committing it to memory (Gibbs and Nortledge, 1977).

Gibbs's work is not confined clinically to the Open University. He has given generously of his expertise to counsellors and teachers in a wide variety of higher education institutions, and his recent research reflects his wide experience.

Gibbs, who now directs the Educational Department Unit at Oxford Polytechnic, sets out what he now believes should be the aim of all who attempt to help students:

> adopt a more purposeful and effective approach to their learning...

1) the development of students' conceptions of the learning process. By this we do not mean theoretical teaching or learning, but a student-centred facilitation of students' own awareness.
2) the development of students' awareness of the nature and purposes of study tasks. By this we do not mean training in the use of specific techniques.
3) the development of autonomous flexibility in adopting learning approaches appropriate to particular study tasks and learning intentions and the emancipation of students from habitual and limiting approaches (Gibbs, Morgan and Taylor, 1980).

Educationalists, as a whole, are disenchanted with psychologists and feel that most so-called research on learning is unrelated to teachers' or students' problems. This view is discussed by Laurillard (1979) and expanded by Cronbach (1975), who sees the theoretical input from psychology into the understanding of the educational concept as negligible.

Laurillard believes that learning should be understood in its educational context and focuses on what students actually do when they learn. She, like Gibbs, feels that the 'execution of the task is at least partly dependent on the nature of the task, the style it demands and partly in the student's perception of the teaching that is relevant to it' (Laurillard, 1979). Neither of them however, give weight to the factors of self-identity and personality that determine the way students learn.

But first let us consider what Gibbs refers to as 'the nature and purpose of the study task' and Laurillard calls the 'nature of the task'. We have been told by Main (1980) that 'there is no systematic research available on the demands generated by different subjects', so that the students can only experiment with no clear aims.

Cyril Weir, from the Associated Examinations Board, has been carrying out research in this field over the last two years at the University of Reading and other institutions of higher education, and this is described by him in Chapter 6. He outlines the format of the new Associated Examining Board's English for Academic Purposes test. It is hoped that, as a result of his work, it will be possible for the 'nature of the task' to be defined.

The second area where there is some common agreement between researchers in learning is in what Gibbs refers to as 'the students' conception of the learning progress' and what Laurillard calls the 'students' perception of teaching'.

Marton and Säljö (1976) showed that students who gave a 'deep-level' processing account of their approach to a task scored better on tests of understanding than students who described a 'surface-level' processing approach, but Laurillard (1979) found that the same students can be both 'surface-level' and 'deep-level' processors depending on 'the different requirements of assessment by considering what they themselves want to achieve by doing it'.

It is important that all students are capable of deep-level processing in the 'holistic approach' described by Svensson (1977), which is 'characterised by students' attempts to understand the overall meaning of the passage, to search for the author's intention, to relate the message to a wider context and/or to identify the main parts of the author's arguments and supporting facts'.

The main difficulty students face is that the 'surface-level', or what Svensson refers to as the 'atomistic' approach - which has been effective for the school examination-orientated learning experience - can only lead to academic under-achievement or failure in higher education.

If one also believes that learning in higher education is to have an effect on the student after leaving university, we may also echo Svensson's words, that

> it is essential to help students who adopt alternative approaches to recognise the importance of interacting actively and critically with the information and ideas presented in the course of higher education. Otherwise it is difficult to see what lasting effects the experiences of higher education could have (Svensson, 1977).

The third vital factor that seems, understandably, to be ignored or seldom referred to directly by the educationalists is self-identity or the personality factor. This relates to the students'

1. Sense of identity and, in particular, work identity and level of self-confidence
2. Motivation
3. Emotional and psychological state - high level of anxiety, depression, obsessive compulsive states, relationships and marital difficulties, 'cultural shock' states
4. Physical factors - physical handicaps of varying kinds
   - loss of energy resulting from, for example, glandular fever
5. Home influences - attitude of parents to higher education
   - the effect of emotional blackmail on the student
6. Developmental stage - attitude to authority - acted out in this context in attitude to the teacher
   - ability to exercise verbal control.

How Personality Factors Can Affect Academic Studies

Our first example of how personality factors can affect academic studies is a second-year female student studying English, well motivated but with a lonely recently divorced mother who expects to be visited each weekend and would prefer her daughter to leave university and live at home. The physical time taken in travelling and the effect of the emotional blackmail is destructive to the student's work pattern.

The second example is a first-year male student studying physics. He has no sense of his own identity and lacks self-confidence. He has recently met an extrovert, well-adjusted girlfriend and become dependent on her - fitting his 'time-table' to hers and not spending enough effective time at his studies.

Not all psychological or emotional states affect learning. Motivation and the 'will to succeed' can often overcome quite severe states for a limited period. Crown, Lucas and Supramaniam (1973) point out that 'many studies have attempted to examine relationships between personality variables and academic success. Furneaux's research showed that moderate neuroticism and introversion relate positively to success, at least in some contexts' (Furneaux, 1962).

Conversely, the loss of a supportive relationship at a point of academic crisis, such as during revision before finals, can lead to a complete cessation of studying.

As it can be shown that institutional as well as personal factors affect the way that the student learns, then the institution must address itself to the needs of the individual learner. Administrators, teachers and counsellors must develop together an eclectic approach.

REFERENCES

Beatty, L. (1978) The Student Study Contract, Lancaster 4th International Conference on Higher Education, also 'Higher Education Bulletin', no. 8 (1979) as quoted in Gibbs, Morgan and Tayler, p. 11

Borgen, R. and Seaborne, A.E.M. (1969) 'The Psychology of Learning', Pelican, London

Cheetham, B. (1981) Towards Specification for Self Access Study Facilities in a Multi-cultured Academic Community, unpublished dessertation, University of Reading

Chibnall, B. (1979) The Sussex Experiment in P.J. Hills (ed.), 'Study Courses and Counselling', SRHE, Guildford, Surrey, p. 37

Cofer, C.N. and Appley, M.H. (1968) 'Motivation: Theory and Research', John Wiley, New York, p. 588

Cronbach, L.J. (1975) Beyond the Discipline and Scientific Psychology, 'American Psychologist', pp. 116-27

Crown, S., Lucas, C.J. and Supramaniam, S. (1973) The Delineation and Measurement of Study Difficulty in University Studies, 'The British Journal of Psychiatry', vol. 123, p. 383

Deese, J. and Deese, K. (1979) 'How to Study' 3rd edn, McGraw-Hill, New York, p. 11

Entwistle, N.J. (1977) 'The Academic Achievement Game',

Hodder and Stoughton, Sevenoaks, Kent, pp. 119-20
Entwistle, N.J. and Wilson, J.D. (1977) 'Degrees of Excellence', Hodder and Stoughton, Sevenoaks, Kent, pp. 49, 52, 75 and 111
Erikson, E.H. (1959) Identity and the Life Cycle in G.S. Klein (ed.), 'Psychological Issues', vol. 1, no. 1, International Universities Press, New York, as quoted in Perry
Farber, L.H. (1966) 'The Ways of the Will', Constable, London, p. 71, as quoted in I. Singer 'The Goals of Human Sexuality', Wildwood House, London, 1973
Freeman, R. (1972) 'How to Study Effectively', National Extension College, Cambridge
Furneaux, W.D. (1962) The Psychologist and the University, University Quarterly, vol. 17, pp. 33 and 47
Galbraith, J.K. (1980) 'The Nature of Mass Poverty', Pelican, London, pp. 58, 78, 83
Gibbs, G. (1977) Can Students be Taught How to Study?, 'Higher Education Bulletin', vol. 5, no. 2, pp. 107-8
Gibbs, G. (1980) Can Students be Taught How to Study, 'Teaching News' (University of Birmingham), no. 11 (November), p. 13
Gibbs, G., Morgan, A. and Tayler, L. (1980) Understanding Why Students Don't Learn, Study Methods Group Report, no. 5, Institute of Educational Technology, Open University, Milton Keynes, p. 11 and pp. 18-19
Gibbs, G. and Nortledge, A. (1977) Learning to Study - a Student Centred Approach, 'Teaching at a Distance', no. 8, p. 4
Glock, M.D. (1949) The Effect of Eye Movements and Reading Rate at the College Level of Three Methods of Training, 'Journal of Educational Psychology', vol. 40, February, pp. 95-105
Goody, J. and Watt (1962) The Consequences of Literacy in P.P. Gigliodi (ed.), 'Language and Social Context', Penguin, Harmondsworth, 1972
Hilgard, E.R. and Bower G.H. (1975) 'Theories of Learning', 4th edn, Prentice Hall, New Jersey, pp. 352 and 609
Hodgins, R.C. (1971) The Text is the Adversary in G.B. Blaine and C.C. McArthur, 'Emotional Problems of the Student', Butterworth, London, pp. 208-9 and 213
Hounsell, D. (1979) 'Learning to Learn - a Critical Introduction to the Work of Graham Gibbs', EARDHE Congress, Klagenfurt
Hudson, L. (1972) 'The Cult of the Fact', Jonathan Cape, London, p. 98
Hudson, L. (1979) 'Contrary Imagination', Penguin, London, p. 125
Hunter, I.M.L. (1957) 'Memory, Facts and Fallacies', Penguin, Harmondsworth, pp. 161-2
Johnson, P. (1977) 'Enemies of Society', Weidenfeld and Nicolson, London
Kelly, G. (1955) 'A Theory of Personality: The Psychology of

Personal Contacts', Norton, New York
Kuhn, T.S. (1962) 'The Structure of Scientific Revolution' (6th edn 1968), The University of Chicago Press and Chicago, London, p. 158
Laurillard, D. (1979) Research Methods in Student Learning, Institute of Educational Technology, University of Surrey, Paper for Conference of the European Association for Research and Development in Higher Education in Klagenfurt, pp. 11-12
Lavin, D.E. (1965) 'The Prediction of Academic Performance' (Science edn), John Wiley and Sons, New York
Mace, C.A. (1973) 'The Psychology of Study', Pelican, London, p. 103
Main, A. (1980) 'Encouraging Effective Learning', Scottish Academic Press, Edinburgh, p. 12
Marton, F. and Säljö, R. (1976) On Quantative Differences in Learning: 1 - Outcome and Process, 'British Journal of Educational Psychology', vol. 46, pp. 4-11
Marvel, J. (1959) Acquisition and Retention of Reading Performance on Two Response Dimensions as Related to Set and Tachistoscopic Training, 'Journal of Educational Research', vol. 52 (February)
Mathias, H. (1978) Science Students' Approach to Learning 4th Lancaster International Conference on Higher Education, as quoted in Gibbs, Morgan and Tayler, p. 11
Miller, L.L. (1970) 'Increasing Reading Efficiency' (3rd edn), University of Wyoming, Holt, Rinehart and Winston, New York
Mowrer, O.H. (1939) A Stimulus-Response Analysis of Anxiety as it Rates as a Re-inforcing Agent, 'Psychology Review', vol. 46, pp. 553-65
Perry, W.G. (1970) 'Forms of Intellectual and Ethnic Development in the College Years', Holt, Rinehart and Winston, New York, pp. 59-170
Robbins, Lord C. (1964) 'Higher Education: Report of the Committee', Cmd. 2154, HMSO, London
Rogers, C. (1969) 'Freedom to Learn', Columbus Ohio, Melville
Rosen, C.L. (1967) Mechanical Devices for Increasing Speed of Reading, University of Georgia, Research for the Classroom Education Series edited by Albert J. Kingston, 'Journal for Reading' (May)
Roueche, J.E. and Snow, J.J. (1977) 'Overcoming Learning Problems: A Guide to Developmental Education in College', Jossey Bars, San Francisco
Ryle, A. (1969) 'Student Casualties', Allen Lane, London, p. 50
Ryle, A. and Lunghi, M. (1968) A Psychometric Study of Academic Difficulty and Psychiatric Illness in Students, 'British Journal of Psychiatry', vol. 114, p. 57
Sexton, V.S. (1965) Factors Contributing to Attrition in College Populations: Twenty-five Years of Research, 'Journal of General Psychology', vol. 72, pp. 301-26

Svensson, L. (1977) Symposium: Learning Processes and Strategies - III on Qualitative Differences in Learning: III Study Skill and Learning, 'British Journal of Educational Psychology', vol. 47, pp. 238 and 243
Voeks, V. (1979) 'On Becoming an Educated Person', W.B. Saunders Co., London, p. 31
Wankowski, J. (1973) 'Temperament Motivation and Academic Achievement', University of Birmingham Educational Survey and Counselling Unit
Willis-Lee, R. (1981) A Survey of the Provision of Facilities in Institutes of Higher Education Through Which Students May Obtain Help and Advice With Study and Learning, unpublished thesis, University of Birmingham
Wilson, R.C. and Einbecker, P.G. (1974) Does Reading Ability Predict College Performance?, University of West Florida, 'Journal of Reading' (December), pp. 235-6
Yi-Guang, L. and McKeachie, W.J. (1970) Aptitude Anxiety Study Habits and Academic Achievement, 'Journal of Counselling Psychology', vol. 17, no. 4, pp. 306-9

4 INDIVIDUAL AND GROUP METHODS

In order to look at the development of more effective learning to learn methods in any one institution, it is necessary to look at where that university or college is at any one time and what its strengths and weaknesses are.

Each institution is unique. It depends on the attitude of its academic staff, the method of assessment, the social environment, the interest of the students' union and many other factors. What is right for one college is wrong for another so there is no one method of learning to learn to be indiscriminately applied with vigour throughout all colleges and all cultures. The way that many teachers teach, many psychiatrists practise psychiatry, and many counsellors counsel, betrays a great deal about their training and research interests, but often derives very little from the needs of the individual client or learner.

Another complicating factor is whether we are helping students to learn to cope with their academic course or whether we are helping them to develop learning skills that might be useful to them throughout life. I hope that it does not have to be an either/or situation. So often the student who is 'interest' not 'course' bound can read widely but may fail to meet his course commitments. In addition, the students who have developed a mature critical self-questioning approach to their learning and learning strategies will adopt the same approach to their curricula and their teachers. One must be aware of the academic consequences of this, as students should not forget that, however knowledgeable about their subject, teachers can feel very vulnerable human beings and - as Bligh (1980) says - 'have a very real fear of criticism':

> What are we afraid it will destroy, our public or our private image, our promotion chances or our self-confidence? If there is a popular belief that teaching does not count too much for promotion, it seems more likely that it is our image of ourselves that is threatened. Similarly, we are free to record or examine our teaching techniques, not so much for fear of what others might think - they need not know - but because we might have to face ourselves. The intense feelings that are sometimes aroused when the privacy of teaching is challenged could come from either fear. So too could our reluctance to try new methods or to share periods of teaching with a colleague.

I would disagree with these latter statements knowing of academic staff who have recorded their lectures on video so that they can critically appraise their own work. I have also run workshops with academic colleagues who have exposed themselves to, and enjoyed, the new experience of group teaching in an informal setting.

As Hudson (1972) points out, lack of conformity can have far-reaching consequences. 'Students who wish to question the prevailing orthodoxy tend in practice to receive poor degrees. And those who get good degrees, but still wish to question, are edged - indeed move of their own volition toward peripheral positions in their profession.' It is also more subtle and insidious, as Hudson goes on to say:

> There is too an assumption made by the tough minded and to a lesser extent by the rest of us on their behalf, that they are somehow in the right: but these who accept a particular intellectual discipline are, in some subtle respect, legitimate, whereas those who do not are free-boaters or dilettantes.

A professor may be enthusiastic for creativity and experimentation but he is aware of the need to conform to the academic system.

Snyder (1971) in discussing the 'hidden curriculum' says:

> It is easy to view the existence of the hidden curriculum as an accidental design, one in which the academic process has somewhat managed to thwart the real interest of the university. Professors and students, presumably, are interested in learning, growth, and intellectual excitement. But instead they find themselves unexpectedly trapped by grades (and grading), competition for success and the rewards that accompany it, and institutionalisation. Everyone may profess to know better but the self esteem of teachers and students alike is tangled in the process; and it is difficult to cut out and ignore the grades, competitions and rewards which have been so internalised.
>
> This view of the situation, however, ignores the fact that the academy has itself created the system and that it serves a protective function, permitting a minimum amount of risk taking and protecting the maintenance of the educational status quo. It's not that students necessarily want to avoid academic risks; it's just that they learn early in their educational career that few rewards justify such risks.

THE OBJECTIVES OF LEARNING TO LEARN

Despite this it is important that learning to learn should have as its objectives:

1. To develop a learning strategy that will enable them to carry out the study task that the course demands.
2. To develop a 'deep-level process of learning'. This includes the development of critical and creative faculties.
3. To develop motivation, decision-making, relationship skills and to increase commitment.
4. To develop skills for future employment arising from a particular discipline. An example of this is the very comprehensive communication skills programme run as part of the General Studies course at the University of Surrey by Aurielle Earle for future scientists.
5. Learning the skills required to 'play the academic game' - for example, 'how to cope with examinations'.

It is my belief that the present learning to learn workshops and individual help as carried out in some higher education institutions in some measure is failing to meet this criteria.

LEARNING TO LEARN METHODS THAT ARE PRACTISED IN EDUCATIONAL INSTITUTIONS

The approaches to learning to learn, whether individual or group, can be set out on a spectrum, where it is then possible to associate them with learning theories and to consider if these various methods are likely to meet the objectives of an effective learning to learn intervention.

Certain cultures tend to favour particular methods. Most reading and study counselling centres in the United States favour the use of study manuals, study tapes and books as part of a programme of instruction. Middle East countries would be more comfortable with lectures and lectures with exercises. Within Great Britain all methods may be experienced; normally dependent on the theoretical background and personality of the study skills counsellor when it should respond to the needs of the student. As overseas students represent approximately 18 per cent of the intake in most British universities, coming from a wide variety of countries (114 countries were represented at the University of Reading for the academic year 1979-80), the study skills counsellor faces the same dilemma as the teacher.

Leaderless Discussion Groups or Tutor-led Seminars

Gibbs (1980), whose learning to learn groups come out somewhere on the spectrum between leaderless discussion groups and tutor-led seminars, has carried out research into group work run by one or more tutors, educationalists or counsellors. His instructional manual has become a model for staff to copy and react against. Academic staff often initially feel uncomfortable about taking part in a workshop instead of the lecturer's

Table 4.1: Instructional Study Skills Method and Associated Learning Theory

Explanatory learning emphasising freedom and self-expression:
evaluation
retrospective and subjective

Method of Instruction	Associated Learning Theory	Type of Theory
Leaderless discussion groups	Rogers	Humanist
Co-operative projects	Maslow	Humanist
Individual project work lecturettes - learning through theory	Bruner	Cognitive
Tutor-led discussions	Perry	Developmental
Tutor-led seminars	Morton	Cognitive
Lectures and lectures with exercise	Broadbent	Cognitive
Study manuals	Lindsay and Norman	Informative
Study tapes and tape booklets		Processing
Study contracts	Skinner	Behavourist

Tight control of content and method: outcome measured psychometrically and related to predetermined specific objectives.

situation and some counsellors, who may themselves be more experienced in group methods, do not always allay their feelings of discomfort. Whilst understanding Gibbs's fear that 'Lecturers will stop caring about student learning if some specialist body or organisation (such as counsellors) takes over the responsibility for running study skills courses', I feel that lecturers do need counsellors in a consultancy role. Several times, in my experience, lecturers have also expressed their views that lecturing is a lonely business and they have enjoyed the planning of the learning to learn group workshops as a joint exercise with the counsellor. There should be at least two course members of academic staff involved so that the counsellor can gradually become simply 'a resource'. It is always more effective in any field for the direct teachers to be introducing new concepts to students as part of their regular curriculum. An an analogy, I would take my clinical experience in other fields, for example in sex education and drug education in schools. It has always been found to be more natural and effective for information and guidance to be given by the normal teaching staff than for the outside expert. The ideas then reach all students as a matter of course, and the regular teaching staff do not feel their role is usurped.

The effective and positive power of groups for good has been well documented. Lamm and Myers (1978) in focusing on the effect of group interaction referred to: 'Malamuth's (1975) peer counselling experiment, which was an analog to actual peer counselling programs, [and] indicated that "such group counselling experiences result in a more extreme advice than that given to individuals". Toch (1965) "describes additional examples of the power of mutual assistance in small self-help groups"'.

Gibbs worked with groups of varying sizes in a 'snowball' design. First, each member was required to carry out a task - such as taking notes from a 15-minute (as opposed to a 50-minute) lecture - then they were asked to work in pairs and later in groups of four and perhaps subsequently eight, explaining to the other group members why they had taken their notes in a particular way. This culminated in a plenary session at the end where each small group contributed ideas on good or bad methods of note-taking which the leader wrote up for the entire group to digest.

This format was repeated for other appropriate study activities. The amount of time spent in the small groups, and the amount of leadership involved in plenary sessions, varied. It depended on how comfortable the academic staff were with the workshop format and whether the student participants were from an English educational system. If students had recently arrived at a British university from countries such as Bangladesh, Thailand or Greece where their educational experience had been very different from the British system, the staff would need to structure the sessions more formally. This is why the Gibbs's method would not, as is the case with any method, transport itself to another cultural environment without some shift of emphasis.

In inviting the students to take a self-critical approach to a variety of alternative methods, the Gibbs' learning to learn methodology meets most of the criteria of objectives. Since Gibbs ran a learning to learn workshop with academic staff participating as students at the University of Reading in November 1978, about a third of the participants have continued to run workshops with their own students.

Co-operative Projects

Studdent-Kennedy (1981), in a letter in the University of Birmingham's 'Teaching News', draws attention to the alternatives to lecturing and mentions that:

> Courses structured in an uncompromising manner around case studies and project work of various kinds have achieved impressive results in fields as far apart as economics and medicine in this country, in Israel and in Australia... they make no use of the familiar formula of lecture - class - traditional examination...the success stories come from

relatively new institutions, physically and organisationally designed for purposes freshly conceived. It is claimed that these developments have established greatly improved structures for those involved in teaching/learning in which fresh energies are tapped because students find themselves as producers of knowledge rather than passive consumers.

In helping students individually with their learning problems, Wankowski (1981), at the University of Birmingham, asks students to prepare lecturettes and deliver them to him in the counselling sessions. He tells us that:

> It seems that a student preparing a talk for an interested but non-competitive listener can relax his apprehensions and concentrate on clarifying his concepts without fear of appearing ignorant in the face of an expert. The preparation of the lecturette enables the student to sort out his material, classified in order of importance, to formulate clear statements, to explain technical points and create simple models of presentation which should help the layman to understand such instruction. This experience gives the student an opportunity of reorganising his own knowledge of the subject and thereby induces deeper understanding (Raaheim and Wankowski, 1981).

This is probably one of the most effective ways of developing the deep-level or holistic process of learning and, in addition, developing a mutuality between teacher and student.

The Open University has been using a similar method for some years either in their study centres or in students' homes, but McIntosh (1976) writes:

> One of the best ways of learning about a new subject is to try teaching it to other people...carefully prepared study materials, duly backed up with annotated discussion, notes and easily accessible follow-up reading, can enable students to hold profitable small group discussions even when no counsellor or teacher is present.

Jackson and Van Zoost (1974) enrolled 'thirty students in an eight session study skills programme... Fifteen were required to teach the contents of each session to a friend and then to reassess and monetarily reinforce their teaching competence'. All subjects improved their study habits with greater gains for the teaching subjects. This is using similar methods to Wankowski but involves several students and may be a better use of teaching and counselling provision. It's a method which I have often suggested that students use to good effect as a useful revision technique.

Individual Project Work

Individual project work, I would suggest, is one of the most fruitful ways of combining learning and learning to learn - 'skills' and 'content'. As Nelson-Jones and Toner (1978) point out:

> There needs to be a specific training in the skills and attitudes of being more effectively responsible for learning. Attention could be paid to the skills of being creative, such as the origination of ideas and risk taking and of critical thinking such as the gathering and analysing of evidence.

It may be a project, a piece of creative work, combines many of the criteria of learning to learn intervention that relate to the personality of the student.

Watts (1977) in a recent paper discusses ways 'To assist the student in gaining experience in the important competence that defines maturity - "decision making" (Daws 1968) and also to help to develop a sense of commitment to a personally-made decision which will increase his motivation.'

I have found that several senior members of academic staff have, in the course of their duties as personal tutors, often encouraged students to carry out projects which are in addition to the course work, indicating that they would be quite happy to discuss and supervise the projects with the students. The student becomes aware of and benefits from the interest that the member of staff is taking in him, rather than the notion that he is going to be involved in work that will not be directly assessed as part of his degree.

Lectures and Lectures With Exercises

In 1974 Tony Buzan published a book 'Use Your Head' which accompanied the BBC series on study skills. It introduced the 'organic study method' and sought to increase awareness. Buzan's aim was to make: 'Study a personal, interactive, continuing, changing and stimulating experience, rather than a rigid, impersonal and tiresomely onerous task'.

Arising from the series and the book, Buzan formed a company, a team of enthusiastic and technically skilled colleagues, and ran a series of study skill courses in a wide variety of settings. One such one-week course was regularly run in an academic environment at the University of East Anglia by Brian Helvig Laarsen. The participants were by no means all students, but the content of the course, which consisted of lectures with exercises and practice for the comprehensive study technique course, was suitable for a university student. Many of the special features such as the organic or pattern note-taking, mnemonics and rapid readings were featured as part of the course.

Buzan's concept of pattern note-taking, which can be used

for planning essays or speeches ('organic maps' as one student calls them), can develop creativity. On several occasions I have introduced them to highly academic finalists who have become bored with their revision and they have found them intellectually revitalising. Some students often find that mnemonics arouses their curiosity. Hanf (1971) points out how important symbolising and labelling is: 'The importance of this action is that the label or symbol is given a general label...and therefore acts as a trigger for all the information stored in the mind under that label.'

George Miller in 'Information and Memory' explains this concept:

> Our memories, he tells us, are limited by the number of units or symbols we must master and not by the amount of information that these symbols represent. Thus it is helpful to organise the material intelligently before we try to memorise it. The process of organisation enables us to sum the total amount of information into far fewer symbols and so ease the task of remembering (Miller, 1956).

Pattern note-taking is creative, and academic staff, I find, like including it in their learning to learn workshops with their own students as it excites the participants. In my work as a counsellor with students, I found that in the main they prefer to retain the linear form of note-taking for the initial note-taking from lectures and texts, and during the first revision of these notes transpose them into patterns.

THE CONTROVERSY OF RAPID READING COURSES

There is great controversy about rapid reading courses. The learning methods' courses introduce the techniques of rapid reading and expect the student to practise them but have many protagonists who are still convinced that the increase of reading speed is off set by considerable loss of comprehension.

Carver (1972) suspects that one major reason that students are dissatisfied with the rapid reading courses in general is the nature of the tests used to measure comprehension. In the United States he studied one test and found that it did not: 'Measure the improvement a person makes in reading rate or comprehension as the result of taking a training course or measure the percentage of material that he actually comprehended whilst he was reading.'

Graf (1973), in a test designed to look objectively at the controversy of speed reading and comprehension, listed 31 students who had enrolled in a privately conducted speed reading programme at the University of Redlands in South California. He used four different types of literature for his tests. He concluded that:

> The average speed reader cannot triple his reading speed, or even double it, without missing out large chunks of the message in front of him; perhaps some of the industries' techniques can be valuable for some people and certain purposes. Moreover, the ability to skim literature intelligently (if that is what speed readers do) may be a very useful skill! In view of the large number of students who fail to 'attack' their reading lists effectively, this ability to skim is a much needed skill.

Perhaps we are asking too much of any rapid reading course to take students of mixed discipline and mixed ability and expect them all to benefit.

Alec Main asks students who come to him with difficulty in reading comprehension:

> 'Would you like to tell me about the different kinds of reading your course demands?' and offers him a formula.
>
> There are five levels of reading skills
>
> a) Reading for <u>enjoyment</u> - light reading
> b) Reading for <u>overview</u> - getting a general idea of the gist of the topic
> c) <u>Search</u> reading - looking for some specific piece of information
> d) Reading for <u>mastery</u> - to get detailed information or understanding of a topic
> e) <u>Critical</u> reading - reading for stimulus, for challenge, to assess values and ideas (Main, 1980).

THE CHOICE BETWEEN DIVIDED AND GROUP METHODS

It is quite clear from my work with students that to work with the individual learner (as Alec Main does) is very effective, but in university campuses of between 4,000 and 20,000 students, the amount of one-to-one help that can be offered is very limited.

Buzan has sometimes been criticised and his techniques referred to scornfully as tricks. One example of this is his treatment of mnemonics which can be taught to large audiences. Many students find it helpful as an aid to memory.

In summing up, I feel that the study skills technique concept of Buzan as opposed to the learning to learn workshop methods of Gibbs has only limited effectiveness for university students, but having said that, part of the courses (such as the pattern note-taking) meet many of my criteria of objectives for learning to learn intervention. Patterns fit more comfortably with the way that the brain functions and have a number of advantages over the more conventional forms of linear note-taking. They clearly state the central theme, show the relative importance of each idea and enable links to be made between them. They are open ended, allowing for new ideas to be added. The pattern is an expression of creativity and can easily be remembered. In addition, students who have taken part in these courses have added 'it has been fun'.

Perhaps learning is a painful process but the joyful participation of students in Buzan-style study courses has side effects that may continue into the learning process long after the course ends.

Study Manuals, Study Tapes and Tape Booklets

Study Manuals

To read a study manual that tells you how to read a textbook has always seemed to me to be a pointless exercise. It has a limited use and often serves only to put the student in touch with the 'hidden curriculum' and to give specific advice about study techniques, as the titles themselves suggest: 'Making the Grade - The Academic Side of College Life' (Becker and Hughes, 1968) and 'Up to the Mark - A Study of the Examination Game' (Miller and Parlett, 1974).

In defining students as 'cue seekers' or 'cue deaf' and relating this to examination techniques, Miller and Parlett (1974) are getting students to examine their own attitude, but this has limited long-term effectiveness compared with participation in a discussion group. As Miller and Parlett tell us: 'Cue consciousness is a concept that extends previous ideas of the "hidden curriculum" in a useful way.'

Study Tapes

Study tapes, whilst still being a passive information processing experience, have the advantage of introducing a voice, the voice of a teacher or counsellor, and this results in a more effective outcome. A good example of this is the tape book 'Effective Learning' (Haynes, Groves, Hills and Moyes, 1978). This resembles the lecture-library study situation with which students can identify.

There are many occasions when a student with examinations a few weeks away seeks help from the counsellor on the last day of term when the student is returning home. It is far better for the student to have a copy of a tape such as Robert Sharpe's 'Pass That Examination', which includes relaxation training and advice on examination techniques, than being told that no help is available.

The Study Contract

Lastly I would report on the contract for academic improvement which was used with students at the Ohio State University in

1972 and has been used since then. This is a behavioural approach. The contract is mutually negotiated and renegotiated between counsellor and student. It focuses on the demands of the course and the institution, and does not encourage the student to develop as an autonomous learner. Most of the initiation of ideas is coming from the counsellor and it does not meet many of the objectives of the ideal learning to learn intervention. The effect of not meeting a predetermined sub-goal on a student who already lacks confidence and who has a poor sense of his own identity could be quite disastrous. It is reminiscent of the Phoenix approach to drug rehabilitation which set goals and sub-goals for drug addicts: nothing succeeds like success but the failure to succeed can be destructive as opposed to being merely non-effective.

CONCLUSION

I am disquietened by the great store that teachers and counsellors place on the method they use and the need for them to assert its superiority over all other methods. If we are asking the academic staff at higher education institutions to focus on the needs of an individual learner, then it behoves all connected with education and counselling to do the same.

It is also necessary, particularly in times of financial stringency, for counsellors and teachers to work closely and co-operatively in developing an eclectic approach. The role of the counsellor as consultant to the academic staff, the role that I have always advocated at the University of Reading, is the story of a co-operative effort.

REFERENCES

Becker, J. and Hughes, E.C. (1968) 'Making the Grade - The Academic Side of College Life', John Wiley and Sons, New York

Bligh, D. (1980) Openness and Approach of Personal Difficulties in Teaching, 'Teaching News' (University of Birmingham), no. 11 (November), p. 8

Buzan, T. (1974) 'Use Your Head', BBC, London, pp. 61 and 140

Carver, R.P. (1972) Speed Readers Don't Read they Skim, 'Psychology Today' (August), p. 30

Daws, P.P. (1968) 'A Good Start in Life', Cambridge Careers Research and Advisory Centre, p. 22, as quoted in Watts

Gibbs, G. (1980) Can Students be Taught How to Study, 'Teaching News' (University of Birmingham), no. 11 (November), p. 13

Graf, R.G. (1973) Speed Reading: Remember the Tortoise, 'Psychology Today', vol. 7, part 7, pp. 112-13

Hanf, M.B. (1971) Mapping a Technique for Translating Reality into Thinking, 'Journal of Reading' (University of Berkeley) (January), p. 230

Haynes, L.J., Groves, P.D., Hills, P.J. and Moyes, R.B. (1978) 'Effective Learning' tape booklet, TeFradon Ltd, University of Aston, Birmingham

Hudson, L. (1972) 'The Cult of the Fact', Jonathan Cape, London, p. 101

Jackson, B. and Van Zoost, B. (1974) Self Regulating Teaching of Others as a Means of Improving Study Habits, 'The Journal of Counselling Psychology', vol. 21, no. 6, pp. 489-93

Lamm, H. and Myers, D. (1978) Group Induced Polarization of Attitudes and Behaviour, 'Advances in Experimental Social Psychology', vol. II, pp. 163-5

McIntosh, N. (1976) 'A Decree of Difference' SHRE, Guildford, Surrey, p. 17

Main, A. (1980) 'Encouraging Effective Learning', Scottish Academic Press, Edinburgh, pp. 39-40

Malamuth, N.M. (1975) A Systematic Analysis of the Relationship Between Group Shifts and Characteristics of the Group Dilemmas Questionnaire, unpublished doctoral dissertation, University of California, Los Angeles, p. 53, as quoted in Lamm and Myers

Miller, C.M.L. and Parlett, M. (1974) 'Up to the Mark - A Study of the Examination Game', SHRE, Guildford, Surrey, p. 53

Miller, G.A. (1956) Information and Memory, 'Scientific America' (August), as quoted in Hanf

Nelson-Jones, R. and Toner, H.L. (1978) Counselling Approach to Increasing Student's Learning Competence, 'British Journal of Guidance and Counselling', vol. 6, no. 1, pp. 123-4

Raaheim, K. and Wankowski, J. (1981) 'Helping Students to Learn at University', Sigma Forlag, pp. 126-7

Sharpe, R. (1981) Pass That Exam, tape on examination techniques, Lifestyle Training Centre, 23 Abingdon Road, London W8

Snyder, B. (1971) 'The Hidden Curriculum', The MIT Press, Cambridge, Mass., p. 18

Studdent Kennedy, G. (1981) Letter from University of Birmingham's 'Teaching News', no. 12 (February)

Toch, R. (1965) 'The Social Psychology of Social Movements', Bobbs-Merrill, Inneapolis, as quoted in Lamm and Myers

Watts, A.G. (1977) A Rationale for Guidance on Higher Education Choices, 'British Journal of Guidance and Counselling', vol. 5, no. 1 (January), p. 61

5 IMPROVING LEARNING COMPETENCE - WITH PARTICULAR REFERENCE TO THE UNIVERSITY OF READING

AN ECLECTIC APPROACH

This chapter sets out to look at the various ways that higher education institutions approach 'learning to learn' and the factors that govern their choice. It then focuses on the University of Reading which has taken an eclectic approach, which includes a Learning Resource Centre (LRC).

I would agree with Ramsden (1974) that:

> European Universities are less heterogeneous than American ones. Students in British Universities rarely have contact with more than one or two academic departments. The relevant focus of analysis in this case is probably the main discipline they study, or the one department in which they spend most of their time, rather than the University as a whole.

Students taking a combined course suffer particular problems due to their difficulty in experiencing two separate, and quite distinct, learning environments concurrently.

THE VARIATION IN POLICY BETWEEN UNIVERSITIES AND POLYTECHNICS

The other important issue is the view of 'study skills' in the various official bodies responsible for higher education in Britain.

The University Grants Committee has always as a body expressed a deep interest in 'learning to learn' interventions and, as I personally experienced in November 1978, showed approval for joint counsellor and academic staff activities. But, as some vice-chancellors would be quick to point out, no separate sum of money has been specially allocated for future development. The polytechnics, on the other hand, are obliged to develop 'study skills' advice for all CNAA courses, and the activities now taking place in various polytechnics reflect this official view. This is particularly interesting when one realises that the CNAA is staffed by university academics who are, in fact, pontificating about what should happen in polytechnics whilst not making the same conditions for their own institutions.

The Attitude of Universities

The difference in attitude is shown in the comments made by various higher education institutions. One university states:

> A year ago, there was an attempt to introduce 'learning to learn' based on 'The Art and Science of Getting a Degree' (Thomas and Harri-Augstein 1077). It was hoped that all first year students might be introduced to this approach through a series of seminars run by interested members of staff. However, this project is at present in abeyance.
>
> All new students are given a leaflet on techniques of study, together with an information booklet on welfare facilities available to students. These leaflets are made available to all students at registration.

It is clear from these and other similar comments that individual academic staff, counsellors and administrators have tried to develop courses and materials to assist student learning. Unfortunately, they have not first had the opportunity to establish their aims, or to attempt to change the attitudes of their academic colleagues.

The Library as a Learning Resource Centre

In some instances, the only source of study skills help is the library. One university, speaking for several, reports that 'The library, in conjunction with the School for Materials, runs courses in library skills for undergraduates. Some of the material covered in the library's courses involves other study skills.'

It has been my experience that the libraries are now often short of staff and not able to undertake courses on library skills for all freshers, having to leave this to individual academic staff in departments. With very few exceptions their 'study skills' material amounts to copies of study manuals and a selection of research papers on learning. This might interest teachers but would hardly assist students.

The Attitude of Polytechnics

Polytechnics seem to accept that study skills have an accepted place in the institution. One polytechnic reports that 'A great deal of support is available to students from a number of sources within the Polytechnic.' Another polytechnic states: 'Any learning difficulty which arose from individual students during the year, that a department feels it cannot deal with satisfactorily without more specialised assistance, are usually referred to the Student Services Unit.' And another that

> Guidance on study methods is available within most subject departments to help new students who are academically successful, and therefore had effective study skills for 6th form, but who have to re-examine their learning strategy to cope with the higher education institution.

Raaheim (1981), writing in the University of Birmingham's 'Teaching News', feels that new students' experience is

> at root, some sort of confusion rather than a lack of maturity and that a high degree of uncertainty on the part of the beginning student about what it means 'to study' can, in fact, be an advantage and even lead to rapid progress because there is no debilitating background of regularly received average or low marks in 'study skills' at some pre-university school!

The Approach to New Students

My experience is that initially, far from being confused, students have well-established school study habits, which have been rewarded by high academic grades (the 'A' level). The initial problem is to develop a self-questioning, self-analytic approach when they first arrive at university, before their confidence is affected by the reality of poor academic results. New students are aware that they need to adapt to a different social environment, but often fail to realise that they will also need to adapt to a new learning environment. This may be due to a basic misunderstanding of what is involved. As Ausubel and Youssef (1963) illustrate: 'The discriminability of new ideas from related previously learned ideas, and hence the efficiency with which they are learned and retained, is a function of the clarity and stability of the previously learned ideas.' This may be true for learning, but it is not precisely true for learning competence.

Bannister and Fransella (1977) suggested that it 'might be possible to devise circumstances in which inadequacies and inconsistencies in students' existing approaches become apparent and possible advantages in methods used by other students also come to light'. This happens only when students view their colleagues on the same course as friends rather than competitors and regularly participate in informal group discussions.

'Is it not possible that students are quite capable of analysing for themselves the shortcomings of their own study habits?' Gibbs and Nortledge (1977) ask. I disagree with the idea of leaving this to chance. Students do not realise that they have problems until several pieces of course work have been marked, and a whole term has passed.

It is necessary to draw on Mowrer's theory of fear (1960) as a motivating factor and the need, discussed in Chapter 3, to arouse the low-anxiety learners to a greater awareness of his minimally effective learning methods. The analogy of Galbraith and overseas aid in Chapter 3 showed us that educating those who accommodate to the 'status quo' can bring about change.

THE LEARNING RESOURCE CENTRE (LRC)

Purpose

At the University of Reading a learning resource centre was set up in the counselling service as a self-directed 'learning to learn' facility - a form of study skills library where students could drop in at any time and use a wide range of books, leaflets and audio-visual materials on study methods. It consists of two rooms. The larger one, 30' x 10', is used for the viewing of video tapes that the students select and obtain from the secretary to the counselling unit. The tapes, tape books and study manuals are all used in the smaller office which is furnished in a manner that is both restful and functional. Tapes on relaxation and examination techniques can be borrowed from the centre, and also certain study manuals.

The principles on which it is run comply with Carver's and Dickenson's (1980) definition of self-direction

1. The learner is responsible for selecting the aims and objectives
2. He monitors the
   2:1 development
   2:2 and its common relevance to his objectives
3. He assesses himself
4. He takes an active role
5. He is prepared to be selective

Cost

The cost of establishing the LRC has been set out in Appendix II (pp. 184-6). As one can see, the cost of publicity far outweighs the cost of equipment. The publicity is necessary as students would not expect to find a LRC at university. The generous co-operation of academic colleagues in other universities made it possible for the centre to be comprehensively stocked from the outset.

Contents

The LRC contains videos, tapes, tape slides, tape books, work books and study manuals covering the following topics:

1. Learning in Seminars
2. Interview Technique
3. Organising Time

4. Note-taking
5. Reading
6. Essay-writing
7. Problem-solving
8. Improving the Memory
9. Report-writing
10. Revision
11. Examinations.

The audio-visual equipment shows alternative approaches to the same topic so that 'note-taking', for example, may have several different presentations. This gives the student the opportunity to choose a learning strategy that suits his self-perception and cultural identity as well as his academic level and perception of the task. In the process he learns to look critically at his own study habits and to develop flexibility.

Use of the Centre

During a typical afternoon in the LRC there might be several students present who had separately either 'walked in' or been referred from an individual counselling interview, seeking help in 'speaking-up in seminars'. They might select and watch the appropriate video recording and then sit around discussing it quite heatedly, as an undirected group which would in itself contribute to their 'treatment process'. At the same time, individual students, who had been watching the video recording on pattern note-taking and listening to the audio recording discussion on linear note-taking, might be having an informal wide-ranging discussion with several teachers who had come to look at material they wanted to borrow.

There is a need for students to be able to work in groups - few jobs expect people to work in isolation. Therefore learning to function well in seminars and informal discussion groups has vocational relevance as well as academic importance.

The LRC as a 'Sheltered' Study Area

The LRC is used as a sheltered study area for students revising for examinations or writing essays - students who have fallen behind with their academic studies for personal or psychological reasons. At the centre the student concerned can re-establish an effective work pattern, which would not be possible in the general academic environment.

A particular case is the student who has suspended his course for psychological or psychiatric reasons, and who has returned to live in the area before recommencing his full-time studies. Previously one would have said that a period of regular employment was a prerequisite to returning to a demanding course of academic study. The present unemployment situation makes that unrealistic.

It has proved useful for such students to be introduced to the study skills work books in the LRC, to help them re-establish a regular pattern of work before commencing full-time study.

Publicity

Research carried out by the National Union of Students, in 1979, showed that the most efficient way to publicise information in descending order of effectiveness is:

1. By word-of-mouth
2. Loud-hailers
3. Badges
4. Posters.

Yet, despite this, posters still seem to festoon the university campus.

The students are informed about the LRC primarily by means of a bookmark, which is distributed by the Students' Union inside their handbook at the commencement of the academic year.

The message is that the LRC is a place for students who might want to improve their learning skills, rather than being 'problem orientated'. This does not dissuade students with problems from consulting the service but in addition attracts a large number of first-year students when they arrive at university, perhaps out of curiosity. A typical example is an overseas postgraduate student from Bangladesh interested in dissertation writing but unaware of the difference in the way students learn at university in the two countries. After his first visit, he might request individual help from the counsellor and thereby avoid working inefficiently and ultimately being referred to the counsellor by his supervisor.

It also acclimatises students to the Counselling Office (they may even meet the counsellor in passing) so that if at a subsequent time they need a counselling appointment, they feel more at ease. This is particularly important for the overseas student who is not conditioned to the concept of 'welfare'. This has been confirmed by the Grubb Report (Reed, Hulton and Bazalgette, 1976) and Healey's (1977) subsequent research at the University of Sheffield.

Academic Staff Use

The academic staff borrow various items of audio-visual material to use in the 'learning to learn' workshops they run in their individual departments. In addition to using the material in stock, senior academic staff have made their own videos, which can subsequently be shown to teachers or students in the LRC, or borrowed by other colleagues for departmental use.

It is by members of staff being innovative and prepared to

expose their strengths and weaknesses to their colleagues in this courageous manner that real change can come about in less progressive departments. An example of this has been the video, made by a senior member of the academic staff, showing his 'study skills' seminar with overseas postgraduate students who have recently arrived at university. This was shown to academic staff in other departments who discussed it critically and, as a result, developed study skills seminars with their own overseas students.

At the weekend workshop in 1980 organised by Sturtridge and Bolitho (for people working with individualised and self-access material) the participants set out the main points of a learning resource centre as shown in Figure 5.1.

Cataloguing for Learner Access

The catalogue, which keeps the academic staff informed of what is currently available, needs to be regularly updated. This is of particular interest to those responsible for first-year students.

The needs of staff and students have been regularly monitored so that new material can be pertinent to their needs.

THE UNIVERSITY COUNSELLOR

Despite the overwhelming evidence that the student's academic success depends, in part, on his stage of personal development and his personality, some academic colleagues, not realising the connection, still feel that the counsellor should not be involved with developmental problems. In practical terms, counsellors give individual and group help with study, emotional and psychological problems on a tutor or self-referred basis, and, in addition, run the LRC, the English Conversation Scheme and undertake the role of consultants to academic staff and student organisations. The LRC, with its emphasis on self-direction, helps to develop the student's sense of identity and self-confidence as well as helping him to develop appropriate learning skills and improve academic standards.

Evaluation

Evaluation has the dilemma of either (a) being too soon after the 'learning to learn' experience, when it is accepted that if change is taking place the students' learning strategies may initially get worse; or (b) being too long after the 'learning to learn' experience when a number of students may have left university and severed all connections.

These facts are borne out by many researchers. In particular, Geerlafs and King (1968) in investigating 'the relationship between current objectives and practices in adult development

Figure 5.1: The Learning Resource Centre

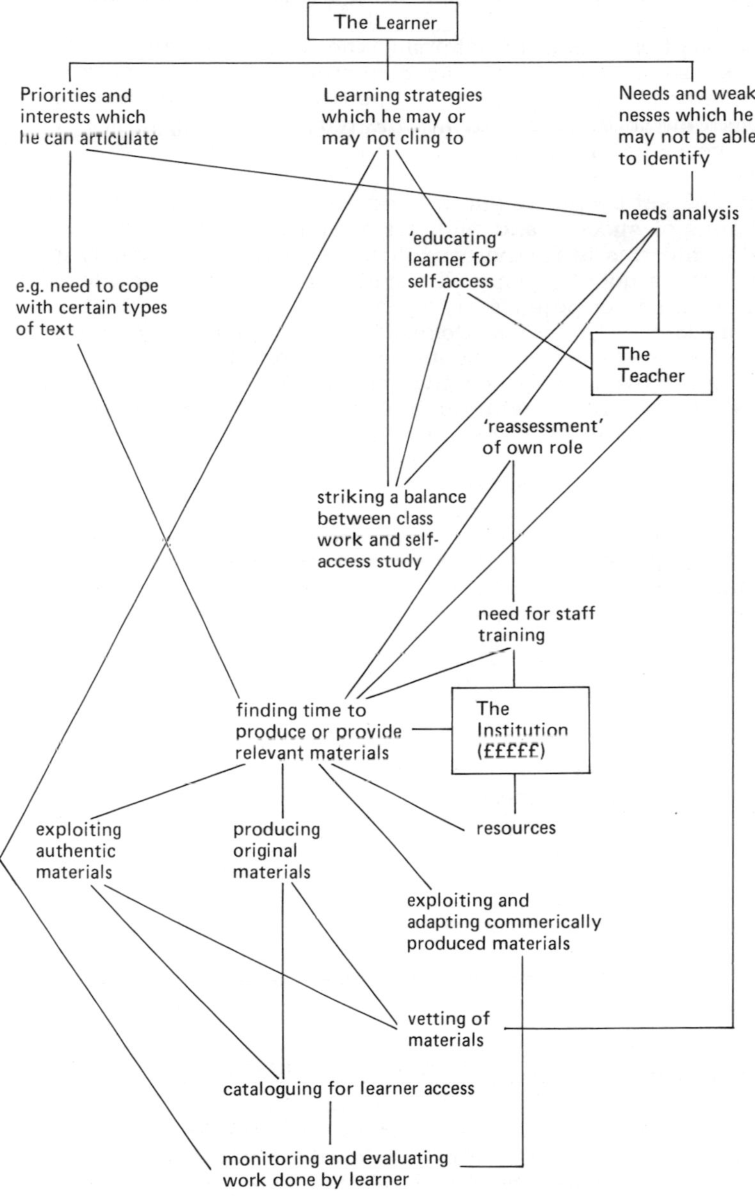

Source: Sturtridge and Bolitho (1980).

reading programmes' - when they had a 73 per cent response rate from 46 states and the District of Columbia - found that:

> No attempt was made to determine the long range effects of the course so that any research showed how the students assessed the course content and possibly the personality of the Course Director but not the permanent long term improvement in reading.

Self-evaluation by participants is rarely accurate since it relies on feelings of success and failure rather than on objective criteria, and this is further complicated by the discrepancy between the student's sense of learning competence and his actual learning competence.

Nelson-Jones, Toner and Coxhead (1979) explored the student's sense of learning competence, and found 'a possible discrepancy between self-image and achievement on the part of many students'. But Covington and Berry (1976) suggested an explanation for the discrepancy. They assert that 'it is the students self standards of level of aspiration that determines feelings of success or failure'.

More worrying than the students who lack self-esteem and feel less academically adequate than the actual results show, is the student who over-estimates his actual competence and, therefore, does not avail himself of the opportunity to learn 'how to learn' more effectively.

THE DEVELOPMENT OF GROUP WORK

My interest in learning to learn workshops arose from a need to try and meet the ever-increasing demands on a counselling service that could not increase its personnel. Sensitivity and social skills groups had been instituted to meet some collective needs of students, and I felt that the skills component of educational counselling could be approached in the same manner.

As time has continued, academic staff and myself have run regular learning to learn workshops in the Student's Union, mainly in the autumn term. In addition, I act as a consultant to academic staff running their own learning to learn workshops in their individual departments.

Learning to Learn Workshops in the Students' Union

The learning intervention that the counselling service provided, when I originally started the service at the University of Reading in 1973, was individual work with students and study skills lectures - using the Students' Union for the latter. It was attended, as most lectures of this kind are, by small groups of highly anxious and over conscientious students. They probably absorbed the generalised remarks about revision and examination techniques, but I suspect that their learning habits did not significantly change.

As McLeish (1968) observed, the lecture 'pays little regard to individual differences among the students'. Conversely, lectures to academic staff by the counsellors, discussing the affective as well as cognitive factors affecting examinations for example, went a small way to informing and changing attitudes. The main result was further tutor referrals to the counselling service rather than encouraging the teachers to develop their own learning to learn group.

Counselling Resource Papers

Occasional papers have been written by myself and distributed to all the teaching staff to sensitise wide areas of the academic community, and this has in turn resulted in individual tutor referrals to the counselling services for treatment. An example of this is the paper on Examination Anxiety which resulted in 22 students being referred with examination phobia in 1980. All the students were successfully treated and passed their examinations. The words 'referred to the counsellor' are inaccurate, however, for much of the treatment of individual students is the joint concern of teacher and counsellor.

Learning to Learn Workshops

The present 'learning to learn' workshops in the Students' Union, whilst attended by students from every faculty, act as a consciousness-raising exercise throughout the university and this leads to greater development of departmentally run workshops.

Normally, each workshop takes a topic 'in depth', such as 'note-taking' and consists of exercises in note-taking from the text, from practicals and from lectures, exploring both pattern and linear note-taking. In this way it aims to interest each and every one of the students attending.

As we have seen, 'learning to learn' intervention involves affective and cognitive factors so that counsellors and teachers combine naturally to plan and run these workshops.

The Policy of the Students' Union on Study Skills

The National Union of Students produced a document which was sent to all student union executives in Britain in 1980, calling on them to promote and develop study skills in each higher education institution. The Students' Union at the University of Reading has now appointed a Students' Union Officer for Academic Affairs (a non-sabbatical post) for the first time.

The workshops have implications for staff development. Although the focus is on students and learning, the staff find themselves questioning the way they are teaching.

Learning to Learn Workshops in Departments

The 'learning to learn' workshops in departments may be run singly or by two teachers during a lecture-free afternoon, or more effectively as part of the syllabus, a combination of 'skill' and 'content'. They meet all the objectives for 'learning to learn' intervention as set out in Chapter 4, except for the skills required for future employment, which would normally be covered by specialist teachers.

In his original 'Guide to Running Group Sessions', Gibbs (1977) makes two remarks which experience has shown are very pertinent. In the introduction, in discussing the plenary stage, he comments: 'There is often a very natural tendency to use this stage for a minor lecture, which I find difficult to resist' and 'It is sad to see a critical, creative, enthusiastic workshop sink into passive inertia as the Workshop tutor begins to speak'. It is just as sad to see recently arrived overseas students who find the informality of the workshops increases their anxiety and who long for more structure. It is important for the teacher to be aware of the needs of <u>each</u> individual learner. Again Gibbs says: 'One way I feel students <u>have</u> appreciated my contributions is when I make disclosures about my own studying.' Students tend to follow the teacher's lead in this respect and by taking this approach Gibbs built up trust.

The Individual Eclectic Approach

Students who are unable to study consult the counselling service or are referred by their teachers. First, their problem needs to be diagnosed. The problems fall under one of two headings.

1. A psychological or emotional problem exists that may inhibit study, or
2. 'study skills' help may be needed.

Even if it is the latter situation there are affective as well as cognitive issues that may need treatment.

Approaching the problems as a counsellor and not as a teacher, I would first diagnose the student physically, psychologically and intellectually before focusing on the study skills problem. In my opinion it is useless to treat a study skills problem without treating the psychological or emotional problem concurrently, which is what a teacher might tend to do.

Wankowski (1979) describes his approach at the University of Birmingham where he is the Educational Counsellor 'as basically that of a tutor'. He reconstructs the picture of past competence by examining the history of schooling.

> I begin with the mid-school career at what was happening up to 'O' level stage...an examination of the sixth form

> tuition and learning procedures is a more precise exercise. More detailed analysis of feelings and attitudes are carried out in the counselling dialogue since the areas of studies of the G.C.E.'A' level subjects bear more direct relationship to the University course!

In order to establish new mastery, the ways of past competence must be discerned, the present possibilities of becoming competent must be explored and the future hopes or fears of mastery or helplessness considered. True, relapses are frequent and many, as all therapists know only too well, but these tend to re-occur with the most highly anxious students. This anxiety requires treatment, at the same time as the study problems.

In reporting on some practical approaches to increasing students' learning competence Nelson-Jones and Toner (1979) stated that

> Mitchell et al (1975) reports a study in which the subjects were bright, failing college under-achievers, high on test and academic anxiety, and low on study skills competence.
>
> The subjects who received desensitization for anxiety followed by re-educative study skills training performed significantly better than those who only received study skills training. 93% of subjects given both anxiety and skills treatment changed from failing to succeeding and 73% were still succeeding when followed up two years later. Success was determined on course average, achievement score and number of pass grades.

There is further evidence of significant improvement when study skills training is combined with relaxation. Katahanm, Stengers and Cherrym (1966)

> treated fourteen highly test-anxious college students in a programme that combined discussion, study skills advice, reading, and systematic desensitization for a total of eight sessions, each approximately one hour in length. Post test results indicate a significant decrease in test anxiety and a significant increase in grade-point-average.

As a final example, Alpert and Haber (1960) produced evidence

> that both their facilitating and debilitating anxiety scales, especially the facilitating scale, were able to contribute to variance in academic performance other than that accounted for by a measure of aptitude. The student sees his feelings of anxiety, his lack of self confidence, his lack of identity, his lack of motivation very much as HIS PROBLEM as he also finds it impossible to concentrate or to write essays, without understanding the interrelation.

It is essential that he can be treated by a counsellor who is competent at treating 'the whole person' (i.e. the affective and cognitive issues) concurrently.

It causes more anxiety and loss of time if he has to take his essay-writing problem to his teacher, his anxiety to the Health Centre, and his lack of identity to the University Counsellor. This does not, however, prohibit the counsellor and academic teaching staff working concurrently and co-operatively to help the student.

Let us imagine a case of 'Examination Anxiety' - a mythical first-year student referred by her teacher in January - to illustrate the eclectic approach. By means of a relaxed interview, I would try to investigate the following:

1. How the student is feeling at the moment - and how she felt about being referred to the counselling service by her teacher.
2. The nature of the problem - as she understands it.
3. An Intellectual Profile:
(a) Sense of learning competence at school
(b) Learning strategies adopted at school
(c) School term grades
(d) 'A' level grades
(e) Feedback on university term work
(f) Results on any university term tests
(g) Ability to achieve 'deep-level' processing
(h) 'Interest' or 'course'-based attitude
(i) Ability to cope with examinations.
4. A Physical Profile:
(a) Physical hardships
(b) Chronic ill health - at school
- at university
(c) Medication for psychiatric or psychological disorders - with particular reference to side effects.
5. A Personality Profile
(a) Attitude to authority - parents
- school teachers
- academic staff
(b) Relationship with peers - before university
(singly or groups) - since coming to university
(c) Relationship with family - prior to university
- at present time
(d) Relationship between parents
(e) Parents' attitude to higher education
(f) Student's attitude to higher education
(g) Sense of vocation
(h) Short- or long-term goals - motivation
(i) Sense of identity
(j) Cultural identity
(k) Level of self-confidence
(l) Hobbies - Individually run by herself
(m) Active involvement in religious or political groups

(n) Ability to organise 'work' and 'play'
(o) Personal or emotional problems that might affect study
(p) Psychological problems that might affect study
(q) Feelings about course at the present time
(r) Perception of the learning environment
(s) Feelings about examinations - at school
- at university.

The diagnosis is then made and discussed with the student. The teacher who referred the student would be informed by the student that she had visited the counsellor and of the proposed treatment plan. In this way confidentiality is maintained, whilst the teacher is kept informed.

In this case the referral of 'examination anxiety' was in fact diagnosed not as normal anxiety about examinations but as 'examination phobia' with previous evidence of this at 'A' levels.

In addition, there was a lack of motivation. This student was found to be studying this course only because she got good 'A' level grades and her parents and school teachers expected her to go to university. She thought that 'she might like English [one of her three first-year examination subjects]... she enjoyed some of the Authors...if she left University she had no idea what she would do'.

The eclectic treatment for examination phobia would then be explained in detail to the student - the method, commitment of time, effective outcome, and the need to identify academic interests more clearly in the hope the motivation might be improved (see Figure 5.2) In some cases it might be necessary to consider vocational counselling with the possibility of course change if she is no longer motivated to study her particular subject.

Each counselling session would allow for time for the behavioural and psychotherapeutic treatment models to proceed concurrently. In addition, the student would make use of the self-directed audio facilities in the LRC and possibly decide to attend a 'learning to learn' workshop run by the teacher and counsellor.

To reinforce the treatment, the Robert Sharpe tape, 'How to Pass Examinations', could be borrowed and taken home for the revision period in the Easter vacation.

Factors that Affect Treatment

The student has teacher contact with the 'learning to learn' workshop and in the setting and marking of mock examinations.

The student has contact with other students on her course in a variety of social and academic settings during the 'learning to learn' workshops, possibly in the LRC and in the peer revision groups.

The student has counsellor contact in the regular treatment

sessions.

Figure 5.2: The Eclectic Treatment Model

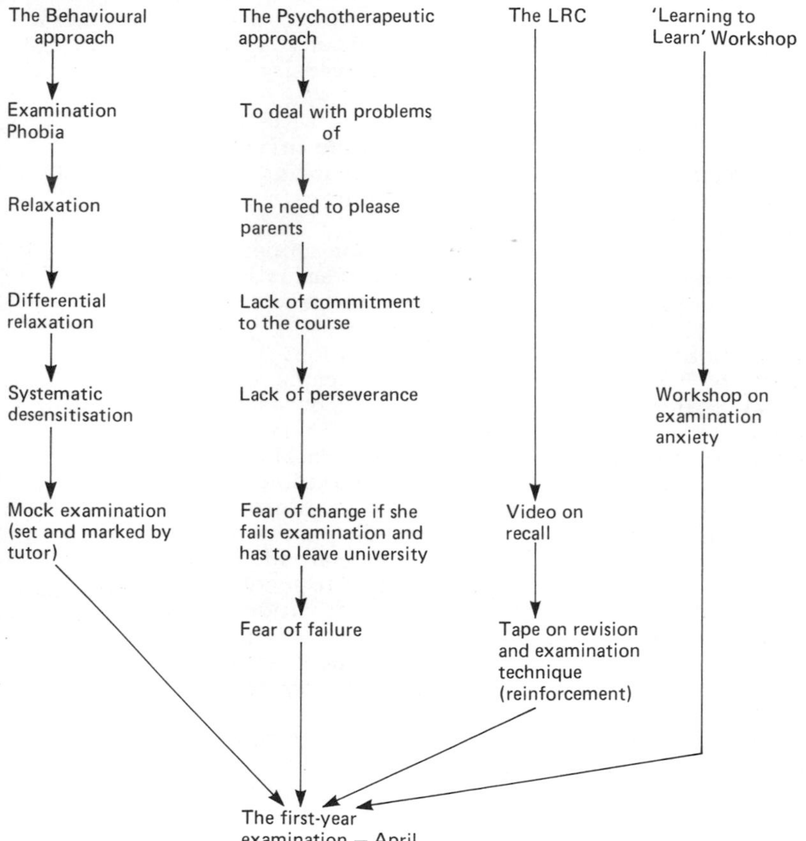

The eclectic approach, which has been called a 'jack of all trades' approach, requires the counsellor to be an expert in a wide variety of theoretical counselling approaches. It makes use of all the appropriate expertise in the institution. It takes into account, as Entwistle and Hanley (1978) point out: 'the very different personal goals, previous knowledge and learning strategies of the student and the context in which learning takes place'. The focus is, as I submit it should be, on the learner rather than on the teacher or the institution.

In the next chapter we shall consider overseas students, looking at the language/cultural/study skills interaction and the difficulties that arise for them in an academic situation. The chapter is written by Mr Cyril Weir, who, for the last two years, has been working on a research project established by the Associated Examination Board to analyse the language needs of overseas students following academic courses in Science, Engineering, Technology and Business Studies at institutes of further and higher education in the United Kingdom, with the aim of producing a series of modular English for specific purposes tests.

REFERENCES

Alpert, R. and Haber, R.N. (1960) Anxiety in Academic Achievement Situations, 'Journal of Abnormal and Social Psychology', vol. 61, pp. 204-15

Ausubel, D.P. and Youssef, M. (1963) Role of Discriminability in Meaningful Parallel Learning, 'Journal of Educational Psychology', vol. 54, no. 6, pp. 331-6

Bannister, D. and Fransella, F. (1977) 'Inquiring Man', Penguin, Harmondsworth

Carver, D. and Dickinson, L. (1980) 'Autonomy, Self Direction and the Affective Domain in Language Teaching in Schools', Report by the British Association for Applied Linguistics on Workshops in Self-Directed Learning (September), Scottish Centre for Education Overseas, Moray House College of Education, p. 5

Covington, M.V. and Berry, R.G. (1976) 'Self Worth and School Leavers', Holt, Rinehart and Winston, New York, as quoted in Nelson-Jones, Toner and Coxhead

Entwistle, N. and Hanley, M. (1978) Personality, Cognitive Style and Student Learning Strategies, 'Higher Education Bulletin', vol. 6, no. 1, pp. 23-43

Geerlafs, M.W. and King, M. (1968) Current Practices in College and Adult Developmental Reading Programmes, 'Journal of Reading' (April), p. 517

Gibbs, G. (1977) 'Learning to Study: A Guide to Running Group Sessions', Institute of Educational Technology, Open University, Milton Keynes

Gibbs, G. and Nortledge, A. (1977) Learning to Study - A Student Centred Approach, 'Teaching at a Distance', no. 8, p. 4

Healey, B. (1977) 'A Review of Student Welfare Services', University of Sheffield, Report no. 15

Katahanm, M., Stengers, S. and Cherry, N. (1966) Group Counselling and Behaviour Therapy with Test Anxious College Students, 'Journal of Consulting Psychology', vol. 30, pp. 544-9, as quoted in Nelson-Jones and Toner, p. 123

McLeish, J. (1968) 'The Lecture Method', Cambridge Institute of Education, Heffers of Cambridge, p. 47

Mitchell, K.R., Hall, R.F. and Piatkowska, O.E. (1975) A Group Programme for the Treatment of Failing College

Students' Behaviour Therapy, 'Behavioural Therapy', vol. 6, pp. 324-6
Mowrer, O.H. (1960) 'Learning Theory and Behaviour', John Wiley, New York
Nelson-Jones, R. and Toner, H.L. (1979) Counselling Approaches to Learning Competence in P.J. Hills (ed.), 'Study Courses and Counselling', SRHE, Guildford, Surrey
Nelson-Jones, R., Toner, H.L. and Coxhead, P. (1979) An Exploration of Student Sense of Learning Competence, 'British Educational Research Journal', vol. 5, no. 1, p. 181
Raaheim, K. (1981) Improving Student Learning Techniques, 'Teaching News' (University of Birmingham), no. 12 (February)
Ramsden, P. (1979) Student Learning and Perceptions of the Academic Environment, 'Higher Education Bulletin', vol. 8, Elsevier Scientific Publishing Co., Amsterdam, p. 413
Reed, B., Hutton, J. and Bazalgette, J. (1976) Freedom to Study: Requirements of Overseas Students in the UK', a report published by the Grubb Institute for the Overseas Students Trust, London
Sturtridge, G. and Bolitho, R. (1980) 'Individual and Self Access Materials', a report on weekend workshop at Bell College, Saffron Walden (May), p. 5
Wankowski, J. (1979) Counselling the Individual Student in P.J. Hills (ed.), 'Study Courses and Counselling', SRHE, Guildford, Surrey, pp. 85 and 89

6 THE PROBLEM FOR OVERSEAS STUDENTS AND FOR THE INSTITUTIONS WHERE THEY STUDY

C.J. Weir (Associated Examining Board, English for Overseas Students Project)

The ability to operate successfully in an academic context is a difficult enough process even for native speakers of English as, quite often, they do not possess academic study skills to the extent that they are assumed to. The problem is compounded for those overseas students who experience a shortfall in specific language skills. Inadequacies in listening, speaking, reading or writing skills often come to light only when students are called on to perform the academic tasks arising out of the courses they are enrolled on

This chapter sets out to survey the problems that overseas students have encountered in an academic context due to lack of proficiency in various crucial skills areas.

IS IT JUST A LANGUAGE PROBLEM?

Studies of overseas students in Britain date back to 1907 with the report of the Lee Warner Committee on Indian students, and the point emerges clearly from subsequent studies that language is only one of a myriad of problems overseas students face on entry to this country. This point is emphasised in Singh (1963), Burns (1965), Davies (1965, 1977), PEP (1965), Dunlop (1966), Morris (1967), Daniel (1975) and Walker (1978).

A composite picture of the overseas student's situation is presented by Sen (1970) who carried out, by questionnaire, English test and interview, an extensive study of 2,367 overseas students and 553 nurses from 130 countries studying in Britain from 1964-6. Amongst other things she investigated their academic and language difficulties and the problems they encountered in adjusting to English society. She subsequently followed up this work with a study of how successful they were on their courses. She was not concerned solely with the language difficulties they encountered as her aim was more to describe the interaction of the general criteria: academic ability, English language proficiency, adequate financial resources and adeptness in adjusting to new social situations. Like Larter (1962), Davies (1977) and Mackenzie (1977), she considered academic study and welfare problems inseparable for most students. She also raised the important question of the extent to which language is criterial to a student's academic success.

Davies (1977, p. 34) notes that Sen (1970) found English language to be non-significant as a predictor of academic success. Sen (1970, p. 113) claimed, on the basis of evidence from her follow-up study,

> that the extent of the use of and familiarity with the English language has little relevance to their final performance. This seems to contradict the experience of teachers in this country and in the United States who have placed great emphasis on the English language proficiency of overseas students.

She seems to arrive at this conclusion (pp. 153-4) from the results of student performance in five sub-tests of the shorter version of the Davies test. She found that these tests did not discriminate between the passes and failures for the qualification courses considered, and so she argues (p. 154): 'for practical purposes the tests do not, alone, provide a useful guide to final performance in these courses. Of course, the diagnostic - as against the predictive - value of the tests is a different matter.' However, she does qualify these remarks (p. 163):

> the criteria of final performance used in the present survey i.e. success or failure, is crude. Certain modifications of the test in the light of the present results and its validation on the basis of actual examination marks with larger samples for each type of course might provide a useful instrument for the selection of overseas students.

As well as considering the effectiveness of language testing as a predictor of academic success Sen also sought to establish the extent of the language problems students faced and she mentions (pp. 161-2) an important caveat:

> the relative proportions of students who are willing to admit difficulties - whether academic or personal - may not always give an accurate picture of the extent to which such difficulties are encountered. It is our impression, supported we believe by the general tenor of the figures reported, that the picture these students and nurses present of themselves is unduly favourable and optimistic. This suggests that where problems appear or criticisms are voiced, they deserve more, rather than less, attention than the cold tabulations would imply.

Earlier in the study (pp. 57-60) she drew attention to the serious nature of some of the problems. Over a third of the 2,367 students found writing essays difficult, and a large number had difficulties in following lectures and tutorials. If one examines her relative figures for different national groupings they point to what may be an even greater cause for concern in the future, namely the worse plight of the foreign as compared to Commonwealth students. She notes that the Middle Eastern students, who scored fewer than the other groups in the Davies test: 'on the whole seem to find most difficulty with their studies. Only few expressed no difficulty with lectures, tutorials and in contacting their teachers, and a high proportion found writing essays and reference reading "very difficult".' She noted (p. 59) 44 per cent reported taking notes in lectures as a difficulty and 40 per cent had difficulty with the speed at which the language was spoken. Over a third had difficulty with 'accent' and just under a third had difficulty in understanding idioms and phrases.

A majority of the students in her survey were from the Commonwealth and in terms of their previous use of English as a medium of instruction, the earlier age at which they had begun to learn English, and their use of English at home, Sen found they had had considerably more exposure to the language than their foreign counterparts. This is a real cause for concern, for the balance between foreign and Commonwealth students coming to study in this country changed in the early 1970s and now there are considerably more foreign than Commonwealth students.

The English ability of the foreign students will, in all probability, be lower because of a much more limited exposure to the taught language, and it might be reasonable to infer that these students are likely to encounter language difficulties proportionate to this in their academic courses. The extent of the language problems brought to light by Sen's study of predominantly Commonwealth students was bad enough, but a similar survey carried out today might well reveal an even greater incidence of problems in the academic context occasioned by language disability.

Davies (1977, p. 36) raised this question of how serious a problem language is on the basis of his findings in a survey completed for the Scottish Education Department on the English proficiency of foreign students in Scotland in the non-university sector:

> it would be a mistake to exaggerate the place of language among foreign students' problems. To do so can be a means of evading the examination not only of other problems of learning and teaching but also of welfare problems. What all foreign students require is a minimum general English, a language core. Thereafter other factors (e.g. academic ability) are important in contributing to students' performance, their welfare and their success.

Davies found in his survey that students ranked English language as being the most serious problem, followed by academic status, social contacts and accommodation, which seems at least to contradict the findings of Stevenson (1974), referred to in the same article (Davies, 1977), who carried out a survey of the welfare problems of overseas students at Edinburgh University in which language was placed very low in the rank ordering of difficulties encountered. Davies (1977, p. 35) admits the view that language is not a significant factor, but this is not borne out by the NAFSA (1961) survey which found language to be criterial, as apparently did Hebron's (1967) survey (quoted in Walker, 1978) of overseas students at Rutherford College. Ryan (1979) quotes similar evidence from Campbell's (1974) study of undergraduate and post-graduate students following courses in technical subjects at the Loughborough, City and Birmingham universities. Campbell concluded that difficulties students had in communication were not solely attributable to an insufficient proficiency in English, but more to a complex mixture of linguistic, academic, socio-cultural and practical problems. However, a majority of the students in Campbell's study did indicate that writing, speaking and understanding lecturers were areas where they had particular difficulty. Walker (1978, pp. 80-8) found that in the interviews he carried out with academic staff at the technical college level, the study skills area was often cited as presenting a major problem for the overseas student.

Walker (1978) also pointed out that student awareness of language inadequacy is often lacking and that there was a general tendency for students to over-estimate their own language ability. This is borne out by Sen's (1970) work on this subject, and by Jordan (1977, p. 14) who found:

> in 1972-73 and again in 1974-75 students' self assessment ratings were examined and compared to the students' scores in the Chaplen test. Overwhelmingly the results showed that the students at the lower end of the scale in the test grossly over-estimated their language ability.

This is an important factor to be borne in mind when looking at surveys carried out by questionnaire and interview which report that language is not seen by students to be a problem.

The extent and nature of the language problem will be discussed below, but first the socio-cultural problems which often compound language difficulties will be briefly considered.

SOCIO-CULTURAL PROBLEMS

Haigh (Dunlop, 1966, pp. 7-8) remarked:

> It soon became clear that young people from one European country seeking education or training in another, met with fewer difficulties than those coming from another continent, and particularly than those whose cultural background had not fitted them for conditions of life and study in a European country.

Whether this is due to problems of 'cultural incommensurability' (Edwards 1978, p. 317) or social pressures due to colour prejudice or xenophobia is difficult to assess. There is obviously a good deal of sensitivity amongst overseas students about the latter as can be seen in some of their essays in the collection edited by Tajfel and Dawson (1965). The National Foundation for Educational Research (NFER) enquiry (Burns, 1965) into the adjustment and attitude of overseas students holding Commonwealth bursaries in England and Wales discovered that a majority felt some sense of handicap because of a difference in race or colour. The 1965 PEP report based on interviews and questionnaires conducted with students from former colonies concluded that the attitude of the British to overseas students came in for some strong criticism. Reed, Hutton and Bazalgette (1978, p. 5) mention that the overseas visiting student often felt he was being treated as an intruder and confused with immigrants.

Both Holes (1972) and Edwards (1978) have commented on the problems associated with cultural incommensurability. Edwards instances the 'shyness' of many South-East Asians and Holes suggested this might be due to a combination of factors: lack of confidence in their English and fear of the English students' ridicule of clumsy or ill-formed sentences (especially in the case of the weakest students); a malaise induced by the unfamiliarity of a situation where their judgements might be questioned (particularly true of older students); and last but not least, an ignorance, not so much of the language but of the cultural admissability of interrupting a lecturer or tutor to ask a question and simply how to ask the question. He quotes from Fishman (1972):

> native members of such (speech) networks slowly and unconsciously acquire sociolinguistic communicative competence with respect to appropriate language use. They are not necessarily aware of the norms that guide their sociolinguistic behaviour. Newcomers to such networks or communities ... must discover these norms more rapidly, more painfully and therefore more consciously.

This is evidenced in the way most foreign students ask questions, by approaching members of staff after the class. This is a strategy which is perhaps indicative of a gap in their communicative competence, namely ignorance of the socio-linguistic conventions associated with asking questions in public.

Related to cultural problems are differences in previous educational background, and Edwards (1978) drew attention to the difficulties this may cause in terms of non-participation in group discussion and problems arising out of self-teaching. Singh (1963) drew attention to excessive deference to staff and it would seem many overseas students have been taught to venerate their teachers, speaking only when spoken to or not answering for fear of losing face. Edwards cites previous exposure to didactic teaching methodology and Singh mentions previous training by rote methods as factors influencing the students preference for being told what to do rather than organise their own study. On the basis of observations in the classroom Edwards notes (p. 321): 'the tendency to rote memorisation and regurgitation was apparent in some overseas learners' answers often with little cognisance of the question asked'. Many of these problems are also referred to by students themselves in the collection of overseas student essays entitled 'Disappointed Guests' (Tajfel and Dawson, 1965).

NATURE AND EXTENT OF LANGUAGE PROBLEMS

The NFER survey quoted above (Burns, 1965) concluded that none of the students admitted any sense of handicap (except for a small number of difficulties arising from local usage) either in the use of English in their studies or in communication. This would seem to be at odds with nearly all subsequent research in the field. It may well have been an exceptionally gifted or well-screened group, but some doubts must be expressed concerning the questionnaire used, as some students misunderstood individual questions (p. 43), and it was not completed by several of the students.

Once we examine the literature concerning the academic language needs of overseas students it soon becomes evident that we cannot describe the language proficiency of some overseas students as adequate when they embark on courses in this country. The inadequacies detailed below might well be merely the tip of an iceberg, as for the most part they emerge from the work done in those institutions that are fortunate enough to have language-servicing facilities which can provide remedial English language tuition.

Rogers (1977, p. 37) discovered in the courses he ran for post-graduate students in science and technology that despite much previous work in the language: 'students have developed certain skills to the virtual neglect of others'. Though they might be able to cope with the reading and writing demands of their courses: 'they were unable to participate in academic discussion: even less were they able to take part in social activities outside the company of other foreign students in the same plight as themselves'. McKenzie (1977, p. 4) discovered for the Latin-American students he taught that: 'lack of oral fluency often proves an insuperable obstacle to effective participation in seminars and tutorials'.

Johns and Johns (1977) looked at the problems faced by students in seminars and found that the sheer variety of teaching situations labelled seminars hampered attempts to devise suitable teaching strategies for remedial work. UKCOSA (The United Kingdom Council for Overseas Student Affairs) (1974) found a common problem was 'reluctance to ask questions due to a fear of using English. This contributes to the formation of nationality groups where students hardly ever speak in English.' Jordan and Mackay (1973) noted: 'one of their biggest problems was to find the opportunity to practise speaking English with native English speakers ... Consequently they made slow progress with their spoken English.' And Edwards (1978, p. 314) found a similar pattern in her study of overseas nurses coming to study in the United Kingdom and concluded that the overseas learners' language problems lay mainly in the field of spoken English, 'in both understanding and speaking. Over 78% admitted to having difficulties of some kind with this.'

Jordan (1977, pp. 15-16) described how post-graduate students at Manchester and Newcastle heard most spoken English in a passive listening role, i.e. in situations where they were not called upon to respond at all, e.g. listening to lectures, the radio etc., and therefore with no check on comprehension. In his study, 70 per cent listed understanding spoken English as their biggest difficulty on arrival in the United Kingdom and 50 per cent mentioned their own speech problems of fluency and self-expression with most speaking for a maximum of an hour a day, but 40 per cent for half an hour or less. Fifty-six per cent found it difficult to meet British people to converse with and this led to restrictions on opportunities for practising spoken language. Davies (1965, p. 235) took a group of students studying overseas through the medium of English and compared them to an equivalent group in the United Kingdom, to see if any difference due to a short period of residence over here showed up. He discovered that in non-contextual listening tests the overseas group were inferior and concluded that this 'could only be accounted for by their lack of exposure to everyday British English in Britain'. Sen (1970) also found that 25 per cent of the students surveyed admitted to having listening comprehension difficulties. It would seem likely, therefore, as Morrison (1974) argued in his thesis, that lack of exposure to natural-spoken British English accounts for the initial difficulty that many experience on arrival.

Rogers (1977) carried out a survey in which students assessed their own language difficulties and produced results which were largely confirmed by Jordan's (1977) experiences at Manchester. The difficulties, in descending order of severity, noted by Rogers (1977) were with:

(a) Fluent conversation at an informal level. McKenzie (1977) pointed out the serious problems Latin-Americans have particularly at the phonological level and Larter (1962, p. 121) provides evidence of this amongst the African students he taught at the technical level.

(b) Informal social interaction. Edwards (1978, p. 319) noted that students had difficulties here: 'with a high rate of mutual misunderstanding between overseas and indigene learners'.

(c) Formal subject discussions and seminars. Johns and Johns (1977) refer to this and Edwards (1978) notes instances where: 'they had difficulty in remaining linguistically coherent when attempting to answer at length or when joining in discussions'. Edwards (pp. 314-26) comments that if one adds to this difficulty problems with accent and general difficulties in understanding the teaching staff: 'the indigene learner's near total ellipsis when answering questions and the speed at which they do so', one has some idea of the factors which might inhibit participation. Edwards concludes that: 'what learner-initiated participation there was in the classroom activities was dominated by indigenes'.

(d) The expression of personal viewpoint.

Rogers (1977) also conducted a series of interviews with members of staff who remarked on the following specific difficulties:

(a) Not knowing the meaning or appropriate use of many colloquial idioms. Edwards (1978, p. 315) also emphasised the difficulties caused by the casual style of discourse of certain tutors: 'The use of slang or allusive language, which excludes the outsider, causes the overseas student to miss a lot of what goes on in the classroom.' Holes (1972) drew attention to the difficulties caused by the employment of excessive colloquialisms, slang and register switching, and quotes (p. 33) Winter (1971):

> the distinctions between formal and informal language may be blurred in a lecture situation where there may be drastic change from formal to informal language when giving explanations ... it may be disastrous for the foreign student who may have been taught English in a combination of literary and formal English.

These difficulties in comprehension are often compounded, as Edwards (1978) observed, by the teaching staff themselves (p. 316):

> The instances of inappropriate methods of presentation of practical procedures, inadequate explanation of theory and lack of advance organisation of material - which were disturbingly frequent - observed in the classroom would almost certainly compound the initial problems of overseas learners and may well account for the difficulties in understanding experienced by some indigenes.

(b) Not playing an active part in discussion: restricted answers to questions (see Jordon, 1977).

(c) Too formal and polite.
(d) Little knowledge of topics of current interest commonly discussed by educated speakers.
(e) Difficulties with 'openers', 'closers' and 'topic change'.
(f) Difficulty with humour of all kinds.
(g) Did not understand various conventions of non-verbal behaviour.

In addition to these, Jordan (1977) drew attention to difficulties in:

(a) Understanding the variety of native-speaker accents (see also Larter, 1962, Sen, 1970, UKCOSA, 1974, Jordan and Mackay, 1973, p. 45, Edwards, 1978, p. 314 and Walker, 1978, pp. 94-103).
(b) Communicating functionally especially in asking questions for appropriate purposes (Holes, 1972).
(c) Understanding lectures in general and taking notes (Sen, 1970, UKCOSA, 1974, Holes, 1972, pp. 29-30 and James, 1977).

One of the most serious problems for English servicing agencies in the universities is the disparate composition of the students they have to cater for as a result of different language backgrounds, different abilities in different skill areas, different subjects being studied in courses which make demands on different ranges of language skills, different previous learning experiences, different learning styles, etc. (see Morrison, 1974, pp. 5-6 and Jordan, 1977, p. 15).

It soon became apparent that no even demand is made simultaneously on all the different English language-based academic study skills, and at different times in a course a different variety of skills is called for. Straker-Cook (1977, p. 5) holds the view that: 'At least for post-graduates, attendance at initial lectures and talks, and participation in seminars and discussion groups, place a heavy demand on oral/aural skills in the earlier stages of their study.' Jordan (1977, p. 17) agrees with this and for his 'typical' student:

> understanding native speakers of English will be his first major problem on arrival in Britain; the next major problem will be personal fluency and self expression in English ... the latter will still be a problem after a few months mainly through lack of practice.

As the course develops writing skills will eventually become more important and will generally (p. 18) 'supersede understanding as a cause of major difficulty as written work has to be submitted' (see also Jordan and Mackay, 1973).

Jordan (1977, p. 14) points to a general inability on the part of the overseas student to:

(a) Write academic English (noted also by Larter, 1962, p. 121 and UKCOSA, 1974). Edwards (1978, p. 316) refers to this but suggests: 'indigenes probably had difficulties as well'.
(b) Write short reports.
(c) Write concisely.
(d) Write quickly.

Holes (1972, p. 57) found that overseas students admitted to having a lot of difficulty in writing essays and reports on their own work. Nearly half of the post-graduate students in Jordan's survey wrote an average of five essays a term, each of about 2,500 words, and one-third wrote between two and five reports per term, each of about 4,000 words. As Larter (1962, p. 121) pointed out though, particular difficulties in this area may only surface when writing has to be done under the pressure of time constraints as in examinations and by then it may well be too late for remedial action.

The skill of reading is likely to remain important through most courses. Straker-Cook (1977, p. 45) noted: 'the reading of specialist literature in English is the one skill that most students seem to have maintained prior to their arrival in Britain'. However, Jordan (1977) still cited a general inability on the part of the overseas student to read quickly or understand the complexities of academic prose. He (p. 16) found that the average student had only one speed (i.e. slow) for silent reading - about 150-60 words per minute. Edwards (1978, pp. 316-17) noted similar difficulties with reading comprehension and adds that of reading aloud, e.g. the ward reports some nurses have to make. UKCOSA (1974) cited 'difficulty in reading effectively' as a common problem and also 'difficulty in understanding examination questions'. Holes (1972) referred to slow reading as a universal complaint as well as a widespread lack of guidance in what to read. He got the impression that the cause of low reading speeds was:

> in some measure due to a reverential attitude to books in general: each one read must be summarised with a great expenditure of time and effort. There was no skimming of books for ideas and information. This was the first time for some students that they had had to read books in any quantity, with specific aims in mind.

He adds (p. 66) that it was not the actual level of linguistic difficulty in the text which caused problems, but 'terminological difficulties in new subjects [which] were the biggest obstacle in reading, as is shown by the large number of students (among them the most fluent) who read their textbooks with a dictionary at hand'.

Morrison (1974, p. 6) also drew attention to the possibility that the crucial factor might be the individual's language ability when starting the course and that average improvement during a one-year course is insignificant when compared to differences between individuals on starting. He refers to work done by Binyon (1972) at Gothenburg who commented that some students were better on starting than others were after a year's study. This may, in some cases, indicate the low value to be placed on any remedial teaching they receive (Mason, 1971). Mason's (1971) argument is that 'at least for many intermediate to advanced foreign students ... intensive E.F.L. work may be a waste of time'. Morrison (1974) argues that improvements in students' performance, as a result of learning experiences evidenced at the Universities of Leeds and Lancaster, would tend to emphasise that it is the difference between students' abilities at the start of the course rather than a question of the extent or lack of any improvement in language ability due to remedial English courses which is of central importance.

Evidence is available that universities have in the past accepted students with critically low scores on the Davies Test and the English Language Battery (ELBA) test. In these cases the width of the gap at the start would certainly seem to be the crucial factor governing a student's relative performance rather than any limitations on achievement due to the nature and amount of remedial assistance received during the course.

THE NEED FOR REMEDIAL ENGLISH

In view of the many difficulties in English for academic purposes faced by overseas students, in June 1972 a group of lecturers formed the Special English Language Materials for Overseas University Students (SELMOUS) group. Their aim was to share experiences in dealing with overseas students' English language difficulties on the basis of investigation of language needs and the production of relevant teaching materials for use in any necessary remedial work. This group is very much aware of the extent of the language problems involved, as one of its members, Jordan (1977, p. 13), stated:

> Once a student has been accepted and arrives at the university, no matter how poor his command of English, he is rarely asked to delay his academic course of studies in order to attend a full-time course of English. Yet S.E.L.M.O.U.S. members estimate that about 30% of those students that they teach are in need of full-time English tuition ranging from 3-12 months.

SELMOUS have been prominent in highlighting the particular language needs of overseas post-graduate students, and Price (1977) described how they have been instrumental in setting up pre-sessional courses to try to improve the language performance of students before their academic studies get under way. Given that present language entry requirements are not uniformly applied and vary as between institutions, and given that present attempts to assess student language ability are not satisfactory, then there is a serious possibility that remedial teaching either pre- or in-sessional will be necessary because of a shortfall in some of the overseas students' language abilities.

The very existence of the SELMOUS group in the universities adds weight to the contention that language problems amongst overseas students are a cause for concern, and there is a felt need for better testing procedures which will point to areas where remedial work is needed. Language disabilities do not necessarily entail failure for the overseas student, but it is likely that the more proficient he is in the language, the more he will benefit from his course.

THE NATIVE SPEAKER NORM

Perren (1963, p. 14) commented: 'often we take it for granted that the British student has acquired the skills he needs with his G.C.E. But we know that the foreign student who has the same G.C.E. has not necessarily acquired the skills he needs.' One of the areas that needs to be considered is that of 'the native speaker norm'. We shall attempt to establish how far, in practice, overseas students experience language-based problems in their academic work in excess of their British counterparts. Very little work would seem to have been done in comparing the two groups' relative levels of language difficulty in the various academic tasks they have to perform, and all too often the false assumption is made that the native speaker has no problems, with the result that the overseas student is expected to reach the standard of a mythical norm.

Austin Ward (1979) examined the competence of a sample of British craft-level students from a variety of courses in the further education sector. He comments (p. 424) that only 17 per cent of these demonstrated any 'satisfactory' competence in their written work: 'The analysis of the scripts for "mechanical competence" revealed that the majority of students found great difficulty with spelling, punctuation and grammar.' He quotes (p. 427) from the Bullock Report (DES, 1975): 'Many allegations about lower standards today come from employers who maintain that the young people joining them cannot write grammatically, are poor spellers and generally express themselves badly.' One would expect a higher standard than this from the native speakers in the range of courses we are surveying, from GCE 'A' level to post-graduate level, but evidence from questionnaires which the Associated Examining Board administered in 1980 does indicate the extent and gravity of the language-based problems for some of the British students even at these levels.

CONCLUSIONS

The evidence from the literature would seem to suggest that serious language problems do exist for some overseas students. Though these problems may vary from student to student, it is by no means an inconsiderable minority who suffer from such problems in one form or another. It is our contention that however much some surveys may downgrade the relative weighting of language as a problem, as against say social and welfare difficulties, there is no question of the pervasiveness of its existence. Because it exists and because it manifests itself in the forms outlined above, there is a strong case for attempting to devise better methods of establishing the extent and nature of any shortfall there might be between a student's proficiency in terms of academic language skills and the demands made in terms of these by the course of study he is undertaking.

In response to requests from receiving institutions for a more comprehensive profile of a student's language proficiency, in terms of the demands that would be placed on him in respect of a particular course of study, the Associated Examining Board set up its English for Overseas Students Project in 1979.

The first two stages of the project have now been completed. In Stage I, we established the levels, the discipline areas and the institutions where overseas students were enrolling in the further and higher education sectors. On the basis of the information gathered during this stage, we focused our research on students following courses in the general subject areas of science, engineering and social, business and administrative studies.

In Stage II, we sought to ascertain the language demands that are made on students following courses in these general discipline areas. Two methods of enquiry were employed to determine the language tasks facing students in a number of different academic contexts.

During 1980, we carried out a series of visits to educational institutions in different sectors of tertiary education. Observations of science, engineering and social science courses were made at the Universities of Exeter, London and Reading and also at colleges in Farnborough, Bradford, Newbury and Padworth. During these visits, the general language tasks facing students taking part in lectures, seminars and practical classes were recorded using an observation schedule derived from the Schools Council Science Teaching Observation Schedule (Egglestone, Galton and Jones, 1975) and from John Munby's Communicative Needs Processing Model (Munby, 1978). The data generated by these exercises provided us with the framework for our second method of enquiry: the questionnaire.

We contacted all the university and polytechnic science, engineering and social science departments and colleges offering GCE Advanced Level science, where we knew from earlier research that there were large numbers of overseas students studying, and asked them to assist us in our project. We then asked those who were willing to co-operate to let us have details of the numbers of overseas students, for whom English was not the first language in the country of origin, enrolled on specific courses within their departments, together with numbers of the staff who taught them. Questionnaires were then sent to staff and through them to both British and overseas students. The responses to these questionnaires enabled us to establish a wider basis for our description of the language tasks facing students in a variety of subject areas and provided us with information on the extent of difficulty both overseas and British students encountered in coping with a variety of tasks and constraints in the academic context. Completed queston-naires were received from 940 overseas students, 530 British students and 559 staff in respect of 43 postgraduate courses, 61 undergraduate courses and 39 'A' level centres.

The information gathered through these two methods of enquiry has provided us with a set of general descriptive parameters which will help us to construct a test battery to assess a student's ability in performing language tasks relevant to the academic context in which he or she has to operate. During the third stage of the project, which is scheduled to continue from September 1981 until September 1982, we will be concerned with designing and validating a variety of test formats to establish the best methods for assessing a student's performance level on those tasks and under those constraints that the research to date has indicated to be important to overseas students following academic courses through the medium of English.

The findings from the enquiry are too numerous to report here so we shall merely attempt a few generalisations. The evidence we gathered indicates that serious problems do exist in the study skills areas for a distressingly large number of overseas students. It would therefore seem imperative to have some kind of early warning system which will enable those receiving institutions, that accept students with a shortfall in language ability in certain areas, to ensure that the necessary remedial instruction is provided. It also emerged from our enquiry that in reading and writing skills over half the British students co-operating in the survey also admitted to experiencing difficulties. The problems of study are inevitably more acute for the overseas students with a language disability in a certain skills area but the research suggests that the British student might possibly be in need of a certain amount of assistance in some areas as well.

REFERENCES

Austin Ward, B.J. (1979) An Enquiry into the Attitudes and Abilities of Entrants to Colleges of Further Education and

Technical Colleges, in Regard to Use and Study of English Language, unpublished PhD, University of London
Binyon, M. (1972) English Language Research at Gothenburg, quoted in Morrison, J.W. (1974)
Burns, D.G. (1965) (ed.) 'Travelling Scholars: an Enquiry into the Adjustment and Attitudes of Overseas Students Holding Commonwealth Bursaries in England and Wales', National Foundation for Educational Research (NFER)
Campbell, V. (1974) 'Pilot Report on the Communication Problems of Overseas Students in British Technical Education', University of London
Daniel, N. (1975) 'The Cultural Barrier', Edinburgh University Press, Edinburgh
Davies, Alan (1965) Proficiency in English as a Second Language, unpublished PhD Thesis, University of Birmingham
Davies, A. (1967) The English Proficiency of Overseas Students, 'British Journal of Educational Psychology', vol. 37, part 2, pp. 165-74
Davies, A. (1977) Do Foreign Students Have Problems? in 'English for Academic Purposes' A.P. Cowie and J.B. Heaton (eds), BAAL, printed by College of Estate Management, University of Reading
Department of Education and Science (1975) 'Language for Life', Report of the Committee of Inquiry appointed by the Secretary of State for Education and Science under the Chairmanship of Sir Alan Bullock, FBA
Dunlop, F. (1966) 'Europe's Guests, Students and Trainees: a Survey on the Welfare of Foreign Students and Trainees in Europe', Council of Cultural Co-operation of the Council of Europe
Edwards, P.J. (1978) The Problems of Communication Facing Overseas Nurses in Training in England and Wales, unpublished PhD Thesis, University of London
Egglestone, J.F., Galton, M.J. and Jones, M.E. (1975) 'A Science Teaching Observation Schedule' (Schools Council Research Studies), Macmillan Educational, London
Fishman, J.A. (1972) 'Language in Sociocultural Change', Stanford University Press, Stanford, California
Hebron, C.C. (1967) The Performance of Overseas Students in Rutherford College (Newcastle-upon-Tyne), unpublished MSS, July
Holes, C.D. (1972) An Investigation into Some Aspects of the English Language Problems of Two Groups of Overseas Postgraduate Students at Birmingham University, MA Thesis, University of Birmingham
Johns, T.F. and Johns, C.M. (1977) The Current Programme of Materials Development in English for Academic Purposes at the Universities of Birmingham and Aston, in A. Cowie and J.B. Heaton (eds), BAAL/SELMOUS Publication, University of Reading, pp. 127-30
Jordan, R. (1977) Study Skills and Pre-sessional Courses in

S. Holden (ed.), 'English for Specific Purposes', Modern English Publications, London

Jordan, R.R. and Mackay, R. (1973) 'A Survey of the Spoken English Problems of Overseas Postgraduates at the Universities of Manchester and Newcastle', University of Newcastle, Newcastle-upon-Tyne

Larter, J.K. (1962) English Language Problems of Overseas Students in Technical Colleges, 'The Vocational Aspect of Further Education', vol. 14, pp. 117-35

Mackenzie, J.G. (1977) Some English Language Problems of Latin-American Post-graduate Students, in A.P. Cowie and J.B. Heaton (eds), 'English for Academic Purposes', BAAL, printed by College of Estate Management, University of Reading

Mason, C. (1971) The Relevance of Intensive Training in English as a Foreign Language for University Students, 'Language Learning (Michigan)', vol. 21, no. 2, pp. 197-204

Morris, B.S. (1967) 'International Community?', National Union of Students and the Scottish Union of Students

Morrison, J.W. (1974) An Investigation of Problems in Listening Comprehension Encountered by Overseas Students in the First Year of Postgraduate Studies in Sciences in the University of Newcastle upon Tyne, and the Implications for Teaching, unpublished MEd Thesis, University of Newcastle upon Tyne

Munby, John (1978) 'Communicative Syllabus Design', Cambridge University Press, Cambridge

NAFSA (1961) 'Research in Programs for Foreign Students', NAFSA Studies and Papers: Research Series No. 2, National Association for Foreign Students' Advisers, New York

Perren, G.E. (1963) 'Linguistic Problems of Overseas Students in Britain', British Council ETIC Occasional Paper No. 3

PEP (Political and Economic Planning) (1965) 'New Commonwealth Students in Britain: With Special Reference to Students from East Africa', PEP

Price, J. (1977) Study Skills - With Special Reference to Seminar Strategies and One Aspect of Academic Writing in S. Holden (ed.), 'English for Specific Purposes', Modern English Publications, London

Reed, B., Hutton, J. and Bazalgette, J. (1978) Requirements of Overseas Students in the UK in 'Freedom to Study', Overseas Students Trust, London

Rogers, S. (1977) The communicative needs of some overseas postgraduate students in A.P. Cowie and J.B. Heaton (eds.), 'English for Academic Purposes', BAAL, printed by College of Estate Management, University of Reading

Ryan, M. (1979) English for Academic Purposes, unpublished MA Thesis, University of Wales Institute of Science and Technology

Sen, A. (1970) 'Problems of Overseas Students and Nurses',

NFER
Singh, A.K. (1963) 'Indian Students in Britain', Asia Publishing House, New York
Stevenson, R.W. (1974) 'Welfare Problems Facing Overseas Students', University Students' Association, Edinburgh
Straker Cook, R.H. (1977) A rhetorical-communicative approach to syllabus design in ESP in A.P. Cowie and J.B. Heaton (eds), 'English for Academic Purposes', BAAL, printed by College of Estate Management, University of Reading
Tajfel, H. and Dawson, J.L. (1965) (eds), 'Disappointed Guests', Oxford University Press, Oxford
UKCOSA (1974) 'Guidance Leaflet 14'
Walker, D. (1978) The Integration of Overseas Students into a College of Education, unpublished MEd Thesis, University of Sheffield
Winter, E.O. (1971) Connection in Science Material. A Proposition About the Semantics of Clause Relations, 'CILT Reports and Papers', no. 7, pp. 41-52

7 STUDENTS WITH SPECIALISED LEARNING DIFFICULTIES

INTRODUCTION

Particular sectors of the university student population may present specific areas of learning difficulties, the types of problem being a reflection of the definition of each student type. Overseas students meet a cultural and linguistic barrier as well as alien concepts such as competitive indecision and the pressure to work independently in academic isolation. This latter concept is even more pronounced for the post-graduate who faces a totally new structural approach from the more cloistered academic environment of the undergraduate. Returning to a formal learning institution can present a great personal and social as well as intellectual crisis to the mature student, changing as he does from a stable high-status job to the ignominious status of an undergraduate. Few universities make physical provision for disabled students and fewer still recognise the increased personal and academic pressures on such students, who feel they have to prove themselves and achieve a higher level of attainment in order to qualify for the same respect accorded to fellow students. Each of these groups experiences some degree of isolation on entering the university system and the interacting web of all these pressures produces specific and common learning difficulties which need to be examined in detail.

OVERSEAS STUDENTS

The student from Venezuela who is studying Food Science at the University of Reading, UK, the student from Thailand who is taking the Guidance and Counselling course at Edmonton, Alberta, Canada, and the student from Papua New Guinea who is studying Medicine at the University of Sydney, Australia, all face similar problems of inter-cultural communication.

Young people who intend to work in another country as part of the US Peace Corps Volunteers or UK Volunteer Service Overseas take part in cross-cultural training. Harrison's and Hopkins's (1967) objectives for such training are to:

1) develop in the student more independence of external sources of decision, information, problem definition and motivation;

2) develop in the student the 'emotional muscle' required to deal constructively with the strong feelings which are created by conflict and confrontation of values and attitudes;
3) enable him to make choices and commitments to action in situations of stress and uncertainty;
4) encourage him to use his own and others' feelings, attitudes and values, as information in defining and solving human problems.

The student in higher education does not have this preparation. It is considered that obtaining the satisfactory academic admission standard is all that is required, and no attention is given to the personal adjustment of the student. The exception to this is mainland Chinese who have been handpicked for their personal as well as intellectual attributes.

The Volunteer Service Overseas and Peace Corps training takes place *before* the young person leaves his own country. As Grabowski (1972) goes on to tell us:

> there have been three general types of cross-cultural training which have evolved: *The intellectual model* (consisting of lectures on the host country culture) the *area stimulation model* (placing the trainees in a surrounding which in some way resembles the country in which they will be working), and the *self-awareness model* (providing sensitivity training in the hope that it will make the trainee receptive to a new environment).

In Britain, most higher education institutions have evolved not a cross-cultural training programme but an Overseas Students Welcome Programme. Over the years these have changed from the *intellectual model*, described above, consisting largely of information given in the form of talks to a passive audience, to something approaching the *self-awareness model* in the form of groups exploring such issues as the language/cultural interface.

The students from the host country gain much from being part of a multi-racial society on the campus. It is important that they are also 'sensitised' to the feelings of the overseas students so that they are made aware that many of their well-meaning efforts at welcoming and integrating overseas students could smack of 'paternalism'.

Culture, language and learning is so interrelated that it is first important to understand the ways that different cultures perceive their learning environments. Howell (1979) points out that:

> The ability to choose to exist in the present and respond to it in context, spontaneously, varies from culture to culture. Creativity cannot happen in communication unless interacting persons rid themselves of their scripted expectations

> and become free to respond as the circumstances of the moment dictate.

An American reacting with a Japanese is rigidly inflexible, relatively speaking. He can only deal with what he anticipates, in ways he has rehearsed, by rearranging and replaying the past. The Japanese can drift into the here and now much more easily, maintaining his ability to adjust to changing circumstances sensitively. In an effort to cope with the difficulties that arise when these two patterns of behaviour come together, Americans have tried to induce Japanese to behave like Americans, while the Japanese have postulated two theories of the lifestyles that produce these dissonent behaviours. These are termed 'erabi' and 'awose'. The 'erabi' view is that, ideally, man can freely manipulate his environment for his own purposes. 'Awose', on the other hand, rejects the idea that man can manipulate the environment and assumes instead that he adjusts himself to it. The mere enunciating of 'erabi' and 'awose' assumptions demonstrates what Watzluwick, Weakland and Fisch (1974, p. 92) term 'the gentle art of reframing'. Until we develop a theory more compelling than the erabi-awose hypothesis, we may well use it to promote deeper understanding and, ultimately, more and better theory.

The British higher education system stifles creativity, imagination and spontaneity so that by the time that overseas and home-based students meet at university they may have many different entrenched positions.

Students from overseas can suffer from 'culture shock'. The onset is usually accompanied by a higher incidence of attendance at the University Health Centre for psychosomatic problems. This culture shock is even more acute if the student's family is living in the host country. When treating a student for 'culture shock' it is important to distinguish between overseas students who intend to return to their country of origin and those who intend to settle in the host country. A period of suspension from the university may be a necessary part of the treatment.

Language

Language is a very sensitive area and, as demonstrated in Chapter 6, is closely linked with study, to become the communication skills needed for particular course.

Cheetham (1981), in an unpublished project, recounts:

> two West African students said that English was their mother-tongue, and rather more students from this kind of background said they considered that they came from an English-speaking country. This comment is not meant to be derisory. What seems important in this case is that the perceptions of the students do not coincide with the

> perceptions of British people, but who are we to say that they are wrong? Similarly in Department A 46% of the overseas non-native speaking students admitted to having language problems, and 55% of students from Department B agreed that they had English difficulties. Again, I do not mean to imply that any students were trying to conceal information consciously, but there are very good reasons why they felt that they had no language problems. I would suggest that these may have to do with the fact that in many countries English has the status of official language in the country, but in fact it is the second language of the vast majority of those who use it. It has therefore been learned with great effort, and in many cases there has been a psychological battle to come to terms with a language that represents the former colonial power. Then, on coming to England, it is a shock to find that many English speakers have an accent that sounds totally foreign, and that the same British speaker may employ a wide range of styles. These are typically missing from second-language varieties of English. In this case, the educated second-language speaker of English convinces himself that his English is right, and dismisses the local British varictics as irrelevant, and deviant.

For example, one could take the case of a second-language student from Hong Kong who arrives at a British higher education institution to find that his first lecture is by a Scotsman whose dialect he cannot begin to comprehend. Cheetham does on to point out that:

> In contrast, <u>foreign</u>-language learners of English generally find it easy to accept a situation where there are many varieties of English, and may even attempt to acquire some of the features of these varieties of styles. This seldom seems to occur with the second-language learner/speaker who possibly feels that he would be betraying his identity if he modified his speech while in Britain.

In practical terms, overseas students, whether second-language or foreign-language learners of English, have been offered the opportunity to take part in pre-sessional English courses prior to commencing their academic studies.

At the University of Reading, <u>all</u> overseas students are required to take an English test and students who require further help are offered remedial English evening classes. These suffer a poor attendance and high 'drop-out' rate. The students with language problems take a long time over their studies due to their poorer standard of English and consequently have little or no time to attend remedial classes. Often this situation reaches a crisis half-way through the academic year and either the counsellor or the teacher arranges private tuition in an attempt to meet the needs of the overseas student. The problems of language are seen to arise in spoken rather than written English and to meet this need the Counselling Service and Students' Union devised the English Conversation Scheme.

THE ENGLISH CONVERSATION SCHEME

The conversation scheme is a way of facilitating inter-cultural communication between British and overseas students. It helps the overseas students' problems with dialect and colloquial English and, if the British students are on the same course, with their technical terminology.

Many British students are quite often not very skilful at initiating contact with strangers, least of all people from other countries, so that they gain immeasurably from the opportunity to meet weekly in this manner. A scheme like this depends on the developing relationships between the participants. It consists of two overseas and two British students. Some groups fulfil their obligations to one another in a term but others develop a group cohesiveness and a warm bond of friendship.

At the University of Reading the scheme has been extended to include the partners of overseas students. The wives may feel very isolated, lacking in language and communication skills and without the institutions that give them support in their own culture. The student husbands may be quite unaware of the function of such institutions in their native country and usually have no training in providing alternatives when they are living in a society where such institutions for women do not exist.

Learning Difficulties

The overseas student sees his role as student to be paramount and his teacher as the figure in authority to guide him.

As the Grubb Report (Reed, Hutton and Bazalgette, 1976) established, the overseas student does not comprehend the meaning of 'welfare'. He will often suffer personal and learning difficulties, which adversely affect his academic studies without seeking wise counsel. This is despite the fact that most of the overseas students are post-graduates and have taken their first degree in a university where there is an established counselling service, e.g. the University of Hong Kong or the Chinese University in the New Territories.

Through the overseas students' use of the LRC - perceived as a self-access facility that is not problem-related - he is 'educated' to explore his learning difficulties.

Counsellors and teachers should become conversant with the cultures and educational systems of the countries of origin of their overseas students. Hopefully, a certain number of counsellors and teachers would themselves be overseas students. I have post-graduate, guidance and counselling students from overseas universities personnel on placement and try to ensure that one of them each year is an overseas student.

The overseas student who comes to the Counselling Service for individual help needs similar investigations to diagnose treatment as I outlined in Chapter 5. In addition, it is vital to have a full knowledge of the student's previous learning environment and education system. In certain overseas countries students learn by the rote method for a first degree, so that an overseas post-graduate student can experience a change in learning strategies as traumatic as a British first-year undergraduate.

Individual departments of British higher educational institutions, in fact all departments where overseas students are accepted, need to devise ways to change the learning environment to meet the needs of the overseas students. Three examples from the University of Reading are given here to illustrate such methods:

1. In one department, overseas students meet for weekly tutorial groups of three, thereby establishing a close student/staff relationship.
2. In another department, two teachers combine in holding joint seminars. One member of the academic staff plays the role of a student, giving the overseas student the confidence to participate in the questioning.
3. A third department has a course of five 'learning to learn' groups specifically designed to introduce overseas students to the learning strategies required for post-graduate work in British universities.

Higher education institutions throughout the world should design a variety of study counselling and learning to learn interventions to meet the needs of overseas students and minority groups. These could take the form of well-planned introductory courses, pre-sessional on-going remedial English courses and an English Conversation Scheme. With the official view that overseas students should be encouraged to study in British universities, it is more likely that administrators and senior academic staff will support counselling proposals to assist the overseas learner.

POST-GRADUATE STUDENTS

Various researchers have highlighted transitional difficulties and suggested ways to alleviate the adverse effects of transition.

> The young graduate may find himself in an alien physical and social environment, unlike anything he experienced in his gregarious undergraduate days. His intermediate status may induce the impression of living in an 'undefined limbo' between the world of undergraduates whom he has outgrown and the staff with whom he may begin to mix on more equal terms (Wason, 1974).

The period of transition from undergraduate to graduate, usually involving a change of university and therefore a change of social as well as learning environment, taxes the personal resources.

In the same way that the academic student's results at 'A' level ensure an undergraduate place, it is the academic level of the undergraduate degree that ensures a research grant and the opportunity to become a post-graduate student. But in order to cope with the problems of 'adjustment to post-graduate study, coupled with intellectual isolation, loneliness, personal difficulties (financial and accommodation) and facilities for study' (Welsh, 1979), the post-graduate student needs to have more than academic prowess. These realities only become 'problems' if the post-graduate student does not have a sense of his own identity, self-confidence and motivation. The criteria for a PhD is a piece of work that is original and publishable, so his research requires creativity. Without the personal attributes, however, the intellectually gifted post-graduate student is not able to achieve his potential.

Terman (1947) made a study of more than 1,500 Californian schoolchildren who had IQ scores of 140 plus, who he longitudinally studied into adulthood. 'Whilst many of the gifted children had become exceptionally successful adults, many others had not; and the differences he was able to discover between the two were not intellectual, but personal and social'.

Hudson (1973), in carrying out his own research, found that 'research students at Cambridge, who later became Fellows of the Royal Society, were no more likely to have First Class degrees than research students who fail to achieve this honour'.

The way that the post-graduate student perceives his learning environment, his personality and his stage of personal development is even more important now that he can no longer be carried along by group support in his social or seminar groups. Post-graduate students who are presented with learning difficulties - after all, they have already achieved high academic status - are reminiscent of the case that Nelson (1971) describes:

> One student had a very specific academic problem as his main symptom and it was clearly related to his basic character problems. He had extreme difficulty in writing papers for his courses, but otherwise did well in his studies. He

was hesitant to offer his thoughts to the criticism of those in authority. This was reflected in his first efforts to move into psychotherapy. He had extreme difficulty in talking about his problems and could express his concern only in the most indirect way. In the course of eleven interviews he was able to gain sufficient superficial insight to accept a move into more intensive therapy outside the clinic. At the same time he became moderately relieved of his academic problems and was able to continue his studies.

In this case the post-graduate needed counselling about his personal problem but he also needed specific encouragement to write regularly - again the eclectic approach.

Welsh (1979) stresses the need for 'the post graduate student to submit written work at regular intervals for assessment and comment by his supervisor'. She says that 27 out of 64 students that she studied during the first year of post-graduate research admitted to having no idea of the standard required for their thesis, and a further 26 stated that they had only a vague idea.

The relationship between the supervisor and the post-graduate student is crucial to the successful outcome of graduate studies. It can begin in several ways:

1. A student wants to carry on in research; generally the topic is suggested by the professor. Welsh (1979) found in her research into the first year of post-graduate study that 24 of the 50 Science students and 5 of the 14 Arts students 'were undecided on their topic at the time of commencement of study'.
2. The student, often from overseas, who submits a topic and starts his research only to find that the supervisor is not very knowledgeable about the subject.
3. The student has decided on the topic he wants to research; he applies and is taken on by a supervisor who is an expert in this area and prepared to see him regularly.

If intellectual and social isolation is coupled with a poor relationship and intellectual disparity between supervisor and student, it is only students with strong motivation, maturity and self-confidence who can overcome these difficulties. These post-graduate students would seek out other academic staff, often in allied departments and disciplines who could share a supervisory role. Often they have gone outside the university to obtain advice from professional research institutes. If a supervisor has academic commitments abroad at a time when the post-graduate is beginning to write up, the effects could be destructive to his academic studies, even to an independently minded post-graduate student.

Post-graduate students are teachers as well as learners - despite a total lack of teacher training. They may be post-graduates demonstrating in Science departments or they may be encouraged by their supervisor to give a colloquial research talk - an example of teaching in a supportive environment.

MATURE STUDENTS

The unemployment and inflation in Western industrial countries seems to have increased the trend for young people to try to obtain work on leaving school rather than go directly into higher education. This is despite the fact that graduate unemployment at 29 per cent in 1981, although rising, is still far below the figure for unemployed youth. The 1978/9 figures for graduate unemployment was 5.2 per cent for all first degree students in higher education, but it was only 2 per cent if one considers university students only. These figures came from the University Grants Committee who base their figures on UK students (not overseas) who have a UK address and are covered by UK grants. The figure rose to approximately 6 per cent in 1980, and 14 per cent in 1981. As the whereabouts of between 14 and 25 per cent of students are 'not known' to careers advisory services, no reliance can be placed on the figures and they can only show trends.

The overall result published last year by the Conference of University Administrators showed that whereas ten years ago more people went into higher education than the number with the formal entry qualification of two 'A' levels, now 13 per cent of those sufficiently qualified stay away. A degree used to be a passport to a good professional job, but increasing graduate unemployment has made would-be students weigh up other possibilities. It is increasingly in the universities' interest to encourage the intake of older students, part-timers and participants in short courses, in order to make full use of the resources.

As a means of giving some official recognition to that interest, a number of universities in Britain, of which Reading is one, have appointed a Director of Extra Mural and Continuing Education. Government policy has encouraged this development by the publication of occasional papers on (a) continuing education, or (b) mid-career training for industry. The University Grants Committee also compiles statistics on continuing education.

The first ever international meeting to study the place of information, guidance and counselling services in adult learning and access to educational opportunities was held at the University of Southern California College of Continuing Education in 1977. The preamble to the report draws attention to 'the significance of adult education within the framework of life long learning which is well-known to all member states of U.N.E.S.C.O. whose General Conference adopted a recommendation on the Development of Adult Education at its nineteenth seminar in Nairobi in November 1976'.

In a paper presented to the 1977 conference, Bertelsen says:

> For the democratization of education and the development of life-long education and learning, it is important to identify such obstacles to the passage of learners from one level of education to another (vertical mobility) and also to the horizontal mobility between different educational paths, eg general education and vocational training so that the necessary 'ladders' and 'bridges' can be constructed in the form of preparatory or intermediate courses, and guidance and counselling can certainly help in the process of identification.

As the British universities develop from extra-mural to continuing education and ultimately to the inclusion of leisure education to meet the needs of the long-term unemployed and those on shorter working hours, educational counsellors will be needed. Bertelsen (1977) goes on to say:

> Furthermore, educational counselling can bring out significant information about the reactions of youths and adults to their previous learning experiences in school and out-of-school. The feedback from adult counselling is thus not only relevant to the planning of adult education, but can also provide valuable insights into the workings of the formal system of education. The conscious development of counselling, both as an integral part of teaching and as a distinct function can help to develop a more diagnostic learner-centred approach to learning, and thus make teaching (as this book has been advocating) more closely related to the situation of the learners.

The Mature Undergraduate in University

Before there is an increase in the admission rate of mature students, which may eventually expand into continuing education, it is important to study the full-time mature undergraduate at present in universities in order to learn from their experience.

If one defines a mature student as one who is aged over 21 on the 1 October in the year of his admission (though local grant-awarding authorities consider 25 as the age of separate financial assessment), there were 1,037 mature students out of a total of 4,100 undergraduates at the University of Reading in 1976.

James (1979) in considering the particular needs and problems of mature learners states that in general

> mature students share the same characteristics:
> i) They have reached a certain state of development, which carries with it a certain social status, e.g.
> a) they are free men able to make their own judgements and choices.
> b) They are mature persons with some experience of life,

whose personalities, attitudes and social roles are becoming fixed, but they may not be irrevocably fixed.

c) They are full citizens (and in many cases parents and the heads of households) with all the rights and duties of such citizens;
ii) they will have a considerable corpus of specialist knowledge arising from their own previous experience of life and work;
iii) they will have a store of general knowledge on which to draw.

d) Considerable variations will exist, however, in terms of, for example:
i) familiarity with methods of study relevant to the course.
ii) ability to participate in seminars, tutorials and discussions and ability to express themselves in speech and writing.
iii) ability to plan and accept responsibility for their own work.
iv) ability to examine arguments, weigh evidence, judge generalisations, ask searching questions, distinguish fact from opinion and example from principle.
v) ability to work alone and in groups.
vi) enthusiasm for study.
vii) pace at which they can work.

Proportionately, many more mature students positively seek help from counselling services, rather than allowing problems to disrupt their studies. McLeish (1968) in a report of his study on the effectiveness of the lecture as a teaching method concludes that:

> It appears that older students, mature students, and tutors, strongly disfavour the lecture. They favour more student-centred teaching methods in a marked degree. The better students, academically speaking, dislike the lecture more than do others. The most interesting features of the Institute group are that it consists entirely of mature and experienced teachers from a variety of backgrounds, and that before being asked to complete the questionnaire they had had considerable opportunities of experiencing in their own skins the specific virtues and weaknesses of the three teaching methods under discussion - lecture, tutorial and seminar.

A teacher will have mature and young students in the same seminar or lecture group, and particularly if he is himself a young lecturer he may need support to create an effective learning environment for such diverse learners.

The mature student will probably be more resistant to change. As James (1979) points out, 'they have been used to real life situations... Once admitted, however, they are presented with academic approaches which they may find difficult.'

It is important that the teacher and counsellor have a thorough understanding of the intellectual, physical and personality profile of the mature student, so that they can foresee the difficulties that he might face. Quite often the mature student who has experienced no problems at previous examinations and who has taught in universities abroad may suffer a work block and examination phobia that is more distressing than it would be for a younger person as it is so unexpected. The mature person feels that he should be able to cope with basic academic and non-academic problems (since he could function well and cope with life as a non-student). The older mature student often comes to university when his personal life is at a crossroads and he experiences an identity crisis as disturbing as any 18-year-old's.

In an unpublished paper that Wright wrote on mature students in 1976 it appeared that the withdrawal rate was not proportionately different from the total university population: 2.18 per cent of the mature undergraduates leaving, as against 2.8 per cent of all students who left. 'Various studies have been done in this country in Australia and in the United States to look at the academic performances, according to the age of the students. Much of the evidence is conflicting and the samples are often small.'

Most of these studies investigate success within the university - the measure of the class of degree obtained and the successful completion of their degree course. Clearly there is a case for including success in chosen employment after leaving university as a test of utility; however, there are less clearly defined benefits which might be considered, such as usefulness to the community, the ability to use leisure time, personality and even personal happiness, though these factors are difficult to assess.

Various research has been done mainly in the USA to explore the reasons why 'older' women become mature students. Often they have touched on issues central to the Women's Movement, such as the study by Harville (1978) on women students in an American suburban community college, where she states: 'The fact that women were enrolling mainly for career reasons suggests a revue of the career programmes offered in terms of whether they meet the needs of women.' She notes that the Women's Movement has developed and grown, 'exerting a significant influence on the thinking of women and their careers'.

Administrators responsible for planning higher education in the 1980s have to be aware of these needs of the mature student learners and consider what changes are needed in their learning environment to help them realise their potential.

DISABLED STUDENTS

In 1981, which has been designated 'The Year of the Disabled' in Britain, there is a growing group of people who have a special interest in the disabled young person in higher education.

The National Bureau for the Handicapped provides a liaison and information service, and the National Union of Students takes a special interest in would-be handicapped students. Students are selected on academic merit and no student is rejected on physical grounds. The special provision that some students need varies greatly from university to university. The academic interview procedure at the University of Reading is the same as for non-handicapped students but in addition they are encouraged to come with their parents for an informal visit to meet the administration and other students and to see the University Health Centre.

A differentiation often needs to be made between students from a protected special boarding school environment and those who have been integrated into normal schooling. For those lacking in social skills and the ability to lead an independent life there is a course at Hereford College which acts as a 'bridging operation'. The nature of some handicaps has cut some students off from normal experiences during school and it may make easy social interaction with teachers and other students difficult.

Some students are very well motivated and self-confident with a sense of vocation and great determination. This type of student makes good use of the help offered by his fellow students but can be very demanding. However, over the years, there have been splendid young physically handicapped students offering help to others with learning or emotional problems, and they see 'handicap' as the 'inability to function'. Certain disability requires specialised help:

1. environmental - lifts and ramps in student accommodation.
2. social - help with reading to a blind student or pushing a chairbound student.
3. learning materials - such as electric typewriters, a personal hearing aid and the visual communication system of Open University summer schools to help hearing-impaired students during group discussion.

It is difficult, as Geoffrey Tudor says, to differentiate between a study and a living aid. This makes for problems in the Open University when students attend summer school, but most other university institutions make generous provision. It is better for handicapped students to integrate fully in halls of residence - rather than to have a hall for disabled students as was generously provided (but under-used) at the University of Sussex. Tudor (1977) makes a case for more appropriate help to be provided:

> Recently the Association of Blind and Partially-Sighted Teachers and Students carried out a survey into the working methods of 27 of its student members in Universities and Colleges of Education. It was found that most of them had muddled through to a working system by a form of trial and error.

As Vida Carver points out, 'Deaf people suffer not only degree and pattern of hearing loss but also they have a low level of linguistic skills.' This is particularly pronounced in those who have been deaf from birth as they have a limited vocabulary and restricted use of techniques such as lip-reading. However, they often have fewer personal problems than those who are categorised as 'hard of hearing' as their deafness is an inherent part of their self-concept and no assimilation process is necessary.

> Many hard-of-hearing people have experienced progressively deteriorating hearing since childhood, sometimes refusing to admit the extent of their disability even to themselves. In many ways their situation is more precarious than that of the prelingually deaf, who tend to retain social links with old schoolfellows and may form close-knit communities of their own, where they can, if they wish to, supplement oral speech with manual signs and finger spelling (Carver, 1977).

Dyslexia and spina bifida can cause certain learning difficulties and the problem can be exacerbated by the lack of reference to the handicap on the UCCA form. It is only when the student physically arrives at university and commences his studies that the learning and other difficulties become apparent.

In summing up, it is apparent that the handicapped student's perception of the learning environment and the skills required for the 'nature of task' may be very different from a non-handicapped student. The third dimension in learning (the personality factors) may vary greatly, depending on the previous schooling and the way that they have been encouraged to develop a sense of their own identity from which comes a sense of self-confidence.

CONCLUSION

The various categories of students with special needs have been arbitrarily divided, but in reality they may overlap. Overseas students are of course generally mature students and often suffer both disabilities. They all suffer some social isolation caused by their handicap. This lack of close staff/student or inter-student relationships affects learning competence so that provisions such as the English Conversation Scheme may have far-reaching effects. It is evident that it is impossible to distinguish between learning difficulties and emotional or psychological problems.

This interrelationship illustrates the interdependence of the academic and welfare aspects of the university system, the two both acting to assist the student's development and his self-concept. In Chapter 8 we shall consider students whose emotional and psychological problems inhibit effective study.

REFERENCES

Bertelsen, P.H. (1977) The Potential of Information, Guidance and Counselling Services for Improving the Access of Adults in Learning Opportunities, the International Symposium on Ways and Means of Strengthening Information and Counselling Services for Adult Learners, held by the College of Continuing Education, University of Southern California, in co-operation with UNESCO, p. 8

Carver, V. (1977) Educational Problems of Hearing-Impaired Students, 'Teaching at a Distance', no. 8 (March), pp. 10-18

Cheetham, B. (1981) Towards a Specification for Self Access Study Facilities in a Multi-Cultured Academic Community, unpublished dissertation, University of Reading

Grabowski, S.M. (1972) Cross-cultural Training Methods, 'Adult Leadership', vol. 20, part 9

Harrison, R. and Hopkins, R.L. (1967) The Design of Cross-Cultural Training: An Alternative to the University Model, 'The Journal of Applied Behavioural Science', vol. 3, no. 4 (October/November/December), pp. 431-60, as quoted in Grabowski

Harville, T.S. (1978) Adult Women in College - What Are They Searching For?, Paper for the International Round Table for the Advancement of Counselling, Oslo, Norway, p. 12

Howell, W.S. (1979) Theoretical Directions for Intercultural Communication, in M.K. Asante, E. Newmark and C.A. Blake (eds), 'Handbook of Intercultural Communication', Sage, London, pp. 36-7

Hudson, L. (1973) 'Originality', Oxford University Press, Oxford, p. 6

James, D. (1979) Counselling the Mature Student, in P.J. Hills (ed.), 'Study Courses and Counselling', SRHE, Guildford, Surrey, pp. 106-7

McLeish, J. (1968) 'The Lecture Method', Cambridge Institute of Education, Cambridge Monograph on Teaching Methods no. 1, p. 23

Nelson, R.L. (1971) Special Problems of Graduate Students in the School of Arts and Sciences, 'Emotional Problems of the Student', Butterworths, London, p. 323

Reed, B., Hutton, J. and Bazalgette, J. (1976) 'Freedom to Study: Requirements of Overseas Students in the U.K.',

a report published by the Grubb Institute for the Overseas Students Trust, London
Terman, L.M. and Oden, M.H. (1947) 'Creativity', Penguin, Harmondsworth
Tudor, G. (1977) The Study Problems of Disabled Students in the Open University, 'Teaching at a Distance', no. 9 (July), pp. 43-9
Wason, P.C. (1974) Notes on the Supervision of Ph.D's, 'Bulletin British Psychological Society', vol. 27, pp. 25-9
Watzluwick, P., Weakland, J. and Fisch, R. (1974) 'Change: Principles of Problem Formation and Problem Resolution', W.W. Norton, New York
Welsh, J. (1979) 'The First Year of Post Graduate Research', SRHE, Guildford, Surrey, p. 32
Wright, J. (1976) Report on Mature Students, unpublished thesis, University of Reading

8 CHANGE IN THE INDIVIDUAL

Counselling is about change - change in the individual and change in his learning environment.

In discussing the concept of 'the counsellor', Halmos (1974) says that he understands 'this term to mean that anyone who uses his own personality professionally to bring about change in the personality of another by modifying the other's self-image is a counsellor'. This definition makes no distinction between 'counselling' and 'psychotherapy' and places all forms of personalised consultations within the 'counselling rubric'.

It has often been said that, in modern society, the psychotherapist has replaced the priest. This rather banal assumption fails to take into account the radical differences between the two roles. As O'Doherty (1974) explains:

> The one aims at the healthy functioning of the psyche and the other at the spiritual well being of the soul... the psychotherapists' role is the healing of the sick mind, the helping of an individual through forces within himself to overcome or remove pathalogical processes, and thus to free his personality from distortions of an emotional or instinctive character. The role of a Minister of Religion on the other hand is to be a minister of grace, to help a person to make right choices, to enable him to salve his conscious moral or spiritual problems, and to choose right means for the attaining of spiritual and supernatural goals. This does not mean that he neglects, depreciates or decries true human and temporal values. It only means that he must integrate these with his formal concerns which is the transcendent.

Counsellors and chaplains co-exist harmoniously on university campuses. They may meet at student welfare meetings and workshops and, when appropriate, as co-therapists in marital therapy. Counsellors would feel that they are not bound by a religious discrimination and can therefore create a value-free environment where students and staff may describe or resolve conflicts. These may concern a decision about whether or not to terminate a pregnancy or how to come to terms with a homosexual relationship, as a practising Christian.

Figure 8.1

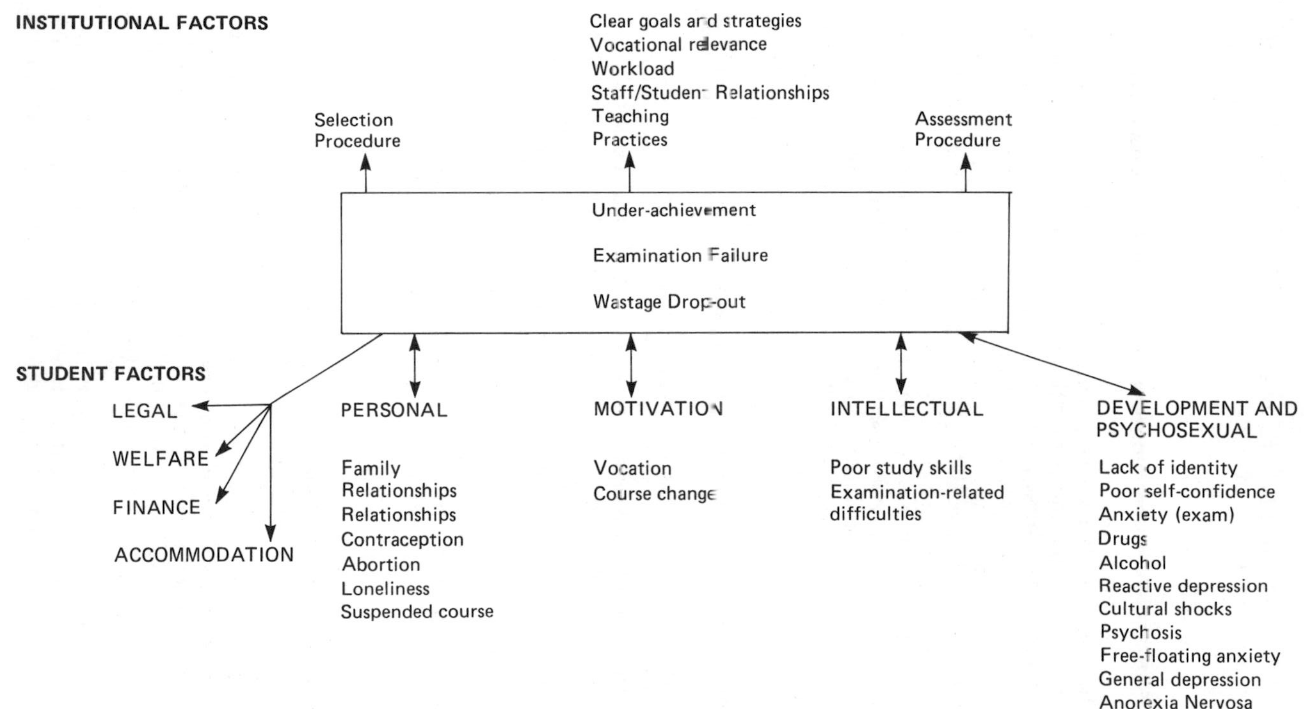
INSTITUTIONAL FACTORS
Selection Procedure
Clear goals and strategies
Vocational relevance
Workload
Staff/Student Relationships
Teaching Practices
Assessment Procedure
Under-achievement
Examination Failure
Wastage Drop-out
STUDENT FACTORS
LEGAL
WELFARE
FINANCE
ACCOMMODATION
PERSONAL
Family
Relationships
Relationships
Contraception
Abortion
Loneliness
Suspended course
MOTIVATION
Vocation
Course change
INTELLECTUAL
Poor study skills
Examination-related difficulties
DEVELOPMENT AND PSYCHOSEXUAL
Lack of identity
Poor self-confidence
Anxiety (exam)
Drugs
Alcohol
Reactive depression
Cultural shocks
Psychosis
Free-floating anxiety
General depression
Anorexia Nervosa
Endogenous depression

THE EFFECT OF THE COUNSELLOR'S PERSONALITY

A counsellor - who needs a theoretical knowledge of philosophy, of ethics, and above all of religion, far more perhaps than a knowledge of medicine or psychology, to practise his skills - cannot fail to influence his clients by his own value systems during the consultation.

Even behavioural psychologists admit that the personality and thus by implication the beliefs and values of the counsellor affect the outcome of the treatment. As the class and nationality of the counsellor and the student may be different, these are important considerations.

THE PROBLEMS OF SOCIETY

Counsellors are dealing with issues that are in a collective sense political and in an individual sense, moral. They are under attack from the establishment to adapt people to 'the system' and maintain the 'status quo', and also under attack from the clients to change 'the system'. The unemployed school leavers whose frustration has erupted into organised violence in the big cities do not need vocational counselling for jobs that do not exist.

Greater Freedom Demands a Sense of Responsibility

The years between the student riots in 1968 and the present time have seen a granting of greater freedom and responsibility to young people, and at the same time a denial of their right to become financially independent and to develop a sense of self-esteem. Four Acts of Parliament have revolutionised peoples' lives:

1. The Abortion Act (1967) which stated that 'A termination may be approved if two doctors agree that to continue would involve risk to the life of the pregnant woman', but in determining risk to the pregnant woman's health, account may be taken of her 'actual or reasonable forseeable environment'. In effect this has led to 'abortion on demand' for the population, provided they seek out the responsible medical agencies and can pay the fee.
2. The establishment of drug addiction clinics in 1968 and the Misuse of Drugs Act (1971) mirrored the more permissive life-styles of young people from every strata of society and the establishment of styles of communal living.
3. The Divorce Laws (1973) have made divorce possible in Britain, after two years' separation with the agreement of both parties or after five years' separation without such agreement. This has led to the 'relinquished role of parents' and a greater emphasis on the quality of relationships rather than the 'institu-

tion of marriage'.
4. The Family Planning (The National Health Service) Act (1974) (Reorganization Act, section 4) allowed contraception free on the National Health Service, and clinics openly give advice to single and sometimes 'under-age' schoolchildren.

People have now to make decisions that fundamentally affect their lives, when they have not established a sense of their own identity and when the rise in unemployment and particularly youth unemployment coupled with prolonged education keeps them financially dependent on their parents. This has to be seen in the wider context of 'the trend to regard society as a business corporation' (Magnussen, 1978).

THE ROLE OF THE SPECIALIST

> Our society also fosters an attitude of deference to and dependence upon specialists. The doctor, the lawyer, the engineer and the teacher are people who do things to us and for us and who tell us what to do and/or how to do it. The relationship is one of dependence, of reliance on authority (Kelynack, 1972).

People are just pawns to be dispensed with as technology advances. This results in low self-esteem. In this new situation, counsellors now have to be concerned with several fundamental issues:

1) Thoughtful people are more concerned about identity than about success. The most urgent question that faces an individual, young or old, in our time is not 'How can I become successful and popular and well adjusted to my social situation?' but rather 'Who am I really and what do I want to become?'
2) In place of vocation guidance, let us set ourselves the more general task of helping people decide what to do with their lives... Decisions about devoting one's life to some important undertaking for human betterment are likely to involve tentative choices and try out perusals even more than decisions about careers do...
3) The counsellor needs to put himself in his clients' place and then make a special effort to think of as many possible courses of action as he can... Too often we assume that a person has no choice in a situation simply because we have not enough imagination to think of something quite different that he might do (Tyler, 1970).

THE LACK OF COMMUNITY PROVISION

If it is agreed that counsellors have something to offer disturbed and troubled people, what is the provision of psychotherapy in the community? The number of psychiatrists in the community is less than 1 per 60,000. This lack of psychiatrists may account for the reliance on chemotherapy. 'In 1971 there were 87,000 re-admissions in England for mental illness - 53% of all mental illness admissions' (National Association for Mental Health, 1974), so it would appear that psychiatry does not have all the answers.

There are few qualified psychotherapists working in the National Health Service and they are virtually unknown outside London. If students were expected to look towards the community for treatment they would find that treatment is almost exclusively available for the professional classes by the professional classes - another example of social advantage. 'The psychotherapists, having surveyed their relatively barren field within the National Health Service have come up with a request for some two hundred extra psychotherapists to add to these fifty or so working wholetime or part-time' (Royal College of Psychiatrists, 1975).

THE COUNSELLOR IN GENERAL PRACTICE

There has been a move in various parts of the country to employ counsellors in General Practice. This is designed to reduce the prescribing of drugs, to reduce the workload of the General Practitioner, and to reduce the dysfunction of the patients.

The Psychosomatic Syndrome

'The Balint Society, for example, claimed that 30% of patients who see a doctor are suffering from psychosomatic disorders and general practitioners have neither the time, nor, generally speaking, the appropriate training to meet the needs of these patients' (Meacher, 1978).

The psychosomatic patient has been studied by various people and they have one fairly common phenomenon. 'This is the pain-prone individual who from early childhood has developed a habit of reporting body pain rather than verbalising feelings of distress including disagreement and hate' (Wilkinson, 1973).

'Professor Neil Kessell in a study of a single general practice, in 1960, reported that when the definition of psychiatric morbidity was based on the International Classification of Diseases, 50 patients per 1,000 per year manifested psychiatric symptoms. However, when patients with 'conspicuous psychiatric morbidity', i.e. conspicuous to the general practitioner, were included, the annual prevalence rate rose to 90 per 1,000. The inclusion of those patients who presented with physical complaints that did not have any detectable organic basis, i.e. psychosomatic disorder, caused the rate to reach 520 per 1,000. Thus, depending on the definition of psychiatric ill-health employed, the rate varied from 1 patient in 20 to 1 in 2 (Clare, 1976).

It is difficult to estimate the number of counsellors working in group medical practices in this country as they have no defined role in the eyes of the Ministry of Health, but the numbers are growing. A survey has recently been carried out by the Royal College of General Practitioners to assess their effectiveness.

COUNSELLORS IN SPECIALISED UNITS IN THE COMMUNITY

Counsellors can also be found in isolated situations in special units or clinics.

1. Pregnancy and abortion clinics:
   - (a) The Marie Stopes Clinic, Camden, London;
   - (b) Pregnancy Advisory Service, London;
   - (c) British Pregnancy Advisory Service, London;
   - (d) The Brook Advisory Centres.
2. Drug addiction clinics in the United Kingdom set up by the Department of Health and Social Security.
3. Family planning clinics throughout the British Isles. The London headquarters has 'advice sisters'. Margaret Pike's clinics have nursing sisters as counsellors.
4. Certain local authorities are concerned with the provision of effective abortion and contraception counselling, notably Aberdeen, Camberwell and Lambeth.

The Counsellor's Paramedic Role

The counsellors in the USA, unlike Britain, have been expected to undertake a paramedical role during abortions. As Simms (1973) reports, 'counselling has arisen as a by-product of the modern technology of abortion. This involvement with the procedure of abortion causes unbearable strain to some counsellors.'

The strain for counsellors in higher education is usually that of working in isolated settings, without support and often grossly overworked.

VOLUNTARY COUNSELLING IN THE COMMUNITY

Britain has a history of voluntary work second to none in the world, which has been firmly established for generations. An example was Octavia Hill who in the last century went among the workers in their back-to-back houses, with her white gloves and her caring concern.

The area of drug dependence was dependent on voluntary day centres, voluntary hostels and voluntary communities, and even a voluntary employment agency to help young people to stay off drugs.

Whilst there is a variety of supportive counselling agencies, the number of counsellors capable of working effectively as dynamic psychotherapists to affect change in the individual are very few.

COUNSELLING IN HIGHER EDUCATION

It may be felt by some administrative and senior academic staff that students should be referred to the inadequate psychological services in the community.

What is the justification for treating students as a 'special case'?

Kelly (1978) makes a case, 'to justify the provision of a University Health Service as providing for the inherent occupational risks of the students...the University of London Central Institute's Health Service has psychologists as members of its staff'. In addition to the 2-4 per cent of the student population who suffer a formal psychiatric illness during the three-year period,

> About ten-twenty per cent of the students suffer from psycho-social disturbances and these disturbances are apt to occur at particular times: in relation to entering University, which may mean being away from home for the first time, often in relation to study or examinations or both, and in relation to important events in personal and family life (Lucas, 1976).

It is unlikely that students will meet a situation in their lives that is more stressful than finals. It therefore seems very reasonable that, if universities insist on retaining the examination system, students should be given support in the shape of counsellors and health centres.

THE NEED FOR COUNSELLORS TO BE SPECIALISED

To meet the needs of students and staff the counsellor should be an expert in a wide variety of specialisations from study skills to marital counselling. The counsellor will usually be working alone when he takes up his first appointment and therefore needs to be competent and effective from the moment he finishes his training.

COUNSELLING TRAINING PROGRAMMES

Unfortunately, counsellor training programmes are normally directed by men who do not have any relevant clinical experience themselves. A great deal must depend on the quality of their counselling placement during training. It will always be difficult to devise a suitable training for the affective work of counselling, within the confines of a cognitive academic department. It is good experience for the counsellor, however, so that he will be able to understand the attitudes of some of his scientific colleagues towards counselling.

THE FINANCIAL JUSTIFICATION FOR COUNSELLING

Students are treated by counsellors on the university campus with minimal interruption to studies. If these students were forced to seek psychological help in the community they would be subject to lengthy hospital waiting lists, six weeks for a first appointment being quite usual. Once in treatment, they would miss essential academic lectures and seminars travelling to and from hospital. Invariably it would necessitate them giving up their academic studies and suspending their course.

ADMISSION TO HIGHER EDUCATION

As Ryle (1969) points out:

> Large scale psychiatric screening, even if the methods available were effective, would have a bad effect. For one thing, the more importance a University placed upon 'good emotional health' in its applicants the more likely it would be that candidates and schools would falsify and suppress any history of difficulty.

He goes on to point out the 'unlikely outcome were the neurotic Darwin and the eccentric Einstein to apply today for a postgraduate grant'.

THE PRESENT POSITION

Student health services are now established in nearly all higher educational institutions. Writing about the development of student health centres, the Committee on Health Services in Higher Education of the Royal College of Physicians, London, points out:

> In 1966 there were no special services for polytechnics. There are now eighteen... Contraceptive services which

> were in their early stages in 1966 are now a major commitment... there is an increased need for psycho-sexual counselling in relation to the physical and emotional problems of greater and earlier sexual activity.

THE TEACHING STAFF'S PERCEPTION OF COUNSELLING

Previously we have looked at the university rewards system which shows that:

> A premium is put on research and publications...the academics' other interests seemed devalued, in effect relative to these particular ones... It is thus pertinent to ask which activities academics in such a context would be most likely to relegate to low priority status. In all probability they would comprise these activities academics themselves queried, these they felt least competent to perform, these which their colleagues did not take very seriously in practice, and these which promised least 'pay-off' in terms of career advancement (Pashley and Shepherd, 1978).

These conclusions come from a study into how students and staff at one English university perceived personal tutoring arrangements or the role of personal supervision.

The personal tutoring role is only part of the occupation of the teaching staff. How then can the counsellor expect to be valued by academic colleagues and/or the institution as a whole when his occupation is concerned with pastoral matters? For this reason, if for none other, it is essential for the counsellor to work as part of an eclectic team with teaching staff and administrators.

FACTORS AFFECTING COUNSELLING IN HIGHER EDUCATION

The Time Factor

Counsellors in higher education have to consider the time factor in planning treatment since the year is divided into terms, when the student is available to come for treatment, and vacations, when the student may continue to live locally or, more likely, returns to his parents' home in another location.

The treatment offered for 'examination phobia' must, of necessity, vary if the examination is three days or three months away. It can be quite crucial, such as when anorexia is diagnosed and the student is returning home in two weeks' time at the end of term. It may be better not to commence treatment until the student returns to university next term. Wilson (1972), a psychotherapist working as a student counsellor, refers to the 'time factor' and says that, 'many of the principles outlined by Malon in "A Study of Brief Psychotherapy" have been applied and worked well. He refers in particular to when the "therapist guides the patient towards partial interpretation and exercises selective attention and selective neglect".'

Motivation for Treatment

There is a considerable difference between the student who is self-referred and the one referred by the college authorities. In the latter case much of the first interview is taken up with discussions of how the student feels about being 'sent to the counsellor'. These tutor referrals are in fact extremely important, showing as they do the teacher's faith in the counsellor, and the teacher is often the best person to judge the opportune time when the student might respond to counselling.

Faith in the Counsellor

Many students have consulted a variety of medical or caring agencies before they refer themselves to the counsellor. A typical example of this was a married couple who had a marital and psychosexual problem. They had consulted the home General Practitioner in a vacation, the physician at the University Health Centre and then the Family Planning Clinic, and eventually referred themselves to the counsellor. The treatment had not been successful, they felt very depressed, and much of the first interview was spent in building up their confidence and faith in the counselling treatment situation. The treatment was successfully concluded in five weekly consultations.

Psychosomatic

Physicians have now become more aware of the diagnosis and the underlying cause of a psychosomatic symptom. Counsellors have now to be aware of the developing body of selective knowledge concerning the psychological disturbances which are symptomatic of underlying physical pathology.

> Such a list includes the dementing conditions secondary to arteria schlerosis affecting the blood vessels in the brain, the acute psychoses secondary to the use and abuse of certain drugs, such as alcohol, amphetamines and L.S.D., a number of nutritional disorders with gross manifestations, of which pellagra is a typical example, and certain brain tumours and epileptogenic lesions which are often accompanied by numerous psychological symptoms (Clare, 1976).

Relationships between counsellors and health centre physicians and psychiatrists need to be informal with a positive regard for the contribution of each service to facilitate ease of cross-referrals and 'shared treatment'. An example of this would be the anorexic girl student who is being treated by the counsellor while the health centre physician keeps a check on her weight.

THE LIMITATIONS OF COUNSELLING

The Personality of the Counsellor

It has already been stated that the counsellor needs to be widely experienced clinically in a variety of therapeutic methods. Whatever the size of college where he works there will be a wide spectrum of psychological disturbances and emotional problems. The counsellor needs to be an integrated personality combining non-possessive warmth, genuineness and empathy. 'In a paper given to the 1961 Congress of the International Psycho-Analytic Association, Sacha Nacht laid emphasis on the importance of the analyst's personality and his deep inner attitude towards the patient' (Jehu Hardiker, Yelloly and Shaw, 1972).

A decade ago Rogers (1969) had come to believe 'that the quality of my encounter is more important in the long run than is my scholarly knowledge, my professional training, my counselling orientation, the technique I use in the interview'.

Even writings on behavioural therapy refer to the therapist as a source of reinforcement (Jehu, 1972), and Meyer and Chesser (1970) acknowledge that 'relationship variables (between patient and therapist) may affect the outcome of behaviour therapy'.

Training

Medical training has in the past usually been 'disease' and not 'patient' orientated so that doctors have not been much concerned with the effect of their personality as a factor in the outcome of treatment. An important exception has been the work of Michael and Enid Balint. They focus on the patients who consult their doctors with problems that are emotional rather than physical in origin. They felt that medicine 'must develop a reliable method for coping with this problem' (Balint and Balint, 1961). Over the years, in this country and abroad, they have developed training research seminars for general practitioners and specialists which focus on the doctor/patient relationship. It is unlikely that university health doctors are Balint trained.

There is a need for the trainee counsellor to understand the theoretical assumptions of the main approaches to counselling and therapy, and to have clinical judgement regarding their application in a treatment situation. Too often student counsellors on placement have been preoccupied with their anxiety concerning the 'method' of a particular therapy, one that may run contrary to their own philosophy and personality, and that the anxiety is inhibiting them being themselves in the relationship with their client.

Procter (1978), in her book which describes ten current approaches to counselling, refers to the fact that 'relating to new theories may produce anxiety' but goes on to say: 'The anxious stage of relating to new theories and wider awareness, seems usually to be temporary, provided the encounter is one of choice and not enforced'.

Counsellors in higher education are aware that psychoanalysis 'which long dominated mental health services in America' can only offer substantial help to a limited (and affluent) few (Frederick, 1973). It is not surprising that in the last few years, and particularly in the present financial climate, that the

> Current trend is to aim to help the client develop problem-solving techniques, rather than to cope with specific problems. Its emphasis on process rather than content, its preoccupation with the 'here and now' rather than past history, its emphasis on feelings rather than intellectual understanding ...and its involvement of the counsellor as an active and real person, all combine to produce fast moving and intense therapeutic change (Frederick, 1973).

It conjures up a picture of 'development counselling', a very attractive picture, but one that still dictates what the counsellor shall apply, not necessarily what the student needs.

Meeting the challenge of problem areas that are new to therapeutic interventions, I have found that the method develops from a number of tentative and experimental approaches and the theory is evolved from the practice. An example of this was in drug rehabilitation. It was therefore a delight to hear Gilmore's paper at the last IRTAC Conference in 1980, 'A Comprehensive Theory of Eclectic Intervention'. There is therefore now a theory for the eclectic method that I favour - making it an acceptable and professionally respectable practice.

THE TREATMENT OF EMOTIONAL AND PSYCHOLOGICAL PROBLEMS

The personality factors that affect academic success are as follows.

Motivation and a Sense of Identity

These potential development crises, if not resolved, will limit an individual's academic ceiling. The protagonists for retaining the examination system are those who believe that it is only at the end of the course that there is a coming together of intellect and mature well-motivated personality so that the final examination is a cumulation and a celebration of the total university experience.

Sense of Identity

> If the overtly conforming child accepts work as the only criteria of worthwhileness, sacrificing imagination and playfulness too readily, he may become ready to submit to what Marx called 'craft-idiocy', i.e. become a slave of his technology and its dominant role typology.
>
> It is immediately obvious that for the vast majority of men, in all times, this has been not only the beginning but also the limitations of their identity; or better; the majority of men have always consolidated their identity needs around their technical and occupational capacities. It may be for that very reason that the identity problem in our time becomes both psychiatrically and historically relevant. For as man can leave some of the grind and curse to machines, he can visualize a greater freedom of identity for a larger segment of mankind (Erikson, 1968).

If people give due weight to matters of identity despite its inability to present itself as a precise science, it is usually attributed to the period of adolescence. For some children the need to achieve autonomy is thwarted at an early age, for often the first tentative fledgling-like step might occur in middle age when they become a 'mature student'. At whatever age it is a period of experiment and turbulence of feelings and is often related to the first time one learns to live alone.

The story of Jonathan Livingstone Seagull portrays it so vividly:

> 'Maynard Gull, you have the freedom to be yourself, your true self, here and now, and nothing can stand in your way. It is the Law of the Great Gull, the Law that Is.'
> 'Are you saying I can fly?'
> 'I say you are free.'
> As simply and as quickly as that, Kirk Maynard Gull spread his wings, effortlessly, and lifted into the dark night air. The flock was roused from sleep by his cry, as loud as he could scream it, from five hundred feet up; 'I can fly! Listen! I CAN FLY!' (Bach, 1972).

In 1964, a book was published which records convincingly 'the successful treatment of a boy called Dibs who was rapidly becoming classified at five years old as defective, and who eventually became a boy with an IQ of 168. It is the moving story of a child "in search of self" through the process of psychotherapy' (Axline, 1971). At the termination of his treatment Dibs,

> had become a person in his own right. He had found a sense of dignity and self respect. With this confidence and security he could learn to accept and respect other people in his world. He was no longer afraid to be himself (Axline, 1972).

Many students and older people would like to be able to describe themselves in this way.

I would like to briefly discuss the treatment of two cases of identity crises.

Case A. A married, mature student aged 45 - a first-year Arts student. She lives in a student hall of residence during the week and returns to her husband at the weekend. There is no child from the 20-year marriage. The husband is working as a clerk. The wife overreacts, is emotional and has been a housewife, financially dependent on her husband. The present problem is a poor marital relationship. The husband is reported to be very resentful and angry and has become chronically ill. The student complains of not being able to write essays.

Table 8.1: The Student's Eclectic Treatment Plan for Identity Crisis

The Behavioural Approach to Writing Essays	The Psychotherapeutic Approach to a Crisis of Identity	Subsequent Sexual Problem	LRC
Concurrent in the same consultations		Couple counselling	
Research	Explore idea about value	Role confusion - husband at home ill, wife out studying	
Recording notes	Sexual identity problems		
		Sexual problem - wife's sexual dysfunction	
Planning the essay	Work identity		Pattern note-taking
	Short- or long-term goals		
		Husband sabotages treatment	
Writing an outline			
	The role of men and women in society		
Writing			
	All treatment took place during summer term, first year		

She is excited by the possibility of developing friendships with both male and female students of all ages. She is well motivated to do her course.

The diagnostic interview involving an intellectual, a physical and a personality profile showed that the student is experiencing an identity crisis. The student also needs study skills help in writing essays; she has no confidence to express what she feels.

The behavioural and psychotherapeutic techniques occur in the same single client situation weekly appointments and the student attended with her husband for fortnightly supportive marital therapy. The dynamic therapy focused on the mature student's problems.

At the end of the term the student was studying hard and had decided to move into hall for the next term and go home just occasionally while she continued to work on her own problems. She had expressed a warm positive regard towards her husband.

Case B. A female student, aged 20, brought to the counselling service by three friends, was diagnosed to be suffering from anorexia nervosa. She had been diagnosed two years ago by her home General Practitioner, admitted to hospital and discharged physically but not psychologically 'cured' back to her family. The student had resisted any 'follow up' visits. Anorexia patients are very unlikely to be self-referred.

> The survey by Crisp, Palmer and Kalway (1976) has shown that amongst social Class 1 and 2, it exists in about one in every hundred 16 - 18-year olds in severe form. In social Class 3, 4 and 5 the prevalence is about a third of this. In these days when the emphasis is upon the direct relationship of high morbidity and low social class existence for many diseases it is salutary to find a disorder which, like migraine, afflicts predominantly the middle classes (Crisp, 1977).

As there is a predominance of girl students, there is therefore a high prevalence of anorexia nervosa on the campus.

> In looking for a 'meaning of food' for the anorexic we have to look at the meaning of adolescent body weight and shape, including its sexual aspects for the individual and her family, rather than specifically the nature of her relationships with her mother as is perhaps more valid in, say, the feeding disorders of childhood (Crisp, 1977).

General Practitioners are often alerted to the condition at such a late stage that hospital admission is inevitable or medically advisable. The restoration of body weight to matched population mean levels is not effective unless the patient wishes to see herself as a mature young woman with a sense of her own sexual identity.

There is an analogy with the in-patient treatment of hard drug addicts when they were physically withdrawn off all drugs; the treatment was abortive unless the psychotherapeutic treatment was also completed successfully.

Table 8.2: The Eclectic Treatment Plan for Anorexia

The Behavioural Approach	The Psychotherapeutic Approach	Family Therapy
concurrently in each consultation		
Sensory stimulation sheet - to develop dormant sense	The role of men and women in a man-woman relationship	Family seen as a group on two occasions - mother very defensive - father cared that she should 'get a good degree'
	Parents' marital relationship	
Body image - breathing exercises Exercises involving the senses - homework	Fears and fantasies The integration of the whole person - intellectual - emotional - sexual	
Information regarding the human male and the human female Planned programme of balanced eating		
	This treatment can be completed in approx. 8 weekly sessions	

The particular girl student in Case B had always been seen as the 'academic daughter' - she was to be a bridesmaid at her sister's wedding in three months' time, when her friends brought her in for treatment.

Occasionally the end of term may interrupt or terminate treatment. Restarting treatment after a period when the patient has returned home and often regressed to her former passive and compliant behaviour is sometimes impossible. If the student's attitude has now changed and she wants to take responsibility for herself as a sexual feminine woman, she may need a short period of in-patient treatment in a special unit, to re-establish a normal eating pattern in a controlled manner. It would be almost impossible to do this in the home situation.

Throughout counselling the student will have been physically examined and weighed regularly by the physician in the student health centre. Family therapy is seldom part of the treatment as the student needs to establish herself as a mature responsible person. As Renshaw (1976) states: 'Aware moral responsibility lies in understanding one's own sexuality, obtaining accurate information, recognition of the body's sexual needs, then making a mature choice of comfortable expression or of comfortable control.'

Female students can now combine the serious pursuit of a professional career with the roles of interdependent women, wife and mother.

It is not helpful for the anorexic student to be treated by a female feminist therapist. Holroyd (1976) points out that: 'Dichotomous traditional-liberated formulation which has successfully generated innovative interventions such as consciousness raising groups, carries within it the danger of losing the individual in favour of a new ideology of producing feminist entities instead of individuals.' And Evans (1976) adds: 'The question of whether a liberated ideology simply replaces one set of stereotypes with another and slows down the process of developing a sense of personal responsibility, has also been raised.'

Women's role in society has changed. The women who saw themselves as second-class citizens became feminists and reversed the roles, but many have now achieved a balance between the sexes. Counselling helps them to develop a sense of their own identity and with it a sense of their work identity and self-confidence, so that they can fulfil their academic potential.

Motivation

If a student is well motivated he can overcome any difficulty or disability - poor health, an unsatisfactory learning environment or inadequate study skills - and still achieve a high academic standard.

If one asks a senior member of the academic staff, who sees counselling as a low priority factor, how he selects students for undergraduate courses, he will invariably say motivation first, then a good intellectual standard. He would not be aware that counsellors can motivate students, his own motivation having arisen from his sense of vocation. Motivation, according to Cheetham (1981) 'is best thought of as something that is to be released within the learner, rather than instilled by an enthusiastic but dominating teacher'.

Academic success can be achieved with two quite distinct personality types. One is

> personally emotionally stable and has high access in theoretical and economic values, linked with a tendency to tough

> minded conservatism. This combination of a characteristic suggests a rather cold and ruthless individual governed by rationality and spurred on by competition to repeated demonstrations of intellectual mastery...

The other is described as:

> The main defining features (of the contrasting cluster) were high scores in neuroticism and syllabus boundness. They saw themselves as neither likeable nor self confident. They had no active social life and had few aesthetic interests... It is tempting to see these students as being motivated by fear of failure (Entwistle, 1977).

One of these groups is motivated by hopes of success, the other by fear of failure, but both are able to be academically successful.

Manifest Needs

In Murray's (1938) study of the 'individual person' he 'defines twenty manifest needs and eight latent needs'.

First, there is the need to succeed. This need to achieve has usually been a well-established pattern during schooling, the parents, whether professional or working-class, playing a significant part in its formation.

Reference has already been made to Mowner's work on fear. The student 'seems to regard fear as a highly generalised, motivated state, being involved with the primary, internal drive as well as with noxious external stimuli' (Cofer and Appley, 1968).

Motivation is concerned with personality and environmental factors. Crown, Lucas and Supramaniam (1973) point out that:

> Interactional aspects are of profound importance, so that a factor such as 'motivation' must be viewed as a product of the interplay of forces in the personal environmental attitudes and pressures. This motivation may vary from time to time and from environment to environment.

From the time of the school experience it is looked on as the function of the teacher to use his experience and knowledge to nuture, maintain and develop the pupils' motivation to learn.

In the higher education situation one again turns to the teacher and expects him to create a learning environment with a 'rewards system' that will meet the needs of individual students and thus affect the students' motivation.

THE STUDENTS' ROLE IN INCREASING MOTIVATION

It is essential to focus on the student, the individual learner. We need to understand how to motivate students and how to reinforce such motivation. As far as Skinner (1968) tells us 'education has never taught the self management of motivation very effectively'.

The student, having lost all motivation, who is considering withdrawing from his course, and who is referred by his personal tutor, is a real challenge to the counsellor. In defining the problem great care must be taken to establish the personality profile for this will determine the treatment programme.

If a student has not come to terms with his attitude to authority and his peers this can be destructive. As Mitchell (1975) says:

> The belief that an individual has generalised attitudes towards classes of persons pervades clinical, diagnostic and research practice. Freud, Pioget and Rogers, among others, all persist that reaction towards authority originates in the family situation and manifest themselves as broadly generalised attitudes expressed in many contexts towards supervisors in later social situations.

Students' attitude and behaviour in seminars are affected by whether they have satisfactorily overcome these normal developmental crises. They can receive help from counselling services by taking part in social skills groups or by watching a video in the LRC which is designed to help students overcome their difficulties in seminars.

> The motivating effect of group membership is frequently mentioned in connection with the value of group discussion methods or co-operative ventures such as group projects. Not only does it keep some students motivated who would idle if left to their own devices, it tends to increase understanding and arouse enthusiasm... The Group for Research and Innovation in Higher Education reports on the value of group projects in a number of fields (Beard and Senior, 1980).

Project work for first-year students in Science departments is a contentious issue. It involves and enlists the students' full commitment and energy, but I take heed of senior academic staff who see the students' prime need as the acquisition of the basic body of knowledge through observable experiments and lectures.

Vocational counselling has moved away from interest and aptitude tests and even views the AGCAS (Association for Graduate Careers Advisory Services) - designed computerised

Figure 8.2: Eclectic Treatment Programme for Lack of Motivation

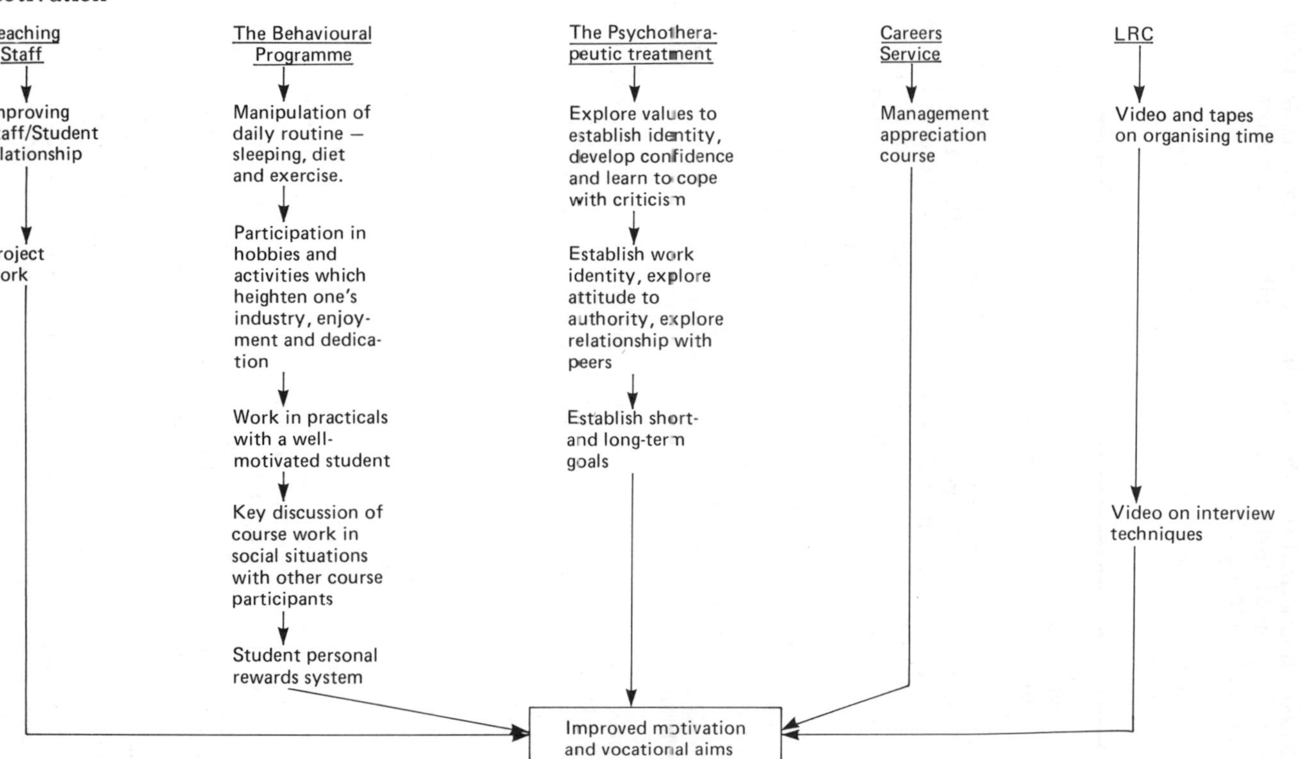

guidance questionnaire with restrained enthusiasm. As early as 1973, the interest tests were being described by Newsome, Thorne and Wyld (1975) as

> by no means the answer to every difficulty nor are they the instant remedy for every recalcitrant client. Used indiscriminantly they can be positively harmful, for they may give the client the impression that he is simply being 'processed' in a way which, far from strengthening his confidence, will tend to reduce the counsellor in his eyes to the rank of a psychological technician of doubtful usefulness.

Work experience, either for a year between school and university or during the university vacation, and field work does not always have the educational effect that might be expected. The students' confidence is increased if he matures through the experience and can set his theoretical concepts in a wider context. But Argyris and Schon (1974) point out that

> Many students learn about their own incompetence, that work in the field is harder than they thought and that they fail. In reaction, they may attack course work with a new energy, or they may express frustration that course work is less responsive to what field work has taught them that they need to know.

Some courses, notably medicine, law and social sciences, have used brief simulated games or case studies. These involve the student increasing his sense of achievement and thereby increasing his motivation.

Relevance of Course to Future Careers

Vocational counsellors are now also using work experience in the form of vacation jobs and management appreciation short courses to show the vocational relevance of courses, which is an important factor in the students' learning environment. The development of experimental and imaginative vocational counselling is particularly important set against the picture of increased graduate unemployment.

Le Blanc (1978) suggests that preventative programmes with unemployed youth such as co-operative education, job sharing and work experience should go a step further and consider the viability of a concurrent training concept.

> By way of example, a concurrent training programme would provide one with the opportunity on the one hand to train in an occupation based on academic skills such as language interpretation and on the other hand in a trade involving mostly physical skills such as woodworking.

The explosion of the frustrations of unemployed young people in the form of outbreaks of violence in big conurbations shows the need for administrators to exercise the imagination and creativity that Hall (1980) referred to, to devise new methods to cope with new situations in an ever-changing technological world. Perhaps at some time the individual will have to take control of the scientific 'progress' that threatens to destroy civilised man. Until such time as schools and universities invest careers guidance and counselling with the value and respect they offered to science and mathematics, the individual will continue to be devalued.

RELATIONSHIPS

The ability to relate to one's fellow men, both individually and collectively, is looked on as a prerequisite of a mentally healthy and well-adjusted human being.

How does one then set this in the context of learning in higher education where research shows that it is the stable introvert who achieves academic honours rather than the extrovert? There needs to be a balance in all things and a responsible counsellor would focus on four basic 'needs' of most students.

1. The need for the student to have a good academic and social relationship with other students. This requires social and individual relationship skills such as awareness and sensitivity.
2. The need for students to be able to function well in 'groups' or 'couple' teaching experiences such as seminars and practicals.
3. The need for students to develop close lecturer/student relationships. It behoves students as well as teachers to develop these relationships.
4. The need for students to be competent in relationships with their work colleagues when they leave higher education.

The changes in socio-economic and moral standards have alienated students from the older generation, not only their parents but also most academic teaching staff. This results from a preoccupation on the part of the media, which since 1968 has brought subjects such as 'drug abuse' and human sexuality into the open. Warburton (1978) says that

> Szasz (1975) is right in pointing out that, at the turn of the century, opiate use was acceptable while most masturbation was not, and that today the reverse is true. That change is a consequence of advancing medical knowledge. Society cannot afford the drug casualties from internal pollution.

Treatment of Drug Addiction

In 1968, 24 drug addiction clinics were set up by the Department of Health all over England - 13 of them being in London. They set out to control the prescribing of 'hard' drugs such as heroin and cocaine, and to stamp out the prescribing of illicit drugs by unscrupulous doctors. Drugs, unlike alcohol, had not been an adolescent experience or threat for the older generation so that they feared what they did not understand.

It was difficult for long-term heroin addicts to come off and stay off drugs but, although the prognosis was poor, a certain number did so and were followed up once a month for periods of up to four years (Oppenheim, Wright, Buchanan and Biggs, 1973). In a study at the Charing Cross Drug Clinic a comparison was made between a follow-up group of the first 40 patients who came off drugs and 40 control patients. It was found that a positive aspect of this study appeared to be the importance of a continuing relationship between the psychiatric social worker and the ex-addict. Regular follow-up domicillary visits aborted several possible relapses. The media continued to concentrate on reports, often visual, of degradation and death.

The Development of Treatment for Psychosexual Problems

In the late 1960s Masters and Johnson (1966 and 1970) made a study of human sexuality which became a subject for laboratory research, comparable to what many scientists were doing in their experiments with the psychology of reproduction among lower animals. I acknowledge the importance of their research but share Singer's (1973) criticism that it 'systematically destroys the normal conditions of coital behaviour', and Singer further suggests that 'the very presence of observers changes the character of female response'.

In 1968 Ted McIlvenna set up the National Sex Forum in San Francisco, which has subsequently developed into the Institute for the Study of Human Sexuality at the University of California. Their SAR (Sexual Attitude Restructuring) process expects each person to take responsibility for his own sexuality. Important further research has also been carried out in the USA by Lo Piccolo on Oregon (1976) and New York (1974), and by Kaplan (1975), and in the UK by Bancroft, Tennent and Cass in Oxford (1974) and Edinburgh (1978), and Gillan in London (1975). The women's groups in America have closely identified with the work of Dobson (1974) and others who have urged women to be responsible for their own sexuality and have freed them from myths about masturbation. The publication of the study and the resulting media coverage brought information about formal sexuality into the public eye.

Other media have been the means of bringing the subject of sexuality into the open:

(a) Articles and surveys in magazines and publications such as the Hite Report on female sexuality (1977).
(b) Books on psychosexual dysfunction and treatment (see Gillan, 1976, and Brown, 1978).
(c) Television programmes on normal sexual development and sexual dysfunction (see Bancroft, 1977).
(d) Sex education in schools. The National Child Development study stated that in 1974 90 per cent of 16 year-olds were taught the psychology of human reproduction in school.
(e) Literature on birth control methods and sexually transmitted diseases distributed free by the Health Education Council and the Family Planning Association.

This openness about sexual matters has helped to dispel ignorance, liberate young women from the folly of double standards, and generally help young people to make responsible personal decisions about matters of premarital sex and birth control.

Most students are at a point where they have a need to establish their own identity. The concept of identity, and in particular sexual identity, has changed dramatically in the last ten years.

Changing Sexual Expectations

Mass media coverage has resulted in changes in attitude. Sensational articles in irresponsible publications and badly controlled advertising have led many sexually inexperienced young people to feel inadequate in a performance-orientated society.

They are inhibited in making relationships based on mutual regard and interests, for fear of sexual expectations. Both young men and women have performance hang-ups in their relationships. This is sad when, in her study of female sexuality, Hite (1977) has shown us that this is not what women want and

> all the kinds of physical intimacy that were channelled into our one mechanised definition of sex can now be re-allowed and re-diffused through our lives, including simple forms of touching and warm bodily contact. Intense physical intimacy can be one of the most satisfying activities possible and an end in itself.

THE GENERATION GAP

The generation gap is very apparent in the area of relationships and sexuality. Parents fear that the earlier physical maturation of women will lead to the development of close emotional and sexual relationships before the student is financially independent, or mature enough to handle his emotions. Also, he may then have less interest in academic pursuits.

Unfortunately, teachers and parents focus on the greater freedom and permissiveness between young people and ignore some of the facts.

Unlike the previous generation, young people see men and women as equal sharing partners valuing one another, and genuine emotional friendship is now possible between men and women, age or sex not being a barrier. Men and women students share communal student flats, caring for one another as friends without being sexual partners. The men do not see the young women as future wives or mistresses nor do the young women devalue men as their feminist sisters would wish them to.

The decision to live together as a couple is taken as seriously as the previous generation entered into marriage, and it is at this stage that a sexual as well as an emotional commitment is likely to be entered into. Marriage is not devalued. It is looked on as a further commitment and usually comes when the degree course is completed or when a family is planned.

There is now more social acceptance of homosexual relationships and they are the natural orientation for some people, whilst others are capable of responding sexually to both men and women. It is therefore now as inconsistent to fear friendship between two students of the same sex as between students of the opposite sex.

This lack of a common language between the generations can cause academic misunderstanding. If a student comes before the Failures committee saying that he is upset because his relationship with his girlfriend has broken up after three years this may mean:

(a) To him - the equivalent of a divorce after a three-year marriage.

(b) To his middle-aged academic tutor - that he no longer has a girlfriend to take out to the cinema.

It is therefore left to the counsellor or to another colleague to 'interpret' the problem.

The Need for Information

Students find it difficult to rectify inadequate or faulty knowledge which they feel they ought to know and are too embarrassed to ask their peers. Sometimes their knowledge is very 'uneven' so that a girl student presenting with vaginismus, who has masturbated to orgasm for the last five years, had never actually looked at her own genitals, and was convinced that she had an intact hymen that would inhibit intercourse - this, despite having experienced an internal medical examination.

If students are considering using a birth control technique, they need informed counselling to discuss the alternatives - abstinence, contraception and sterilisation. Some students think that 'the pill' and contraception are synonymous; others dislike its side effects but are unaware of alternative methods. As Professor Donald (1978) observed, 'Despite the pill, the illegitimacy rate is rising as never before, and the abortion rate per number of live born children continues to rise.'

I would now like to discuss a case that covers many of the problems that we have been discussing. A first-year couple came for treatment of what they presented as a sexual problem. They had become close friends, they lived in the same hall but they did not have a sexual relationship. They told me that the girl was sexually unresponsive and I arranged to see them diagnostically both alone and together.

In the course of the 'diagnostic' consultation it was apparent that both the man and woman were stable, well-balanced, self-confident young people with strong motivation for their course who had a good sense of their own identity. The girl had started a 'break away' Christian group which required the courage to be different from her group of friends and the man student had hobbies and interests that were different from the 'average' student. It appeared that this couple, because of their Christian beliefs, did not want a sexual relationship before marriage. They felt that this sexual part of the relationship was expected of them, in order to conform to the way that other student couples behaved. They both independently said that this friendship was the most rewarding that they had ever experienced.

Through counselling, they were able to come to their own decision to continue to share a close friendship based on mutual trust and empathy but by choice a non-sexual one.

THE NEED FOR COUNSELLING THE PHYSICALLY HANDICAPPED

We now have increasingly better provision for physically handicapped students in higher education, and counsellors must be able to help them with problems concerning their sexuality. Two years ago a research project was carried out by the National Fund for Research into Crippling Diseases in Coventry, to look at the sexuality of physically disabled persons, their sexual needs and the problems that confront them in this area (Stewart, 1975).

The Termination of Pregnancy

Students may think that an abortion is a simple matter, like going to the dentist, but it can have 'after effects' that are not only psychological. Wynn and Wynn (1972) stated that: 'The evidence is clear that abortion frequently reduces a woman's future reproductive capability.' The first report of the British Perinatal Mortality survey concluded: 'Any patient who has a previous history of an abortion should be regarded as a high risk patient and be invariably booked for hospital delivery under consultant care' (Wynn and Wynn, 1972). Their survey showed that 'induced abortion has adverse consequences to the reproductive capability of young women who wish to have children subsequently and increases the risk that such children may suffer perinatal damage'.

Counsellors need to be well informed medically as well as therapeutically in order to counsel effectively in higher education institutions. A student must be able to arrive at the decision of whether to have a termination or not without being influenced by the ethical attitude of the counsellor. He can, however, encourage the student to seek the support of her parents, to make an unhurried decision despite the time constraint and to encourage the putative father (invariably another student) to take a responsible attitude towards the situation.

Drug Abuse

'It is a paradox of our present age that even though many causes of physical disease, i.e. nutrition, sanitation, are being eliminated, our consumption of drugs is increasing' (Klass, 1975, and Illich, 1977). 'Forty per cent of all adults in one comprehensive survey in Britain had taken some form of medication at least once a day for the previous two weeks' (Dunnell and Cartwright, 1972).

'Patients report that around 40% of the central nervous system drugs that they had taken had been obtained on the tenth or more repeat prescription' (Dunnell and Cartwright, 1972). 'Women are more likely to have these repeat prescriptions than men' (Dunnell, 1973). 'The increase in illicit drug taking among young people shocks their middle-aged parents who prefer not to face the fact that they themselves are probably one of the statistics' (Dunnell and Cartwright, 1972).

In the course of domicillary visits to the homes of drug clinic patients I came across many instances of mothers giving their legally prescribed sleeping tablets to their 'addict son' (knowing that he would crush and inject them into himself) as she gave him breast milk when he was a baby.

There have been widespread compaigns by the Ministry of Health aimed at persuading general practitioners to cease prescribing certain drugs and to generally reduce the prescribing of drugs overall. The Committee on the Review of Medicine warned doctors in a report in the 'British Medical Journal' in March 1980 to bring patients off drugs such as Valium, Librium or Mogadon gradually because of the danger of withdrawal symptoms. Research is being carried out at the Institute of Psychiatry into the effects of withdrawal from Valium after long-term prescribing. Despite this, student health centres continue to prescribe Valium for students who suffer from anxiety. It is the students themselves who, finding that the drugs treat the symptom rather than the cause, and that the body builds up a tolerance rendering the drug ineffective, turn to counselling as an effective alternative.

The drug of choice amongst the student population is marijuana or cannabis, often as an initial means of obtaining entry to a peer group when their inadequate social skills make the normal peer group relationship difficult. As the ability to make relationships improves, drugs are used less. Only a very small percentage progress to mind-expanding hallucinogenics such as LSD or mescaline. LSD can cause problems. Students who have given up taking the drug but who suffer from 'flashbacks' are terrified that these will occur during crucial examinations.

Alcohol Abuse

It is difficult for a physically fit young person to understand the physical deterioration of alcoholism. They may, however, want to marry and have a family and not want to run the risk of having a child handicapped by the teratogenic effect of alcohol.

> In humans exposed to alcohol during gestation the effect can range from foetal alcohol syndrome in some offspring of chronic alcholic women to reduced average birthweight in offspring of women reporting an average consumption of two to three drinks per day. The effect of such exposure may range from mental retardation in children with foetal alcohol syndrome to milder developmental and behavioural effects in infants born to the social drinker (Streissguth; Landesman-Dwyer, Martin and Smith, 1980).

Students with a very high alcohol consumption often call themselves 'social drinkers' when by definition of consumption they are alcoholic. Universities condemn heavy drinking whilst encouraging bars in halls of residence, with drinks at advantageous prices. Students reflect the trend in the general population where 'social drinking' has escalated at an alarming rate. 'Between 1965 and 1975 the average amount of alcohol being consumed annually in the UK rose from 210 pints to 269 pints per person aged 15 years or over. Individual consumption of spirits rose from 3.3 to 5.9 proof pints and that of wine from 6.8 to 14.5 pints' (Diggory, 1980).

Suicide by Hire Purchase

Drug and alcohol abuse amount to 'suicide by hire purchase' and 'drugs head the list of methods used not only in suicide attempts but also in suicide' (Stengal, 1973). Baechler (1979) feels that 'Dr. Stengal is probably the first person to put the accent on the "appeal" dimension' (Baechler, 1979). Students often attempt suicide as an <u>appeal</u> for the affection that they have often not experienced from their home situation. Baechler refers to this as 'disappointed expectations... The appeal is addressed to agencies of "social assistance". They are seeking a means of gaining attention and care.'

In the treatment of addiction it is important to treat the cause underlying the symptom of drug or alcohol abuse - the depression, the dependency - rather than focusing on the drug and its effect.

Motivation for Treatment

When students who are interested in their course of studies, are unable to work, due to an emotional or psychological problem, they are well motivated to respond to counselling.

According to Egan (1975) the sources of the client's motivation are as follows.

> 1. The motivation of the client is generally high if he is in psychological pain. The disorganization of his life makes him susceptible to the influence of the helper...
> 2. The client will involve himself in the helping process more fully if he is dealing with issues of intrinsic importance to him...
> 3. The amount of physical and psychological effort demanded of the client by the helping process affects his motivation...

Family Relationships

Some students are still very over-involved with their families, often the widowed or divorced parent who has been 'left behind'. This can be very detrimental to the student's studies. He feels that he should be at home looking after his depressed and lonely parent, often a mother, and in fact often does go home each weekend. He attends lectures, seminars and practicals, but feels guilty that he is not at home, fulfilling all of his parent's expressed and unexpressed needs.

Through counselling, he can begin to separate from home and achieve his own identity. At the same time he can encourage his parent to seek support from close friends and neighbours. If the parent sabotages these ideas the student could inform the parent's General Practitioner of his concern.

In time one hopes that the parent develops new interests and that the student is allowed to lead his own life and pursue his studies.

Such parents could heed the prophet who said:

> Your children are not your children. They are the Sons and Daughters of Life's longing for itself. They come through you but not from you and though they are with you yet they belong not to you.
>
> You may give them your love but not your thoughts. For

Figure 8.3: Eclectic Treatment for Drug Addiction

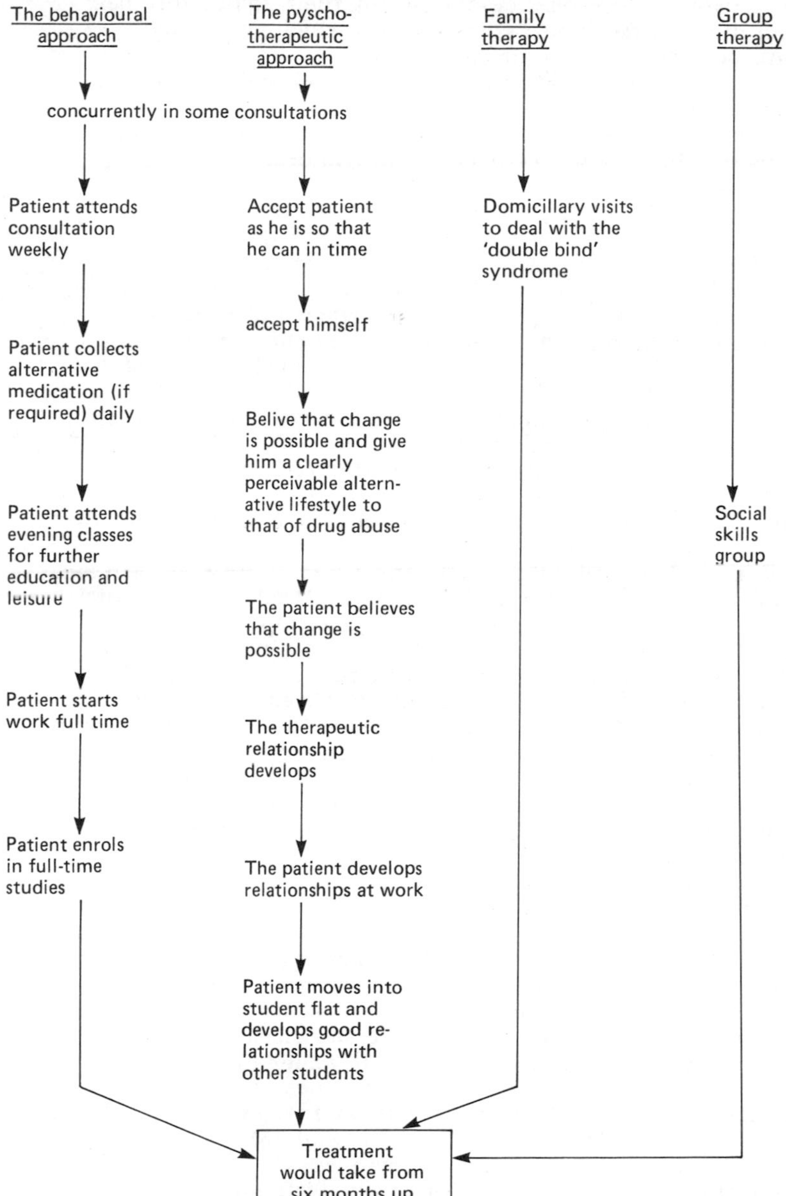

they have their own thoughts.
You may house their bodies but not their souls, for their souls dwell in the house of tomorrow, which you cannot visit, not even in your dreams.
You may strive to be like them, but seek not to make them like you.
For life goes not backward nor tarries with yesterday.
You are the bows from which your children as living arrows are sent forth (Gibran, 1980).

REFERENCES

Argyris, C. and Schon, D.A. (1974) 'Theory in Practice', Jossey-Bass Publications, San Francisco, p. 188
Axline, V. (1971) 'Dibs: In Search of Self', Pelican, London, pp. 8 and 180
Bach, R. (1972) 'Jonathan Livingstone Seagull: a Story', Pan Books, London, pp. 82 and 83
Baechler, J. (1979) 'Suicides', Basil Blackwell, Oxford, pp. 141, 152 and 153
Balint, M. and Balint, E. (1961) 'Psychotherapeutic Techniques in Medicine', Tavistock Publications, London
Bancroft, J.H.J., Tennent, J.G. and Cass, J. (1974) Control of Deviant Sexual Behaviour by Drugs, 'Archives of Sexual Behaviour', vol. 3, pp. 261-71, as quoted in Wright
Beard, R.M. and Senior, I.J. (1980) 'Motivating Students', Routledge and Kegan Paul, London, p. 60
Brock, G. (1979) Drugs: Rising Heroin Threat, 'Observer Review', 'The Observer' (11 November), p. 34
Brown, P. (1978) 'Treat yourself to Sex', Dent, London, as quoted in Wright
Cheetham, B. (1981) Towards Specification for Self Access Study Facilities in a Multi-cultured Academic Community, unpublished dissertation, p. 10
Clare, A. (1976) 'Psychiatry in Dissent', Tavistock Publications, London, pp. 31, 44 and 402
Cofer, C.N. and Appley, M.H. (1968) 'Motivation: Theory and Research', J. Wiley and Sons, New York, p. 504
Crisp, A.H. (1977) Anorexia Nervosa, 'Proceedings of Royal Society of Medicine', vol. 70 (July), pp. 465 and 469
Crisp, A.H. (1978) Anorexia Nervosa - A Disease of our Time (The Need to Make Provision For It), Paper presented at Session 2 of the RIPHH Annual Conference, Eastbourne, 3 October and published in, 'Health and Hygiene', vol. 2, no. 3 (January-March 1979), pp. 149 and 151
Crown, S., Lucas, C.J. and Supramaniam, S. (1973) The Delineation and Measurement of Study Difficulty in University Students, 'British Journal of Psychiatry', vol. 123, pp. 381-93
Diggory, P. (1980) 'Alcohol and the Unborn Child - the Foetal

Alcohol Syndrome', The National Council of Women, London
Donald, I. (1978) After the Pill, 'Daily Telegraph', 10 April as quoted in Wright
Dobson, B. (1974) 'A Mediation of Self-love', Betty Dobson, Box 1933, New York, as quoted in Wright
Dunnell, K. (1973) Medicine Takers and Hoarders, 'Journal of Royal College of General Practitioners', vol. 23, supplement 2, no. 2, as quoted in Warburton, p. 311
Dunnell, K. and Cartwright, A. (1972) 'Medicine Takers, Prescribers and Hoarders', Routledge and Kegan Paul, London, as quoted in Warburton, p. 312
Egan, G. (1975) 'The Skilled Helper', Brooks/Cole Publishing Company, Monterey, California, pp. 113 and 114
Entwistle, N. (1977) Strategies of Learning and Studying: Recent Research Findings, 'British Journal of Educational Studies', vol. XXV, no. 3, p. 227
Erikson, E.H. (1968) 'Identity: Youth and Crisis', Faber and Faber, London, pp. 127-8
Evans, D. (1976) Emerging Truths on the Psychology of Women: As Through a Glass Darkly, 'The Counselling Psychologist', vol. 6, pp. 60-4, as quoted in B. Noonan and L. Wilgosh, An Existential Model for Counselling Women, 'International Journal for the Advancement of Counselling', vol. 4, no. 1 (1981), p. 37
Frederick, J. (1973) 'Changing Professional Roles - a Counsellor's Viewpoint', Counselling Service, University of Melbourne, Australia, p. 6
Gibran, K. (1980) 'The Prophet', Pan Books, London, p. 20
Gillan, P. (1976) Objective Measures of Female Sexual Arousal, 'Journal of Psychology', as quoted in Wright
Gillan, P. (1975) 'Sex Therapy To-day', Open Book Pub., London, as quoted in Wright
Gilmore, S.K. (1980) A Comprehensive Theory for Eclectic Intervention, 'International Journal for the Advancement of Counselling', vol. 3, nos. 3/4, pp. 185-210
Goffman, E. (1971) 'The Presentation of Self in Everyday Life', Allen Lane, London
Hall, P. (1980) 'Great Planning Disasters', Weidenfeld and Nicolson, London
Halmos, P. (1974) The Personal and the Political, 'British Journal of Guidance and Counselling', vol. 2 (July), p. 131
Hite, S. (1977) 'The Hite Report', Paul Hamlyn, Sydney, as quoted in Wright
Holroyd, J. (1976) Psychotherapy and Women's Liberation, 'The Counselling Psychologist', vol. 6, pp. 22-7, as quoted in B. Noonan and L. Wilgosh, An Existential Model for Counselling Women, 'International Journal for the Advancement of Counselling', vol. 4, no. 1 (1981)
Illich, I. (1977) 'Limits of Medicine, Medical Nemesis. The Expropriation of Health', Penguin, Harmondsworth, as quoted in Warburton

Jehu, D., Hardiker, P., Yelloly, M. and Shaw, M. (1972) 'Behaviour Modification in Social Work', The Garden City Press Ltd, Letchworth, Herts, pp. 132 and 156
Kaplan, M.S. (1975) 'The Illustrated Manual of Sex Therapy', The New York Times Book Co, published in London (1976) by Souvenir Press, as quoted in Wright
Kelly, T. (1978) Medical Needs of Young Adults as quoted in 'Students in Need', SRHE, Guildford, Surrey, pp. 182-3
Kelynack, D. (1972) 'Symposium on Problems of Adolescents', Counselling Service, University of Melbourne, Australia, p. 4
Kessell, W.I.N. (1960) The Psychiatric Morbidity in a London General Practice, 'British Journal of Preventative and Sexual Medicine', vol. 14, no. 16
Klass, A. (1975) 'There's Gold in Them Thar Pills', Penguin, Harmondsworth, as quoted in Warburton
Le Blanc, J.P. (1978) Counselling Today's Unemployed Youth, Paper presented to IRTAC Conference, Oslo, Norway, 5 July, p. 14
Lichter, S.O., Rapien, E.B., Seibert, F.M. and Sklansky, M.D. (1962) 'The Drop Outs', The Free Press, New York
Lo Piccolo, L. (1976) 'Becoming Orgasmic: a Sexual Growth Program for Women', Prentice Hall, Englewood Cliffs, New Jersey
Lucas, C.J. (1976) Psychological Problems of Students, 'British Medical Journal', vol. 2, pp. 1431-3
Magnussen, M.D. (1978) New Thinking in Mental Health, paper presented to IRTAC Conference, Oslo, Norway, 5 July, p. 13
Masters, W.H. and Johnson, V.E. (1966) 'Human Sexual Response', Churchill, London, as quoted in Wright
Masters, W.H. and Johnson, V.E. (1970) 'Human Sexual Inadequacy', Churchill, London, as quoted in Wright
McIlvenna, T. (1975) 'The S.A.R. Guide', The Institute for Advanced Study of Human Sexuality, The National Sex Forum, San Francisco, as quoted in Wright
Meacher, M. (1978) 'A Pilot Counselling Scheme with General Practitioners', Summary Report, Mental Health Foundation, London
Meyer, V. and Chesser, E.S. (1970) 'Behaviour Therapy in Clinical Psychiatry', Penguin, Harmondsworth, as quoted in Jehu, Hardiker, Yelloly and Shaw
Mischel, J. (1968) 'Personality and Assessment', J. Wiley and Sons, New York, p. 6
Mitchell, J.J. (1975) 'The Adolescent Predicament', Holt, Rinehart and Winston of Canada Ltd, Toronto, p. 21
Murray, H.A. (1938) 'Explorations in Personality', Oxford University Press, Oxford, pp. 715-19
National Association for Mental Health (1974 o.p.) Psychotherapy: Do We Need More 'Talking Treatment'?, 'Mind

Report', no. 12, pp. 7-8
National Council of Women (1980) 'Alcohol and the Unborn Child - the Fatal Alcohol Syndrome', National Council of Women of Great Britain, London
Newsome, A., Thorne, B.J. and Wyld, K.L. (1975) 'Student Counselling in Practice', University of London Press Ltd, London, p. 75
O'Doherty, E. (1974) 'Religious Therapy', Constable, London, as quoted in V. Varma, (ed.), 'Psychotherapy Today', pp. 213-14
Oppenheim, G.B., Wright, J.E., Buchanan, J. and Biggs, L. (1973) 'Out-patient Greatment of Narcotic Addiction, Who Benefits?', as quoted in 'The British Journal of Addiction to Alcohol and Other Drugs', vol. 68, pp. 37-44
Pashley, B. and Shepherd, A. (1978) How University Members See the Pastoral Role of the Academic, 'British Journal of Guidance and Counselling', vol. 6, no. 1, p. 14
Proctor, B. (1978) 'Counselling Shop', Burnett Books Ltd, London, p. 239
Renshaw, D.C. (1976) Understanding Masturbation, 'The Journal of School Health', vol. XLVI, no. 2 (February), p. 100
Rogers, C. (1969) 'Freedom to be Born: a View of what Education Might Become', Merrill, Columbus, Ohio
Royal College of Physicians (1979) 'College Committee on Health Services in Higher Education', Royal College of Physicians, London
Royal College of Psychiatrists (1975) 'Norms for Medical Staffing of a Psychiatric Service - Psychotherapy', Report to Central Manpower Committee, London
Ryle, A. (1969) 'Student Casualties', Allen Lane, London, p. 41
Simms, M. (1973) 'Report on Non-Medical Abortion Counselling', Birth Control Trust, London, p. 27
Singer, I. (1973) 'The Goals of Human Sexuality', Wildwood House, London, as quoted in Wright
Skinner, B.F. (1968) 'The Technology of Teaching', Appleton-Century-Crofts, New York, as quoted in J. Bynner and J. Whitehead, 'Personality Dimensions and Motivation', Open University, Milton Keynes, 1972
Stengal, E. (1973) To Die or Not to Die, 'New Society', 15 March, p. 579
Stewart, W.F.R. (1975) 'Sex and the Physically Handicapped', National Foundation for Research into Crippling Diseases, Horsham, Sussex, as quoted in Wright
Streissguth, A.P., Landesman-Dwyer, S., Martin, J.C. and Smith, D.W. (1980) Teratogenic Effects of Alcohol in Humans and Laboratory Animals, 'Science Journal', vol. 209 (18 July)
Szasz, T. (1975) 'Ceremonial Chemistry', Routledge and Kegan Paul, London, as quoted in Warburton
Tyler, L.E. (1970) The Social Implications of Counselling, as quoted in 'The World of Guidance Education and Vocational',

IRTAC Report, The Hague, p. 21
Warburton, D.M. (1978) Poisoned People Internal Pollution, 'Journal of Biosocial Science', vol. 10, p. 313
Wilkinson, A. (1973) Psychosomatic Concept and Approach, Paper presented to the Annual Conference of the British Student Health Association, p. 3
Wilson, J.R. (1972) The Psychotherapist as Student Counsellor, Paper presented at IRTAC Conference, Paris and Orsay, France, pp. 10-11
Wright, J.E. (1980) An Approach to Psychosexual Counselling, 'International Journal for the Advancement of Counselling', vol. 3, Martinus Nijhoff Publishers, The Hague, pp. 125-35
Wynn, N. and Wynn, A. (1972) 'Some Consequences of Induced Abortion to Children Born Subsequently', Foundation for Education and Research in Child-Bearing, London, p. 11

9 CHANGE IN HIGHER EDUCATION INSTITUTIONS

In Chapter 8 we considered the change that can occur in the individual student which can lead to an improvement in academic performance. In this chapter we will look at the institutional factors that impede rather than facilitate the students' progress and consider ways in which changes might be introduced into the higher educational institutions.

INSTITUTIONAL FACTORS THAT MAY IMPEDE THE LEARNING PROCESS

First, the aim of the institution on the one hand and the learner and teacher on the other may be at variance. Students and teachers have to work in an educational institution that is geared to the syllabus and to the examination as tangible proof of educational practice. 'The pre-eminent values of this culture are technologically scientific and one consequence has been a high premium placed on knowledge that can be used to change, control, manipulate and order both nature and society' (Emler and Heather, 1980).

However, knowledge is acquired when a person's intelligence is coupled with experience so that learning is a process that goes on alongside the formal syllabus. One learns from family, from friends, from nature, from religious experience and, above all, from good teachers whose value systems may be very different from those of the institution. So knowledge and therefore learning is bound up with meaning, values and social groupings and relationships. We treat matters of learning and teaching as separate entities instead of two halves of the same relationship.

The National Foundation for Educational Research has been carrying out a research project into study skills programmes for 16-19 year-olds in schools. They found that in evaluating different courses and discussing them with the researchers in teacher groups, the outcome was the staff's critical reassessment of their methods of teaching. This also led to innovation in the design of courses. The use of study skills, then, has implications for teacher training.

I mentioned in a previous chapter that university staff participating in 'Learning to Learn' workshops spontaneously and critically re-examined their teaching approaches, and this again has implications for staff initial training courses and staff development. By focusing on the learner and not the teacher, the academic staff did not feel threatened.

Despite evidence that the large, formal lecture encourages passivity, deference to authority and dependency on the ideas that the teacher has extrapolated, most first-year teaching in Arts and vocational courses takes place in this manner.

Most of the teachers in the schools' study skills research project that I referred to gave lectures in study skills by regurgitating chapters of study skills manuals. Some higher education institutions have also committed the same errors initially in their study skills programmes. These methods of learning and learning to learn create dependency. Gibbs (1981) mentions another study skills method which can have an adverse effect on the student. He criticises the 'contract' method of study that Goldman (1979) uses.

> It is largely only the student's dependence on and submission to the counsellor's authority that makes this contract stick at all. Only a relatively insecure student lacking in self-confidence and self-direction is likely to undertake many such one-sided contracts. It is also very time consuming (Gibbs, 1981).

The Mature Learner

The development of emotional maturity and the formation of identity is crucial if the student is to be capable of becoming a mature learner and able to adopt a deep-level approach to learning. Whilst it has been stressed that some students adopt a surface-level and at other times a deep-level approach, dependent on how they conceptualise learning at a particular time, the immature student is <u>only</u> able to be a surface learner. In fact, if the student experiences a crisis of identity, he will be quite unable to work at any level. 'The exigency of this developmental crisis seems to us to impose a profound responsibility on the educator, a responsibility which is no longer a separate moral task like "building character" that was once somehow "tacked on" to regular teaching' (Perry, 1970).

Again, the teacher can do much to help the alienated student by helping him to feel a sense of commitment to his academic group and department, and by displaying a certain openness which shows the teacher's own vulnerability, doubts and personal style.

Many teachers know from wide experience that students who are developing intellectually and personally through their years in higher education need close emotional support when they are taking the greatest intellectual risks. We have an analogy of this in infancy when a one-year-old child who is learning to walk changes from being a contented baby able to be left alone to a dependent child clinging to its mother.

The Need for Change

Higher educational institutions' promotional structures have never rewarded the conscientious teacher. In the present situation of financial stringency, the members of academic staff who concentrate on teaching rather than published research may put their careers in jeopardy.

Now more than ever before, universities need good teachers to cope with the increase in mature students and to assist an increasing number of overseas students who have inadequate linguistic and study skills.

There is a need for innovative experimental teaching schemes but this is discouraged in times of financial stringency. There is also a need for students to be shown the vocational relevance of their courses. This is particularly pertinent in times of increasing graduate unemployment. There are still departments who put students under extreme examination pressure in the final examinations in particular, and they need to change their policy to one of more continuous assessment.

The Curriculum

The curriculum in some departments is concerned with making a fair assessment possible, so that all students have the same chance to learn the same material under the same conditions. This presupposes that there is a body of knowledge waiting to be assimilated instead of acknowledging the 'spirit of inquiry'. This totally focuses on 'the syllabus' leading to 'the examination' and cxcludes consideration of

(a) learning abstract meaning,
(b) learning to interpret processes aimed at an understanding of reality,

and only considers

(a) learning to increase knowledge,
(b) learning for memorising, and
(c) learning as the acquisition of facts and processes.

It hehoves each department to update the curriculum constantly and critically, and to reassess selection and assessment procedures.

The Aim at Universities

In order to understand the resistance to a fundamental change of attitude in universities, it is necessary to realise that the prime aim of universities is research. 'The search for knowledge - "re-search as we call it today" not merely actual discovery, not merely even the attempt to discover, but the creation and cultivation of the spirit of discovery' (Truscott, 1943).

The universities are unlike polytechnics who have always put emphasis on the polytechnic as a teaching institution, as Entwistle and Percy (1973) found in the interviews they conducted in the follow-up study to the Rowntree project. The original idea of teaching in universities was for academics to train the young in the image of themselves so that they could become the researchers of tomorrow. From this, the present situation has developed, when some students come to be taught who are undesirous of becoming researchers and who, in some cases, are undesirous of being taught!

In 1980, the number of Arts graduates continuing into postgraduate studies was 7 per cent; the figure for Science graduates was 19 per cent. This needs to be looked at in the light of research that is actively pursued in universities.

Research in Universities

> A little factual research will make the state of things clearer.
>
> One University has on its official list of Professor Emeriti, four from the Faculty of Arts. Their average age in 1942 was seventy-one; their average length of service, as full Professors, i.e. with adequate salaries and complete security of tenure, was sixteen years; the average number of books they have published, according to their own returns in the current 'Who's Who' is three. (Truscott, 1943).

Truscott then gives figures showing the record of publications of members of an Arts faculty covering one year.

> It includes text books and also reprints and re-editions of books published years before:

Number in Faculty	Number Reporting No research at all	No. of Books Published	Average	No. of Articles Published	Average
20	10 (50%)	Professors 3	$\frac{3}{20}$	20	1
80	56 (70%)	Lecturers 10	$\frac{1}{8}$	35	$\frac{7}{16}$

> Twenty Professors, who in twenty two weeks of vacation produced a single article and three books between them. Eight Lecturers, each the proud author of an eighth of a book and less than half an article. Certainly, if the universities can boast even a few productive workers, they

> must carry an unconscious number of pure passengers (Truscott, 1943, p. 118).

Despite the lack of published research and lack of research students (i.e. post-graduate students) in the Arts faculties, the universities will still consider promotion (or, in the present financial crisis, security of tenure) to be dependent on research rather than on teaching.

The University Grants Committee who in 1981 suggested cuts which have fallen disproportionately harshly on the modern technological institutions, with their greater emphasis on teaching, have reinforced this point of view. In universities, separate departments, some large and some small, that are perceived as good learning environments, will be threatened with closure.

Resistance to Change

Even in the case of recession, resistance to change can be minimised if staff are kept fully informed. In industry,

> the manager needs to be advised in advance as to the reasons for the changes, using audio visual aids if necessary, and to be allowed to discuss his fears and queries with the regional management so that he feels an active useful agent in the change process, rather than just a helpless pawn (O'Connell, Bennis and Mee, 1968).

However, even this procedure of fully informing the staff may fail if the changes threaten valued stable situations or increase the incomprehensibility and non-communicative barriers of the organisation (Hutton, 1972).

Not only is the member of staff likely to lose his job but also his work identity, which is for many professional people their identity per se. It is also important to recognise men's need for affiliation. 'The need for belonging was seen as providing the basic motivation for individuals to work' (Lawrence and Lorsch, 1969). To understand this one must understand vested interests.

Vested Interests

'A vested interest is simply an involvement in an organisation which gives a valued reward to an individual. When the reward is "at risk" the individual will make every effort to retain it' (Gray, 1975). At a time of change, particularly when change is brought about by financial constraints, the reaction of insecure people is to try to hold fast to the familiar.

Civilised society needs institutions but institutions can be remodelled by civilised men - men of vision as well as logic.

THE DEFINITION OF UNIVERSITIES

A university is, after all, an institution and 'our institutions, in the broadest sense in which I am using the term, include the organs of central and local government, government agencies, public corporations, business enterprises, co-operatives, trade unions, Universities' political parties, charitable foundations, churches and clubs' (Vickers, 1965).

CHANGE IN ORGANISATIONS

There have been many books written on changing organisations but many of these are autobiographical, really case studies setting out methods of intervention. Jerome Franklin lists about 200 books, chapters and articles (Franklin, 1973).

Rather than a programme of expansion and determined growth, the main direction of change in organisation at present (shown by Bennis, 1966) is negative: cutbacks of both employees and productivity resulting in union/management problems and strikes, further worsening of the competitive situation and, finally, mergers or even closures.

Much of the present management behaviour is rigid and unstimulating, clinging to petty, departmental, archaic rituals rather than pressing forward to challenge current problems with consolidated company policies.

The Method

There has been a changing emphasis in the last few years from small- to large-scale organisational change reaching into every part of the institution and, if the managing director is wise, into his own office. The choice of method used is often dependent on the character and expertise of the 'change agent', often an outside consultant, rather than what is appropriate to that particular institution.

Change in organisations is concerned with people's attitudes as well as technology. It may take many years to be seen as effective. If evaluation is immediate it may only be an approximation and there is the 'absence of hard criteria of organisational change, productivity, profit, turnover and the like' (Kahn, 1974).

The Successful Method

There are three major approaches to the introduction of organisational change along 'a power spectrum' ranging from unilateral authority (decree, replacement, structure) to delegated approach (data, discussion, T group). Somewhere in the centre is the shared approach which leads to more successful outcomes.

In a survey of 18 studies of organisational change that Greiner (1967) carried out, he showed that:

the successful changes generally appear as those which
- Spread throughout the organisation to include and affect many people.
- Produce positive changes in line and staff attitudes.
- Result in improved organisation performance.

The survey revealed some distinct patterns in the evolution of change.

1. The organisation, and especially top management, is under considerable external and internal pressure for improvement long before an explicit organisation change is contemplated. Performance and/or morale are low. Top management seems to be groping for a solution to its problems.
2. A new man, known for his ability to introduce an improvement, enters the organisation, either as the official head of the organisation, or as a consultant who deals directly with the head of the organisation.
3. An initial act of the new man is to encourage a re-examination of past practices and current problems with the organisation.
4. The head of the organisation and his immediate subordinates assume a direct and highly involved role in conducting this re-examination.
5. The new man, with top management support, engages several levels of the organisation in collaborature, fact-finding, problem-solving discussions to identify and diagnose current organisation problems.
6. The new man provides others with new ideas and methods for developing solutions to problems, again at many levels of the organisation.
7. The solutions and decisions are developed, tested and found creditable for solving problems on a small scale before an attempt is made to widen the scope of change to larger problems and the entire organisation.
8. The change/effect spreads with each success experience, and as management support grows, it is gradually absorbed permanently into the organisation's way of life (Greiner, 1967).

Unsuccessful Changes

Studies of unsuccessful changes show that they start at various points on the continuum after missing out a phase, so that it is no longer a developmental plan. The successful effect of the outcome can often depend on the introduction to the company of an acknowledged expert with the full public approval of the

Figure 9.1: Dynamics of Successful Organisation Change

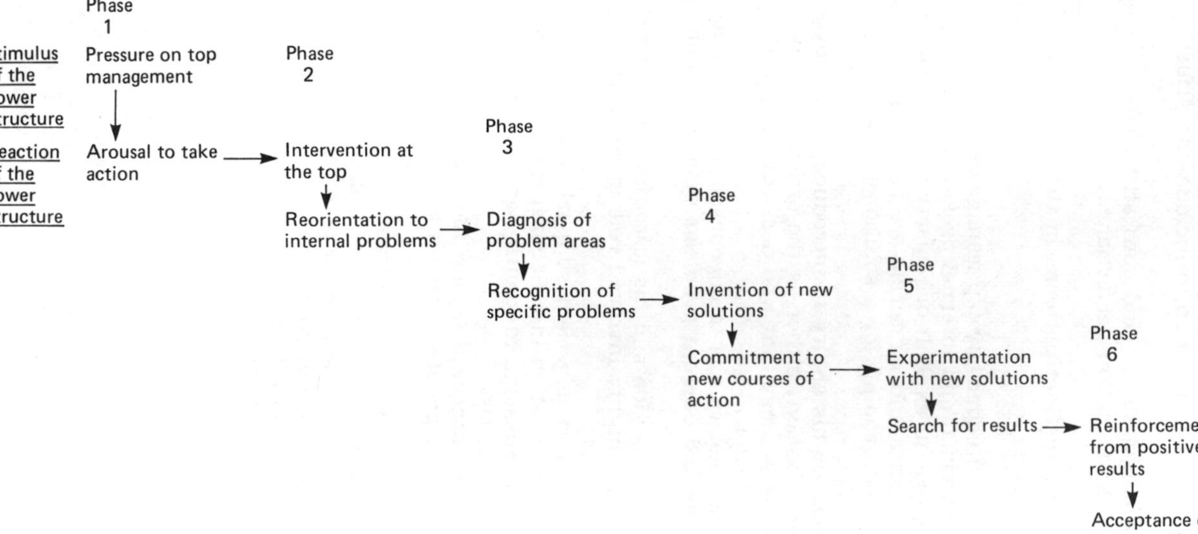

Source: Greiner, 1967.

head of the organisation.

It is for this reason that professional academic staff have more effect as a 'change agent' in an overseas country than in their own university. Unlike business organisations, the vice-chancellor would probably not employ an outside consultant but would expect to be the 'change agent' himself. It is important for him to demonstrate that even his own job is subject to scrutiny.

The paternalistic attitude is an indulgence in modern society, but with what shall it be replaced? It is important to put the 'needs of people' into the design of new technological systems.

The Concern for People

'The intervention strategies currently in use by such social scientists as Argyris, Blake, Bennis, Shepherd, Miles, Schlein and others, quite naturally fit the collaborative change-agent role and the human value focus' (O'Connell, 1968). Social scientists might be acceptable to modern organisations but not to pure scientists in universities, who would not value their intervention. Sensitivity on laboratory training would be even less valued. 'T Groups are seen here as an ideal learning environment that (need not or) can not be duplicated in so many ways in the "real" world of organisations' (Golembiewski, 1972).

The Power of the Head of an Organisation

Unless the top men believe in change in any organisation, it has little chance of succeeding. Argyris (1965) and many others have shown that for any changes in interpersonal relationships, values and norms to be effective they must begin at the top of the management structure.

Organisation change consultants have often found it impossible to affect an organisation which is a power culture, characterised almost completely in terms of power and politics. Reason (1977) in reporting on an abortive exercise in organisation development in a company that was a power culture rather than a role culture, came to the conclusion that: 'since power cultures are such strong competitive self centred and self serving structures (Harrison 1972), they are able to move fast and resist with a cloak of power orientated, politically minded, risk taking individuals (Handy 1976)'. He continues:

> In a power culture, some people are power<u>ful</u>, some are power<u>less</u>; relationships nearly always have a vertical (one-up one-down) character: even colleague (i.e. presumably equal and collaborative) relationships are often arenas for competitive striving and gamesmanship. The power to define reality and to define relationships lies in the hands of a very small number of people at the centre, and the ability of other members of the organisation to raise and

define issues is drastically curtailed (Reason, 1977).

Handy (1976) likens the power culture to a web, depending on a 'central power source, with rays of power and influence spreading out from that central figure ... Control is exercised by the centre largely though the selection of key individuals, by occasional forays from the centre or summonses to the centre.' Harrison (1972) argues that:

> An organisation that is power-orientated attempts to dominate its environment and vanquish all opposition. It is unwilling to be the subject to any external law or power. And within the organisation those who are powerful strive to maintain absolute control over subordinates.

Any change that happens in an organisation or a university that is a power culture comes in the form of a policy statement or verbal command. It assumes that employees are 'highly rational and motivated by authoritative direction. Its expectation is that people will comply in their outward behaviour and that this compliance will lead to more effective results' (Reason, 1977).

The Unilateral Approach

Managers of organisations and vice-chancellors of universities who adopt this unilateral approach seem to presume ahead of time that they know what the real problems are and how to fix them. By avoiding Phase 3 (see Figure 9.1, p. 164), they do not find out where improvements could emerge from the group as a whole. Colleagues at lower levels are aware that they are not valued and this is how resistance to change is developed.

CHANGE IN UNIVERSITIES

Universities are now in a state of enforced change. The changes must reflect not just the financial implications of government but also the need to maintain the best of their traditional heritage, whilst at the same time acknowledging the current social conditions and the needs of the individual learner, so that he may achieve academic excellence. Universities ignore these needs for change at their peril.

THE CAUSES OF STUDENT UNREST

Before trying to find solutions to such conflicting aims for universities in the 1980s, there is a further factor that demands urgent consideration - that of student unrest. We can gain from a study of the problems in 1968 in France, where the obsolete national system of higher education was perhaps the most important single cause of the upheaval. Student revolts are extremely complicated phenomena but one can speculate on causes that can contribute to unrest by taking the case of the University of Berkeley in 1964 as an example. Searle (1972), has investigated both external and internal causes:

1. Affluence. The unparalleled security of the white middle-class student removes his need to strive for success and destroys motivation, but he is also aroused to a fury by the unfairness and injustice of the system that gave him that security.
2. The Style of Upbringing. The way that students are reared as children in a protected child-centred home results in insecure adults with no sense of their identity, unable to cope with the anonymity of a competitive society.
3. The Unresponsiveness or Obsolescence of Institutions. The institution continues to function ineffectively and maintain the status quo in the face of emerging problems and new challenges.
4. The Crisis of Authority. The status quo is being challenged by the students.
5. Sheer Numbers. There is a double reciprocal relation between campus disturbances and the size of universities. This is exacerbated by the fact that universities have not responded to the new challenges and changed to meet them.
6. The Obsolete Structures of Contemporary Universities. The universities as a whole, and the way courses are run in particular, need to be re-examined.
7. The Crisis of Educational Philosophy. The bulk of general courses and service teaching is dull and uninspiring. The talented academic staff do not teach them.
8. Compulsory University Membership and Delayed Independence. University students remain financially dependent on parents and the state at a time when they should be responsible, independent adults.
9. The Service Station University. The professors are often funded by industry and private bodies to conduct research, using the universities' resources, and are little interested in the students.
10. The Reaction Against Technology and Higher Standards. There is a reaction against the era of science and technological education that followed Sputnik.
11. Imitation. Violent outbursts act as a catalyst and are repeated on other campuses.

Prevention Instead of Cure

The United States of America can often be used as a gauge of the way in which the United Kingdom will react a decade later. In 1973 when some young people were taking barbiturates and heroin in London, in New York they had progressed to sniffing glue.

But where is England going in 1981? If one considers the
Affluence
Style of upbringing
Unresponsive or obsolescence of institutions
Crisis of authority
Obsolete structures of contemporary universities
Crisis of educational policy
Compulsory university membership and delayed independence
Service station university
Reaction against technology,
many of these factors could be a description of universities in the UK in the present day, with an additional explosive factor - the escalating graduate unemployment level. This stood at 2 per cent in 1978/9, rose to 6 per cent in 1980 and was approximately 14 per cent in 1981. It has not yet reached the figure for 'unemployed youth' which stands at 29 per cent but that has already erupted into violence. Imitation encouraged by the wide television coverage of outbreaks of violence has multiplied the incidence of violence in many of the big conurbations.

Many of the causes that I have described may only apply to the American universities but they have their counterpart in the British universities. The organisation of English modern universities could be streamlined with no loss of dignity and standards.

RECOMMENDED WAY IN WHICH CHANGES MIGHT BE INSTITUTED IN UNIVERSITIES

Learning to Learn Workshops

Students need to acquire the general skills that are common to all and the specific skills that have been identified as necessary for the course of study that they are following. The general study skills such as
Organising time
Rapid reading - skimming
Note-taking for lectures
Note-taking for the text
Note-taking for practicals (if appropriate)
Creative writing
How to pass examinations,
can be acquired by students from academic staff who run workshops, which counsellors can develop in the first year of all courses. In this way, the material for the workshop will be relevant to the course.

It may be difficult to get students to invest the workshops with the right degree of importance when the experience of a student-centred workshop is sometimes at odds with the teaching on the degree course, and when students are not going to be 'examined' on the study skills course!

As we are aware, e development of worksho takes time.

It is also important to deve shops the specific skills needed been identified by the newly develo mic Purposes Test, based on observab normal study conditions which should the of the scientists. These workshops should a demic staff with the counsellor as consultant, e carried out on a long-term basis.

These workshops can be built into the timetable wh them credibility and ensures attendance from students i need.

The Curriculum

The further development, whether it is in school or higher education, is to look at the ways in which content and method can be integrated by changes in the curriculum. Certain methods of teaching or facilitating learning, such as the project or mini-thesis, fulfil the objectives for developing creative, mature, motivated, deep-level learners. 'Curriculum should give more weight to the teaching of social and interpersonal skills, in particular the skills of dialogue, discussion and argument that are critical to the effective evaluation and sharing of knowledge' (Emler and Heather, 1980).

Changes in Teachers' Attitudes

Fundamental to the learning process is the attitude of the teacher and how he encourages the student to engage with him in a spirit of inquiry.

> both student and teacher are engaged in a two-way process of expressing what it is that they are trying to formulate and grasping those things which the other person is indicating. An idea in this sense is no object to be looked upon, but is a perspective from which the person anticipates ideas in formulation. It takes on a quality of being a sign, a felt indicator of things that are not yet fully expressed, and brings into relation the person's own questions with elements in the discipline or in the world to which that question points. And yet this is only half-true because the idea itself - in that form - is that moment created as an expression of the relationship between the person (his questions) and those things which he is trying to explain or to understand. The teacher engages with the student in the task of exploring a perspective or set of ideas within the discipline in relation to the student's own basis of understanding (Radley, 1980).

part

ulum
ged
of
clearly
opment
on and
ing a
ndably
he study
hom I have
lly effective
d with no
otivation.
me is every bit
as ... elling his own
student ... se, only a widely
experienced ... n the lack of
identity and motiv... one integrated
eclectic treatment prog... outlined in Chapter 5.)

We have already been shown ear... is book that motivation and maturity are important factors ... academic success. Previous writers, who are educationalists or experimental psychologists, have recommended educational innovations that would result in the gradual development of the mature learner, but, understandably, none of them have discussed the importance of treating the lack of identity psychotherapeutically at the same time as counselling the study problems. In my experience, a mature person makes a mature learner capable of a deep-level approach to his studies with the confidence to critically reappraise his own learning methods.

A student who is a mature, self-activating person seeks out new experiences which might differ from the values and viewpoints that he already holds and accepts that there may be different viewpoints. He has the intellectual ability to question what he has already been taught and to propose alternatives which are better suited to the new situation. He takes responsibility for developing his own potential through his own efforts and feels responsible for his decisions. Having a sense of one's own identity is not a static state but a continuous process of becoming, which means not just an on-going intellectual development but also attitudinal, emotional and motivational changes as he meets new experiences and challenges.

The mature student fulfils the definition of a creative person as stated in Chapter 1; that is, a person who is curious, has a spontaneous and imaginative style, an analytical and critical approach, the courage to be independent and different from others, with a commitment to hard and persistent work. Arising from his sense of identity is the confidence that he can bring to his educational task, his work identity and a strong motivation.

To change the attitude of universities towards teaching, to change the selection procedures, the assessment procedures and the curriculum is of little worth unless the student has the personal attributes to make effective use of his learning environ ment. What you know and what you learn is dependent on 'who you are'.

The Implications for Teaching Methods

Many primary and junior schools have experienced in groupings based on division of intellectual ability as defined by tests and examinations and sometimes on the principle of 'family groups' where children of mixed ability and age are encouraged to help one another. The idea of grouping higher education students by developmental stage has not been researched fully but Perry (1970) refers to the experiments of Wispé (1951) and Hunt (1966): 'Wispé grouped students in relation to a concept of personality difference readily translatable into developmental level on our scheme, Hunt in relation to a scheme of development parallel to the early section of our own' (Perry, 1970).

It is here that the good teacher has the job of assisting his students to discriminate between complicated patterns of interpretation.

The Implication of Change in Selection

A head of department recently remarked to me that he is no longer interviewing would-be candidates as they have been so drilled by their parents and teachers in interviewing techniques that they know how to feign motivation and the other worthy attributes that the teacher would be trying to assess. I would argue for longer and more complex interviews, such as the selection procedures for certain management positions or Oxbridge colleges that take place over several days. In this way, a detailed personal as well as intellectual and physical profile can be compiled before the student commences his studies, so that the teaching staff can be aware of his developmental stage and react to him accordingly. Because students do not all progress through the stages at the same rate and may in fact have been very varied at 'A'-level, certain departments, such as the Engineering Department at the University of Reading, have developed formal links with local colleges of technology, which will make transfer between degree and diploma courses easier.

> Students wishing to obtain entrance to a degree course in Engineering can, instead of taking normal Advanced Level GCE subjects, enter a 2-year Ordinary National Diploma

> course at one of the local technical colleges and provided, as with Advanced Levels, the overall standard obtained in the second year is adequate the student can obtain a place at a University to read Engineering through the normal UCCA system... and progress to either a degree or HND programme. By design the syllabus for both of these programmes is similar during the first two terms so that, where appropriate, students on either stream can transfer directly to the other (Department of Engineering, University of Reading).

This course then, is primarily run for the benefit of the learner rather than the academic institution.

Education Counselling Services ensure the development of learning resource centres; learning to learn workshops which teach identified skills; institutional changes that accommodate learning difficulties of special groups, including overseas students. It provides professional diagnosis for the treatment of individual students, using the University College Study Questionnaire (see Appendix 1).

However, there still needs to be a fundamental change in the reward system for academic staff in universities.

REFERENCES

Argyris, C. (1965) 'Organisation and Innovation', Richard D. Irwin Inc., Homewood, Illinois, p. 3

Baskin, S. and Hallenbeck, E.F. (1972) Nontraditional Program of Undergraduate Learning, 'Compact' (October), pp. 21-5

Beckhard, R. (1969) 'Organisation Development: Strategies and Models', edited by E. Scheine, Addison-Wesley Publishing Co., Reading, Massachussetts

Bennis, W.G. (1966) 'Changing Organisations', edited by K. Davis, McGraw-Hill, New York, p. 170

Bennis, W.G., Benne, K.E. and Chin, R. (eds) (1972) 'The Planning of Change', Holt, Rinehart and Winston, London, p. 493

Dalton, G.W., Lawrence, P.R. and Greiner, L.E. (1970) 'Organisational Change and Development', Richard D. Irwin Inc. and the Dorsey Press, Homewood, Illinois, p. 385

Davis, L.E. and Taylor, J.C. (eds) (1972) 'Design of Jobs', Penguin, New York, as quoted in Kahn

Emler, N.P. and Heather, N. (1980) Intelligence: An Ideological Bias of Conventional Psychology in P. Salmon (ed.), 'Coming to Know', Routledge and Kegan Paul, pp. 135 and 150

Entwistle, N.J. and Percy, K.A. (1973) Critical Thinking or Conformity? An Investigation of the Aims and Outcomes of Higher Education, in C. Flood Page, and J. Gibson (eds), 'Research into Higher Education 1973', Society for Research into Higher Education, London

Franklin, J. (1973) 'Organisational Development: An Annotated

Bibliography', Centre for Research on the Utilization of Scientific Knowledge, Institute for Social Research, University of Michigan, as quoted in Kahn

Gibbs, G. (1981) 'Teaching Students to Learn - A Student-centred Approach', Open University Press, Milton Keynes

Goldman, G. (1979) A Contract for Academic Improvement in P.J. Hills (ed.), 'Study Courses and Counselling', Society for Research into Higher Education, Guildford, Surrey

Golembiewski, R.T. (1972) 'Renewing Organisations', F.E. Peacock Publications Inc., Itasca, Illinois, p. 464

Gray, H.L. (1975) 'Exchange and Conflict in the School', Ward Lock in conjunction with the Open University, Milton Keynes, as quoted in V. Houghton, R. McHugh, and C. Morgan (eds), 'Management and Education: The Management and Organisations of Individuals', Reader 1, Ward Lock, London, in association with Open University Press, Milton Keynes

Greiner, L.E. (1967) Pattern of Organisation Change, 'Harvard Business Review' (May-June), pp. 119, 121 and 122

Hall, P. (1980) 'Great Planning Disasters', Weidenfeld and Nicolson, London, p. 252

Handy, C.B. (1976) 'Understanding Organisations', Penguin, Harmondsworth, pp. 178-9, as quoted in Reason

Harrison, R. (1972) Understanding your Organisation's Character, 'Harvard Business Review' (May-June), p. 121, as quoted in Reason

Herzberg, F., Mausner, B. and Snyderman, B. (1959) 'The Motivation to Work', John Wiley and Sons, New York, as quoted in Hill

Hill, P. (1971) 'Towards a New Philosophy of Management', Tonbridge Printers Ltd, Tonbridge, Kent, pp. 10-11 and 14

Hunt, D.E. (1966) A Conceptual Systems Change Model and its Application to Education in O.J. Harvey (ed.), 'Experience, Structure and Adaptability', Springer, New York, pp. 277-302

Hutton, G. (1972) 'Thinking About Organisations', Tavistock Publications, London, p. 141

Kahn, R.L. (1974) Organisational Development: Some Problems and Proposals, 'Journal of Behavioural Science', vol. 10, no. 4

Lawrence, P.R. and Lorsch, J.W. (1969) 'Developing Organisations: Diagnosis and Action', Addison-Wesley Publishing Co., Reading, Massachussetts, p. 63

Nicholls, S.H. and Nicholls, A. (1975) 'Creative Teaching', George Allen and Unwin, London

O'Connell, J.J., Bennis, W.G. and Mee, J.E. (eds) (1968) 'Managing Organisational Innovation', Richard D. Irwin Inc., Homewood, Illinois, pp. 7 and 129

Perry, W.G. Jr (1970) 'Forms of Intellectual and Ethical Development in the College Years - A Scheme', Holt, Rinehart

and Winston, New York, p. 210
Radley, A. (1980) Student Learning as Social Practice in P. Salmon (ed.), 'Coming to Know', Routledge and Kegan Paul, London
Ramsden, P. (1979) Student Learning and Perceptions of the Academic Environment, 'Higher Education Bulletin', vol. 8, pp. 411-27
Reason, P. (1977) 'Centre for the Study of Organisational Change and Development', University of Bath publication, Bath, p. 5
Russell, L. (1973) 'Adult Education: A Plan for Development', Russell Report, HMSO, London
Searle, J. (1972) 'The Campus War', Penguin, Harmondsworth, pp. 142-68
Tichy, N.M. (1975) How Different Types of Change Agents Diagnose Organisations, 'Human Relations', vol. 28, no. 9, pp. 771-99
Truscott, B. (1943) 'Redbrick University', Faber and Faber, London, p. 48
Vickers, G. (1965) 'The Art of Judgement', Chapman and Hall, London, p. 117
Waddington, C.H. (1960) 'The Ethical Animal', Allen and Unwin, London, p. 117, as quoted in Vickers
Waddington, C.H. (1977) 'Tools for Thought', Paladin, St Albans, Herts
Wilson, J.D. (1977) Swots and Slackers: Students' Hours of Study, Paper given at the Scottish Education Research Association Seminar, Scottish Branch of SRHE, St Andrew's
Wispé, L.G. (1951) Evaluating Section Teaching Methods in the Introductory Course, 'Journal of Educational Research', vol. 45, pp. 161-86

CONCLUSIONS

Changes are taking place and these come mainly from individual persons in individual departments rather than in universities as a whole. While there appears to be little attempt to do so, it should be possible for staff/student committees to investigate the learning environment in the way that Gaff, Crombag and Chang (1976), and Hermans (1979) researched departmental environments in the Netherlands. Similar research was carried out in this country by Centra (1976) and Hartnett and Centra (1977).

Having noted that the running of study skills programmes in both schools and universities led to teachers re-examining their teaching methods, it may be that students' assessments of the teaching methods in their departments will act as a consciousness-raising strategy and encourage the students to re-examine their learning methods.

It is important that schools and institutions considering the development of 'learning to learn' programmes should learn from the programmes and the experience of counsellors, teachers, educationalists and psychologists who have been working with students in this way for many years. Third World countries and countries with ethnic minorities, such as South Africa and Australia, want to develop help for students with learning difficulties. I would urge them not to copy the methods of Western countries with sophisticated programmes but rather to study the problems that an individual learner has in their educational institutions and devise 'learning to learn' methods that are suitable to him. In the past this has not been so, and in fields such as education and housing developing countries have copied Western ideas without learning from their mistakes or adapting the Western ideas to their culture. The high-rise dwellings in Hong Kong are a pertinent example of this.

Change has been forced on universities and financial issues are currently claiming attention. This means that administrators and senior academic staff will have to scrutinise not just which departments and individuals are dispensable and cheapest to annihilate but will need to examine critically the very fabric of the way that universities function, not forgetting themselves.

In determining the goals of higher education in the late twentieth century, it is important that financial considerations, the clamour of industry for vocational courses and the development of technological-scientific research does not obscure the needs of the individual learner. With him, we will continue to work in faith, knowing that there is much to discover.

This book seeks to contribute new perceptions to the age-old ideas of learning and teaching at universities and, as such, hopes to contribute to the 'winds of change'.

REFERENCES

Ashman, S. (1980) Focus on Learning, 'Teaching News' (University of Birmingham), no. 9 (February), p. 12

Baskin, S. and Hallenbeck, E.F. (1972) Nontraditional Program of Undergraduate Learning, 'Compact' (October), p. 24

Beckhard, C. (1969) 'Organisation Development: Strategies and Models', Addison-Wesley Series, Massachusetts, pp. 101 and 104

Centra, J.A. (1976) 'Student Ratings of Instruction and their Relationships to Student Learning', Educational Testing Service, Princetown, NJ

Entwistle, N.J. and Percy, K.A. (1974) Critical Thinking or Conformity? An Investigation of the Aims and Outcomes of Higher Education in C. Flood Page and J. Gibson (eds), 'Research into Higher Education', Society for Research into Higher Education, London

Entwistle, N.J. and Hanley, M. (1977) Personality, Cognitive Style and Students' Learning Strategies, 'Higher Education Bulletin', vol. 6, no. 1 (Winter), p. 40

Gaff, J.G., Crombag, H.F.M. and Chang, T.M. (1976) Environments for Learning in a Dutch University, 'Higher Education Bulletin', vol. 5, pp. 285-99

Hartnett, R.T. and Centra, J.A. (1977) The Effects of Academic Departments on Student Learning, 'Journal of Higher Education', vol. 48, no. 5, pp. 491-507

Hermans, B.M.J. (1979) Students and System: Academic Success and Study Problems in Relation with Characteristics of the Academic Environment and of the Students in E.A. van Trotsenburg (ed.), 'Higher Education: A Field of Study', 5 vols, Verlag Peter Lang, Bern

Makinde, O. (1980) Indigenous Counselling Techniques Among the Yoruba and Igala People of Nigeria, Paper presented at the International Round Table for the Advancement of Counselling, Greece, 'International Journal for the Advancement of Counselling', vol. 3, no. 3-4/80, Martinus Nijhoff Publishers, The Hague, p. 183

Nelson-Jones, R. and Toner, H.L. (1978) Counselling Approaches to Increasing Students' Learning Competence, 'British Journal of Guidance and Counselling', vol. 6, no. 1 (January), p. 29

Nicholls, H. and Nicholls, A. (1975) 'Creative Teaching', George Allen and Unwin, London, p. 115

Ramsden, P. (1979) Student Learning and Perceptions of the

Academic Environment, 'Higher Education Bulletin', vol. 8, Elsevier Scientific Publishing Co., Amsterdam, p. 413
Ratigan, B. (1977) Counselling Training for Tutors in Higher Education, 'British Journal of Guidance and Counselling', vol. 5, no. 1 (January)
Stewin, L.L. (1980) A Bird in the Hand, Although Messy, Stills Beats Two in the Bush, Abstract, Paper presented to IRTAC Conference, Greece
Thoreson, R.W. (1974) The Evolution of Counselling, 'British Journal of Guidance and Counselling', vol. 2, no. 2 (July)

'It is in fact nothing short of a miracle that the modern methods of instruction have not yet entirely strangled the holy curiosity of enquiry: for this delicate little plant, aside from stimulation, stands mainly in need of freedom; without this it goes to wreck and ruin without fail.'

Albert Einstein

APPENDIX I

University College London Study Questionnaire

NAME............. FORENAMES................ AGE...SEX...

Below is a list of feelings or reactions which students sometimes experience in relation to study. Please indicate how you stand in respect of each item by circling T = mainly true, ? = neither true nor false, F = mainly false.

1.	I can't stop thinking about work even when trying to relax	T	?	F
2.	I go over work again and again even when I know it	T	?	F
3.	When I start a piece of work I feel inadequate and incapable of doing it	T	?	F
4.	I keep losing the thread of things	T	?	F
5.	I just can't get down to working as much as I should	T	?	F
6.	Thinking about work can make me feel physically ill	T	?	F
7.	I enjoy tackling a difficult topic or problem	T	?	F
8.	I prefer to concentrate on set work, rather than following up my own ideas	T	?	F..
9.	I always feel I have to hurry through work tasks	T	?	F
10.	I can't bear to hand in an untidy piece of work	T	?	F
11.	My tutors overestimate my abilities	T	?	F
12.	I keep changing from one topic to another	T	?	F
13.	I am quickly bored	T	?	F
14.	I often get headaches when trying to study	T	?	F
15.	Some aspects of my subjects are really exciting	T	?	F
16.	I cover assigned work equally well whether it interests me or not	T	?	F..
17.	Sometimes when studying I get downright panicky	T	?	F

18.	I spend too much time on unimportant detail	T	?	F
19.	I often can't be bothered to respond to a question even when I know the answer	T	?	F
20.	I often make silly mistakes	T	?	F
21.	I am always behind in my work	T	?	F
22.	I often can't get to sleep for thinking about work	T	?	F
23.	I often study purely for pleasure	T	?	F
24.	I prefer to restrict myself to recommended reading	T	?	F
25.	I feel guilty unless I am working	T	?	F
26.	I rarely complete my work to my satisfaction	T	?	F
27.	If I get good marks I feel a fraud	T	?	F
28.	I get excited about a topic but soon lose interest	T	?	F
29.	When working I continually break off to smoke, drink coffee, walk about or talk to someone	T	?	F
30.	My hand gets stiff and clumsy so that I can't write properly	T	?	F
31.	I enjoy discussing work topics with others	T	?	F
32.	I consider the best way of learning is by completing the set work and doing the required reading	T	?	F
33.	I get anxious when I hear others talking about work	T	?	F
34.	I am always planning out work schedules	T	?	F
35.	I feel I ought not to be taking up a place in College	T	?	F
36.	I frequently mislay my notes or textbooks	T	?	F
37.	I don't worry enough about work	T	?	F
38.	I am frequently distracted by aches and pains	T	?	F
39.	I look forward to lectures or classes	T	?	F
40.	I find a systematic presentation of a topic more useful than discussion	T	?	F..
41.	As soon as I start one task I feel I should be doing something else	T	?	F
42.	I like doing things thoroughly, or not at all	T	?	F
43.	My thinking about work matters seems very slow	T	?	F

44. My notes get into a muddle T ? F
45. I keep wanting to sleep all the time T ? F
46. I am often handicapped by sheer physical tiredness T ? F
47. I like reading around my subject T ? F
48. I find it difficult to tackle something unless I know just what is expected T ? F..
49. When I try to revise my work, my mind goes blank T ? F
50. I spend a lot of time on making preparations to work T ? F
51. I am often too depressed to concentrate properly on my work T ? F
52. I forget to go to tutorials or lectures T ? F
53. I read automatically without taking things in T ? F
54. I get a feeling of nausea and sickness when there is a lot to do T ? F
55. I would like to continue post-graduate study or research T ? F
56. I don't let myself get diverted onto something that is not strictly relevant to the course T ? F..
57. I am afraid of panicking in exams T ? F
58. I find it difficult to decide which parts of my work are most important T ? F
59. I often feel that others know more T ? F
60. I keep getting out books but never really read them T ? F
61. I often think another subject would be more interesting T ? F
62. I suffer from eyestrain when working T ? F
63. I believe in knowledge for its own sake T ? F
64. It isn't often I try to think of doing something differently from the way described in the lecture book T ? F..
65. When I am asked a question about work I 'seize up' T ? F
66. I force myself to work even if I don't feel like it T ? F
67. I fear exams will expose all my weaknesses T ? F

68. I work in fits and starts T ? F

69. I seem to have no real drive to work T ? F

70. I never seem to be able to get comfortable when trying to study T ? F

71. My interest in my subject grows continuously T ? F

72. I like to feel everything important is contained in my notes T ? F

FOR MEDICAL USE ONLY

ANX___OBS___DEP___DIS___LOM___SOM___WS___SYL___

NAME:__________ FORENAMES:__________ AGE:___ M F

U.C.L.S.Q. Norms

	ANX	OBS	DEP*	DIS	LOM	SOM*	WS	SYL*
Male Mean	1.35	3.07	1.49	2.09	2.40	0.51	4.60	2.30
SD	1.59	1.86	1.44	1.62	2.11	0.77	2.32	1.67
Female Mean	1.60	3.03	2.37	1.97	2.93	1.17	4.23	3.43
SD	2.01	2.14	2.03	1.87	2.49	1.74	2.21	2.37

* = sig M/F mean difference

ANX Anxiety
OBS Obsessionality
DEP Depression
DIS Disorganisation
LOM Low motivation (High score = poorly motivated)
SOM Somatic
WS Work satisfaction
SYL Syllabism (High score = syllabus bound)

The scale items are arranged so that ANX items are 1, 9, 17, 25, etc., OBS items 2, 10, 18, 26, etc., with the remaining scales in similar sequence. Each mainly true response is given one point and the scales totalled separately. Scale maximum is 9.

APPENDIX II

The LRC was part of the Counselling Office so that there was no outlay for furniture, furnishings or tape recorders. The Academic Support Centre loans video equipment for regular use.

The cost of establishing the LRC in the first year at operation was:

	£
Study skills books	35
Tapes and tape booklets	80
Publicity/Stationery	195
Cost of making own videos	22
Total	£ 340

Publicity in the form of well-designed bookmarks, timetables, etc. is expensive, but is considerably more effective than posters. Students may have experienced counselling at their schools but it is unlikely that they will have experienced a learning resource centre so that publicity is essential.

Catalogue: Learning Resource Centre Counselling Service, Palmer Building, University of Reading

Video Tapes (VHS)

'Pattern Note-Taking' - Tony Buzan - Different Techniques
'Organising Your Time' - Tony Buzan - From a BBC series - 'Use Your Head'
'Study Patterns' - Alex Main - A series of five video programmes - Personal Time-tabling, Using Your Time, Note-taking, Recording and Essay Writing (University of Strathclyde, 1977).
'Speak Up, Speak Out' - from the Educational Technology Dept, University of Surrey, made in Australia. This video shows the problems students face in a seminar and how to overcome them.
'An Introduction to Study Skills for Overseas Students - Dr David Lloyd - The Personal Budget and How to Manage It - Exercise and Use of Time - Library and Use of Time.
'The Interview' (U-Matic) - David Huggett, University of Aberdeen (1972) - How to conduct yourself in an interview.

Cassette/Book sets

'Effective study - Dr Phillip Hills, University of Leicester - Effective Strategies for Study, Tools (Materials and Equipment), Lectures, Sources of Information, Resources, Concentration and Memory, Examinations

'Memory Matters' - Mark E. Brown - produced by Sound Thinking Ltd 'Improve Your Memory'

'The Edinburgh University Mathematics Tape-Book' - Elementary Techniques of Integration, Part 1

Cassettes

Relax and Enjoy it! - Dr Robert Sharpe
Control Your Tension - Dr Robert Sharpe
Sleep Well - Dr Robert Sharpe
Diet Effectively - Dr Robert Sharpe
Kick the Smoking Habit - Dr Robert Sharpe
Don't be Shy - Dr Robert Sharpe
Assert Yourself - Dr Robert Sharpe
Do Well in Interviews - Dr Robert Sharpe
Study Effectively - Dr Robert Sharpe
Pass That Exam - Dr Robert Sharpe

Work Books

'Remedial English' - A series of Daily Work Books by Diana Collinson, Open University - Introductory Quiz, Spelling and Grammar, Punctuation, Taking and Making Notes, Essay Writing.

Books Available

Title	Author	Publisher
'Degrees of Excellence'	Entwistle, N.J. and Wilson, J.D.	Hodder and Stoughton
'A Student's Guide to Efficient Study	James, D.E.	Pergamon Press
'The Psychology of Study'	Mace, C.A.	Pelican
'Student's Guide to Success'	Fisher Cassie, W. and Constantine, T.	Macmillan
'Successful Study'	Burnet, J.	Hodder and Stoughton
'Staying the Course'	Gilbert, J.	Kogan Page
'Learn How to Study'	Rowntree, D.	Macdonald and Jane's
'The Success Factor' 'How to Be Who You Want to Be'	Sharpe, Dr R. and Lewis, D.	Souvenir Press

Title	Author	Publisher
'Effective Study Skills'	Hills, P.J. and Barlow, M.	Pan
'How to Be Interviewed'	Mackenzie Davey, D. and McDonnell, P.	British Institute of Mangement Foundation
'Good Style - for Scientific and Engineering Writing'	Kirkman, J.	Pitman
'How to Take Exams'	Pitfield, M. and Donnelly, R.	Institute of Personnel Management
'How to Pass Exams'	Kemble, B.	Orback and Chambers
'How to Pass Examinations'	Erasmus, J.	Oriel Press
'Study Skills in English'	Wallace, M.J.	Cambridge
'Helping Students to Learn at University'	Raaheim, K. and Wankowski, J.	Sigma Forlag
'Forms of Intellectual and Ethical Development in the College Years'	Perry, W.G. Jr	Holt, Rinehart and Winston
'Indicators of Performance'	Billing, D.	SRHE
'Encouraging Effective Learning'	Main, A.	Scottish Academic Press
'Understanding of Non-Technical Words in Science'	Cassels, J.R.T. and Johnstone, A.H.	The Royal Society of Chemistry
'Careers in the 80's	Webb, A. and Montague, A.	The Observer Publication

Pamphlets

'How to Write a Scientific Paper'	Day, R.A.	Reprinted from ASM News
'An Exploration of Students' Sense of Competence'	Nelson-Jones, R., Toner, H.L. and Coxhead, P.	Department of Educational Enquiry University of Aston
'Techniques of Study'	Nisbet, J.	University of Aberdeen

APPENDIX III

(Taken from A. Jenson (1951) Determining Critical Requirements for Teachers, 'Journal of Experimental Education', University of California, LA, vol. XX, pp. 79-85.)

The practical application of the critical incidence technique - this assesses the effectiveness of the teacher's intervention in a specific situation.

The participants were asked to respond to six situations or questions each printed on a separate page of the booklet. The six sets of directions read as follows:

1. Think of the elementary or high school teachers with whom you have been closely associated recently. Of those teachers, think of the one teacher you consider most ineffective. The teacher you are thinking of probably did a lot of things which caused you to feel that he or she was ineffective, but what was the final incident that influenced you? Describe the situation and just what the teacher did that convinced you of his ineffectiveness on the job. What behavior demonstrated the teacher's ineffectiveness?

2. Think of the one most effective elementary or high school teacher with whom you have been closely associated recently . The person you have in mind probably did many things that convinced you he or she was effective, but what was the most recent thing that he did which was outstanding and made you consider him especially effective. Describe some specific thing that he did that makes him stand out in your mind as being particularly effective on the job.

3. Think over the past month or two and recall that last time you observed a teacher in elementary or high school do something especially ineffective (it need not have been done by a generally ineffective person). Just what was done on that particular occasion? What was the act? What did he do? Be specific, and avoid inferences.

4. Think over the last month or two and recall the last time you observed any teacher do something especially effective. Just what was done on that particular occasion? What was the act? What did the teacher do? Be specific, and avoid inferences.

5. Think back about the teachers you had when in elementary school and high school. Try to think of the most ineffective teacher you had. Now try to recall specific incident that stands out in you memory as an illustration of the ineffectiveness of this teacher. What was the situation? What did the teacher do?

6. Think back about the teachers you had when in elementary and high school. These are the teachers who taught the classes you attended when you were in school. Try to think of the most effective teacher you had. Now try to recall a specific incident that stands out in your memory as an illustration of the effectiveness of this teacher. What was the situation? What did the teacher do?

Approximately 500 incidents were reviewed. After some 200 incidents each of effective and ineffective behavior had been analyzed, few new types of behavior were noted.

Personal Qualities

Effective	Ineffective
1. Is alert, cheerful, and enthusiastic in expression and manner	1. Is dull, bored and shows lack of dramatic qualities
2. Exhibits self-control and good organization ability in midst of classroom demands	2. Loses temper, is impatient, disorganized, fault-finding, easily disturbed in face of classroom demands
3. Likes fun and possesses a sense of humor	3. Is serious, too occupied for fun or humor
4. Recognizes and admits own mistakes graciously	4. Is unaware of, or fails to admit own mistakes
5. Is fair and impartial	5. Fails to maintain a fair, impartial objective attitude
	6. Is overcritical and suspicious, showing disapproval of child as a person

Professional Qualities

1. Evidences a planned but flexible procedure anticipating individual needs and interests	1. Shows rigidity of procedure; fails to provide for individual variation or differences

Effective	Ineffective
2. Stimulates pupils through interesting and original and teaching techniques	2. Uses uninteresting materials and poor teaching techniques
3. Conducts well-planned, clear practical demonstrations and explanations	3. Gives poorly-planned explanations, and develops subject matter ineffectively
4. Is clear and thorough in giving directions	4. Is unclear, vague, or incomplete in giving directions
5. Is skilful in encouraging pupils to work through their problems and evaluate their own work	5. Fails to give pupils chance to participate or make choices, and to evaluate their own work
6. Disciplines in a quiet, dignified positive and fair manner	6. Resorts to cruel meaningless forms of physical correction
7. Gives constructive help willingly and enthusiastically	7. Fails to give help or gives it grudgingly
8. Forsees and resolves potential difficulties	8. Evidences inability to see and resolve potential problems
	9. Fails to link course with larger educational objectives or reality

Social Qualities

Effective	Ineffective
1. Shows understanding and sympathy in working with pupils	1. Makes threats, uses sarcastic remarks or in other ways shows lack of sympathy for pupils
2. Is friendly, democratic, and courteous in relations with pupils	2. Is tense, authoritarian, and antagonistic in relations with pupils
3. Helps individuals with personal as well as educational problems	3. Is unaware of pupils' personal and educational needs
4. Commends effort and gives generous praise for work well done	4. Fails to give approval and commendation for pupils' effort and activities
5. Is able to anticipate reactions of others in social situations	5. Is unable to anticipate reactions of others
6. Encourages others to do do their best	6. Fails to encourage pupils to do best work

APPENDIX IV

Bibliography of Study Skills Manuals

Burnett, J. (1979) 'Successful Study - A Handbook for Students', Teach Yourself Books/Hodder and Stoughton, Sevenoaks, Kent

Buzan, T. (1974) 'Use Your Head', BBC Publications, London

Carman, Robert A. and Royce Adams, W. (1972) 'Study Skills - A Student's Guide for Survival - A Self Teaching Guide', John Wiley and Sons, London

Cassels, J.R.T. and Johnstone, A.J. (1980) 'Understanding of Non-Technical Words in Science', The Royal Society of Chemistry, London

Crew, L. and Crew, A. (1963) 'How to Study', Collier Macmillan, London

Deese, J. and Deese, E.K. (1979) 'How to Study', McGraw-Hill, New York

Erasmus, J. (1980) 'How to Pass Examinations', Oriel Press, Stocksfield

Fisher Cassie, W. and Constantine, T. (1977) 'Student's Guide to Success', The Macmillan Press, London

Freeman, R. (1972) 'How to Study Effectively - A 2 Month Course', National Extension College, Cambridge

Gilbert, J. (ed.) (1979) 'Staying the Course', Kogan Page, London

Hills, P.J. and Barlow, H. (1980) 'Effective Study Skills', Pan Books, London

James, D.E. (1978) 'A Student's Guide to Efficient Study', Pergamon Press, Oxford

Kemble, B. 'How to Pass Exams', Orbach and Chambers, London

Kirkman, J. (1979) 'Good Style for Scientific and Engineering Writing', Pitman, London

Mackenzie Davey, D. and McDonnell, P. (1979) 'How to be Interviewed', British Institute of Management Foundation, London

Pauk, W. (1974) 'How to Study in College', Houghton Mifflin, Boston

Pitfield, M. and Donnelly, R. (1980) 'How to Take Exams', Institute of Personnel Management, London

Rowntree, D. (1970) 'Learn How to Study', Macdonald and Jane's, London

Sharpe, R. and Lewis, D. (1976) 'The Success Factor', Souvenir Press, London

Wallace, M.J. (1980) 'Study Skills in English', Cambridge University Press, Cambridge

Wickelgreen, W.A. (1974) 'How to Solve Problems', W.H. Freeman and Co., San Francisco

APPENDIX V

A Humanist Psychologist's Point of View

It makes sense to talk about a normal, mentally healthy person not as a finished product, but rather in terms of becoming that kind of person by means of certain main capabilities which the person develops in order to actualize all of his potentialities.

To become this kind of self-actualizing person reqires (a) an internal kind of motivation where you take responsibility for your own behavior and for developing your own potential through your own efforts; (b) it requires an attitude that allows you to be 'open to your experiences', which means to seek out and accept new experiences which might even be discrepant with the values and viewpoints you already hold; (c) it requires the intellectual ability to question what you have previously been taught to accept as truth or fact and to propose novel alternatives which seem better suited to each situation; and (d) it requires an awareness of your feelings so that you can behave in ways that are congruent (consistent) with how you feel.

From a humanistic viewpoint, this kind of self-actualizing person is on the path to becoming mentally healthy. But this cannot be said to be normal from a statistical viewpoint in that it is not commonly done. It is normal, however, in that everyone has the potential to develop the main capabilities described above (although to different degrees), which can then help the individual strive towards actualizing all of his or her potentialities.

A person cannot become all he is capable of becoming (a) if he blames his environment for what he is rather than taking responsibility to alter his own circumstances, (b) if he rejects all values and viewpoints which are different from his own rather than trying to understand these different viewpoints and trying to accept that there will be different viewpoints, (c) if he totally accepts all he has been taught without questioning its basis or validity in fact, and if he thinks in narrow conventional ways rather than in broader, novel ways, and (d) if he disregards his feelings and behaves in ways that result in emotion upset rather than 'doing what feels right'.

The self-actualizing person is in a continuous process of becoming all he or she is capable of becoming, which means that there will be continuous motivational, attitudinal, intellectual, and emotional changes in this kind of person - changes in the direction of becoming more and more mentally healthy.

APPENDIX VI

Sensory Stimulation Sheet Used in the Treatment of Anorexia

1. Which of the following do you like touching? Tick:

Animals Children Female body Male body Silk Satin Rubber Fur Plastic Nylon Marble Warm sand Velvet Wool Glass Sculpture Sandpaper Seaweed

2. Which of the following do you like the smell of? Tick:

Outdoor Odours: Smoke Cut Hay Grass Earth Sea Manure

Scented Products: Floral Citrus Spicy Exotic Oriental Mossy Pine Leather

Foods: Fish Vanilla Curry Garlic Gorgonzola Beer Cigars Your partner's body without scent Smell of a clean baby Incense Some body smells

3. Do you like listening to:

Music: Classical Modern Pop Soul Rock Drumming the Radio Male voices Female voices Laughter Sighing Groaning Giggling Panting Sex sounds Stories

4. Which of the following do you like tasting

Lemon Candy floss Soups Spicy food Wine Cheese Liqueurs Your partner's skin

5. Do you like looking at:

Blossom A field of corn A rough sea A naked baby A still pond A waterfall Attractive people Your partner's body

INDEX